LEISURE AND URBAN PROCESSES

CRITICAL STUDIES OF LEISURE POLICY IN WESTERN EUROPEAN CITIES

Leisure and URBAN PROCESSES

Critical Studies of Leisure Policy in Western European Cities

Edited by
Peter Bramham, Ian Henry,
Hans Mommaas, Hugo van der Poel

ROUTLEDGE
London and New York

First published 1989
by Routledge
11 New Fetter Lane, London EC4P 4EE
29 West 35th Street, New York, NY 10001

© 1989 European Consortium for Leisure Studies and Research

Wordprocessed by Vibes, Brighton, Sussex
Printed and bound in Great Britain by
Biddles Ltd, Guildford and King's Lynn

British Library Cataloguing in Publication Data

Leisure and urban processes: critical studies
  of leisure policy in Western European Cities.
  1. Europe. Urban regions. Leisure facilities.
  Policies of local authorities
  I. Bramham, Peter
  306'.48'094   790.091732
  ISBN 0-415-01433-6   90517

Library of Congress Cataloging in Publication Data

Leisure and urban processes : critical studies of leisure policy in
  Western European cities / edited by Peter Bramham . . . [et al.].
      p. cm.
    Bibliography: p.
    Includes index.
    ISBN 0-415-01433-6
    1. Leisure—Europe—Case studies. 2. Europe—Social policy—Case
studies. 3. Cities and towns—Europe—Case studies. I. Bramham,
Peter.,
GV73.L45 1989
790'.01'35094—dc19   88-38723
                                                          CIP

CONTENTS

Contents

TABLES

FIGURES

Figures

ABOUT THE CONTRIBUTORS

Franco Bianchini graduated in comparative politics at the University of Florence. He is currently completing a Ph.D. thesis in the Department of Government at Manchester University. He is the author of various articles on the relationship between culture and socialist party politics.

Livin Bollaert graduated in physical education at the University of Ghent and obtained his Ph.D. from the University of Brussels. He also holds a masters degree in leisure studies from l'Université Libre de Bruxelles. He is currently professor at the Vrije Universiteit Brussel, director of the Leisure Studies Department, and president of the Educational Board of the University. He is president of the Dutch-Flemish Working Group in Leisure Studies and a member of ELRA, WLRA, and ICHPER. He has published studies in the field of physical education, leisure studies, education, and strategic planning.

Peter Bramham graduated in economics at the London School of Economics and subsequently received a sociology doctorate from Leeds University. His research interests are in the area of leisure, policing, and deviance and he has published in the fields of criminology, leisure, and leisure policy. He is a member of a collaborative project researching young people in Bradford.

Eric Corijn graduated in science and philosophy at the Universities of Ghent and Brussels, and attended Art School in Brussels. He followed a postgraduate course on futures research at the State University of Utrecht (Netherlands). He is currently working at the Centre for Leisure Studies at the Vrije Universiteit Brussel. He is the author of several articles on leisure theory and leisure education, as well as on such diverse subjects as sociobiology, cultural studies, political economy, and basic education. He has edited books on sociobiology, Marxism, and the future of labour.

Dominique Danau graduated in sociology at the University of Brussels. She is currently working at the European Centre for Work and Society (Maastricht-Brussels). She has published papers in the field of sport, and leisure satisfaction of the elderly.

Jean-Michel Dewailly graduated from l'Université des Sciences et Techniques de Lille in geography. He completed his doctoral thesis at the Sorbonne in Paris in 1984 on the topic of 'Tourisme et loisirs dans le Nord/Pas-de-Calais', which has subsequently been published as a text. He is now maître de conférence at l'Université des Sciences et Techniques de Lille. His primary research interests lie in the fields of tourism and regional planning, and he has published several papers on this topic relating to northern Europe.

Adri Dietvorst graduated in human geography and history in 1964 and is associate professor at the Katholieke Universiteit Nijmegen. His research interests include theoretical geography and spatial aspects of recreation and tourism. He has published on these themes in a variety of German, Dutch, and American academic journals. He has recently published a book on the role of leisure and tourism in the inner city.

Sue Glyptis graduated in geography at the University College of Wales, Aberystwyth in 1974, and obtained her Ph.D. in geography at the University of Hull in 1979 for a thesis entitled 'Countryside visitors: site use and leisure lifestyles'. From 1977 to 1981 she was employed as a research officer at the Sports Council, involved in the management of a wide range of research projects on sport and recreation provision. Since 1981 she has lectured in the Department of Physical Education and Sports Science at Loughborough University of Technology and she is now senior lecturer in Recreation Management and Leisure Studies. She teaches on undergraduate and postgraduate recreation management courses and is involved in research supervision and contract research. Her main interests are leisure lifestyles, recreational deprivation and the leisure needs of particular social groups, and countryside recreation.

Linda Hantrais graduated in French and German at London University, obtained a postgraduate diploma in Social Administration from the London School of Economics and Political Science, and completed her Ph.D. at the Flinders University of South Australia. She is currently senior lecturer in French at Aston University, Birmingham, and associate researcher with the CNRS team, Temps Sociaux, Ages et Modèles Culturels (Paris). Her main research interests are in the methodology and practice of cross-national comparative research, with special reference to time and the family in France and Britain. She has published two single-authored books, and co-edited a third, as well as a series of papers on cross-national research, and has written book chapters and articles, several of which are concerned with leisure values and policies, particularly from a cross-national perspective.

Les Haywood graduated in physical education from St. Luke's College, Exeter, and went on to undertake postgraduate studies in education at the University of Leeds and a masters degree at the University of Manchester. He has published a number of articles and monographs in the fields of sport, leisure, and physical education. He is currently principal lecturer in the Department of Community Studies, Bradford and Ilkley College.

Ian Henry graduated in English and philosophy from the University of Stirling and subsequently received an M.Sc. and Ph.D. in the field of Recreation Management from Loughborough University. His primary research interests are in the area of leisure and the state, leisure policy analysis, and comparative leisure policy, and he has published widely in the fields of recreation policy, planning, and management. He is currently senior lecturer in the Carnegie Department, Faculty of Education and Leisure Studies, Leeds Polytechnic.

Myriam Jansen-Verbeke graduated in human geography in 1965. She is senior lecturer at the Katholieke Universiteit Nijmegen and also lectures at the National Institute for Tourism and Traffic in Breda. She is also research manager of the Research Centre of the Dutch Scientific Institute for Tourism. She has published articles in a variety of Dutch, English, French, and German academic journals. She has just completed her Ph.D., to be published as 'Leisure, recreation, and tourism in inner cities'.

Frank Kew graduated in physical education from Loughborough University and has subsequently received masters degrees in physical education and sociology from the

University of Leeds. He is currently engaged in Ph.D. research at the Department of Social Policy and Sociology of Leeds University, and is senior lecturer in Leisure Studies in the Community Studies Department of Bradford and Ilkley College. He is author of a number of publications on physical education, leisure studies, and the sociology of sport.

Henk Meiburg graduated in sociology from the Agricultural University of Wageningen in 1981. At the moment he is working in the Department of Sports and Swimming Pools for the municipality of The Hague. He has published articles on leisure spending in ethnic minorities, on marginal youth, and on basic education for adults in a variety of Dutch youth and leisure journals.

Hans Mommaas graduated in sociology in 1982 at the Agricultural University at Wageningen and is lecturer in the Sociology of Leisure at Tilburg University. His research interests include leisure and social theory, post-modernity, and changing political and economic relations. He has published mostly on themes such as labour, social order and leisure, unemployment and leisure, leisure and social theory. His articles have appeared in a variety of German, Canadian, and Dutch academic journals.

Fouli Papageorgiou graduated from the Technical University in Athens with a first degree in architecture. She subsequently completed a Ph.D. in recreation planning at the Centre for Urban and Regional Studies University of Birmingham, England. She is now based in Athens, working as a research consultant with government and industry in the fields of leisure, recreation, and tourism.

Sjoerd Rijpma graduated in human geography and planning in 1973 at the University of Amsterdam. He is a member of staff at the Department of Research and Policy Development in Sport and Recreation, municipality of Rotterdam. He has published articles about the development of sports participation and leisure planning in a variety of Dutch journals.

John Spink graduated in geography at Leeds University, gaining an M.A. at the University of Manitoba, Canada and a diploma in Town and Regional Planning from Leeds

Polytechnic. He is currently teaching in the Community Studies Department of Bradford and Ilkley College, and is a Social Science tutor/counsellor for the Open University. He has published studies in the fields of environmental perception and urban structure.

Hugo van der Poel graduated in sociology at the Agricultural University of Wageningen in 1982 and is lecturer in Leisure Studies at Tilburg University. His research interests include leisure theory and policy. He has published an introduction to leisure studies (with Theo Beckers) and several articles in German, Dutch, and Canadian academic journals.

PREFACE

This text represents the first fruits of a European Consortium for Leisure Studies and Research which was established to encourage dialogue among European researchers in this field and to generate literature in the comparative studies field. The process of producing the material presented here was therefore important as it brought together writers whose work has until now largely been concerned with intra-national issues. The first meeting of the Consortium took place in Brussels at the Vrije Universiteit Brussel in July 1987, focusing predominantly on embryonic versions of the chapters of this book. The product of this first collaborative endeavour is a contribution to the field of comparative leisure policy, which has been seriously neglected. As we note elsewhere, the contributions to this text are largely single-nation studies, and there is a need therefore to generate genuinely cross-national studies to build on this initiative, which represents merely the first stages in a programme promoting comparative leisure studies.

We would like to take this opportunity to thank formally the Leisure Studies Department of the Vrije Universiteit Brussel under Professor Livin Bollaert, which so generously hosted the first seminar of the Consortium. In addition we wish to acknowledge the financial contributions made by the various academic institutions to which Consortium members belong, and to the Sports Council, which provided some financial support towards the costs incurred by members at the seminar.

The preparation of the manuscript and illustrations was the work of a number of individuals in addition to individual authors and editors. Thanks are therefore due to Carol O'Connor, Marion Collinson, Sue Davies, Ian Dick, and Lynne Mitchell.

INTRODUCTION

This collection has as its focus urban leisure policy in six of the liberal democracies of Western Europe. There are at least four major reasons why urban leisure policies merit attention. The first is that cities, particularly the industrialized metropolitan areas, have exhibited the most serious symptoms of recent economic political, and cultural change. The economic crisis has struck areas of traditional industry hardest, while at the same time the effects of the sustained growth in the information sector seem to have been concentrated in the more service-oriented and 'attractive' cities. Such phenomena provide the background for the concentration of unemployed, ethnic minorities, and other relatively impoverished groups within certain cities (or certain parts of cities), while elsewhere other urban areas are distinguished by increased prosperity and gentrification. The larger cities form the locale for the expression of new lifestyles and new cultural forms, but they are also the places that seem to experience increasing social disorder and political extremism. In many ways, city life is what modern life is all about, both in its saddest, impoverished forms and in its most elated, carefree forms. City life is both the product and object of local and national socioeconomic and sociocultural policies, and contemporary urban developments guarantee this trend for the foreseeable future.

A second reason for focusing on leisure policy and urban processes is that urban life is increasingly concerned with non-work activities. The domination of the urban landscape by industrial forms of production, factories and offices, is in many cities giving way to 'consumption palaces' to accommodate the leisure consumer, with pavement cafes, museums, cultural events, and a wide range of entertainment facilities vying for the increasing disposable income and time of local citizens and tourists.

On average, people in employment tend to work fewer hours and have smaller households. Those with higher salaries who still work long hours often 'buy leisure' by employing others, predominantly women, to take responsibility for household and childcare duties. The increasing quality and quantity of leisure of these groups is met by a

1

growing 'leisure industry', an army of domestic labourers, many employed on a part-time basis with low incomes.

However, non-work life does not mean a life of unproblematic leisure. The percentages of disabled, elderly, and unemployed in the urban populations have grown in the 1970s and 1980s and on the whole these groups have been experiencing a deteriorating quality of life. There are local policy initiatives directed at some of the problems with which these groups have to cope, but here most local authorities, rightly or wrongly, claim that they have little room for manoeuvre. More basic policy shifts, aiming at structural improvements in the quality of life of under-privileged groups, tend to be hard to accommodate within the mainstream thinking and actions of the 'neo-conservative' national governments that dominate the scene in Western Europe and are more attuned to the caprices of the economics of capitalism.

Thus modern urban life increasingly represents non-work life, but it does so in very different ways and with distinct meanings for different groups, denoting a growing social inequality. Local policy efforts to remedy this are confronted with restraints imposed by national governments and demanding investors. There is pressure, sometimes not wholly acknowledged, to restrict these policies to the treatment of symptoms, not the symptoms of the underprivileged groups themselves, but preferably the symptoms that disturb social order and have a damaging effect on the image of a city. Thus male youth is a favourite target group for local policy initiatives, while women and the elderly are largely forgotten. So far the implications of the ageing of the population in most larger cities, or specific parts of these cities, for the use of all sorts of leisure facilities have not been discussed systematically. Nor do we know of examples of concrete policy initiatives that anticipate this development. The decarceration of the elderly and the mentally ill into the community raises important policy issues not only about their quality of life but also about the nature and provision of leisure in the urban process.

This brings us to the third factor in the decision to focus on this set of issues: the need to evaluate leisure policy in the light of the postwar development of welfare policies and the changed economic and political circum-stances in Western Europe. The particular model of welfare policy adopted in the liberal democracies of Western Europe varies considerably, but together they represent instruments to mediate unequal market opportunities in access to consumption services, such as education, housing, medicine, cultural, and leisure provisions. In recent years welfare policies in much of Western Europe have been subject to attack, particularly from neoconservative governments which have proclaimed a renewed belief in the liberating power of the market. This provides a highly relevant background for the contributions in this collection, raising as it does questions about whether 'rolling back the state' and the privatization of all kinds of leisure facilities really provide increased leisure opportunities for all.

The fourth element of the rationale for focusing on urban leisure policy is attention to the process of 'individualization' or the 'differentiation of lifestyles'. This process has different sources, of which the division of labour is the most widely discussed in social analysis. Since the Industrial Revolution, cities in Western Europe have been subject to physical and industrial restructuring as a consequence of economic developments. Along with this there has been a continual creation and decline of geographical and occupational- or industry-based communities. In the past few decades these processes have been intensified by welfare policies that were intended to create an altogether more flexible and mobile workforce. Housing policies have generated new and more diverse living conditions, as city plans unfolded into industrial and commercial zones, housing estates, recreational areas, and transport channels. The car allowed more geographical mobility and the extension of the educational system was thought to provide more social mobility. Health care and social security made people less dependent on their employers, relatives, and/or neighbours in times of misfortune. The 'expressive' revolution of the 1960s corroded traditional values surrounding music, art, literature, and sexuality; the boundaries of style and taste were redrawn and developed new opportunities for commercialism and distinctive consumption.

Thus both economic developments and different forms of policy feed the process of individualization by the differentiating effects they produce in everyday life. This demands adjustments in policies and economic strategies, for instance in fine-tuning regulations and marketing plans for ever smaller and well defined target groups. The increase in leisure opportunities also contributes to this differentiation process. But at the same time, individual-ization undermines forms of leisure that can only exist in localized community networks, and threatens those forms of leisure that require a particular group of people meeting collectively on a regular basis.

From a policy perspective the differentiation in leisure forms therefore implies two developments that demand attention. First, there is a shift in leisure forms, from soccer to jogging and from cinema-going to video-watching, which necessitates a restructuring of public leisure provisions and regulations in relation to the process of individualization and forms of private commercial leisure provision. Second, the question arises as to whether or not there should be some form of public life or public culture, accessible to all local citizens of the city; and if so, how this can be stimulated by local policies. This last question is particularly relevant in local politics. Is the city a product to be sold on the tourism market and/or as a location in which to invest money? Or is a city a place to live, where people can express themselves, even if it is in terms of resistance to, rather than rejoicing in, the dominant culture?

The aim of this collection is to contribute to comparative analysis in the leisure studies field, and, more precisely, to the topic of urban leisure policy. As such it represents the first stage, the raw materials for such analysis since each of the studies deals predominantly with aspects of policy development in a single nation state, and indeed most focus on specific urban localities.

Each of the chapters of this book has been written specifically for this collection. The interest of this group of authors in developing a collection of studies focusing on urban leisure policy from a comparative perspective derives first of all from the factors outlined above relating to the importance of urban leisure as a site of changing social and structural relations. In our view the subject certainly merits detailed research on urban leisure policy in single nation states or in single cities. It is hoped that one of the results of this collection will be in-depth analyses of urban leisure policy in such individual cases. However, there is also a recognition of the lack of comparative policy analysis in the leisure field, and the conviction that benefits accrue from such comparative analysis, in terms of both theoretical understanding and practical advocacy of policy.

The arguments for cross-national policy research are

well rehearsed in the public policy and social policy literature (Heidenheimer 1973; Rodgers 1980; Jones 1985). Although writers differ in emphasis the benefits and opportunities that are cited include a better understanding of policy within one's own country or city, and material for a discussion of the viability of different policy responses to defined problems. It then may be possible to find answers to the question of whether a certain policy response is more or less necessitated by circumstance, or is a matter of political choice. Of course, in the end it is to be hoped that comparative research delivers more generalized insights in the role of specific contexts, for instance in the shaping of urban leisure policies. However, the state of the art in the field of leisure policy research does not yet allow the more systematic approach which might provide such knowledge. One of the main problems one is immediately confronted with is the problem of conceptualization of the key terms such as urban, inner city, policy, and leisure.

PROBLEMS OF CONCEPTUALIZATION

As Van Moorst argues, with regard to the conceptualization of leisure the problem actually 'is not one of definitions or even concepts but of theoretical frameworks within which meaningful concepts can be developed' (Van Moorst 1982; 161). This, of course, also applies to concepts other than leisure, and the problem of conceptualization is more difficult to resolve in both theoretical and practical terms with the work of a group of authors of different national, language, disciplinary, theoretical, and professional backgrounds.

It should be clear that this text does not solve this problem. On the contrary, the reader will discover that this problem is once more underlined by this collection. Although each reader or reading always makes a 'translation', or an 'interpretation', of texts offered in terms of his or her own 'theoretical framework', in such a collection this interpretative work is complicated by the fact that individual chapters themselves imply different forms of interpretation of (presumably) different empirical realities. ('Presumably', because in the end it is an a priori assumption that national boundaries do make a difference in the making of urban leisure policies, and if so, these differences are important enough to merit a specific kind of research, that is 'comparative research'.) Thus each reader has to perform a double interpretation, or is part of a 'double hermeneutic', estimating, against the background of his or her own theoretical framework, the point of view of the different authors against their specific national, cultural and policy backgrounds. We will return to these methodological intricacies in our concluding remarks.

Having made this point, the editors still feel that by way of introduction to this collection, they should say something about its key concepts, to give the sympathetic reader some clue of what this book might be about. We will concentrate on the two most problematical concepts, 'urban' and 'leisure', and briefly discuss the ways they are most commonly used in this collection.

Most of the authors have not gone to great lengths to clarify what in their opinion constitutes a legitimate definition of 'urban' (or, for that matter, 'leisure'). Elsewhere different research traditions in urban studies have been discerned and discussed (Saunders 1981; Dunleavy 1982). Most authors in this collection more or less implicitly use a concept of the urban that does not belong so much to one or other of these research traditions, but combines elements of these various traditions. Thus, certainly in this collection as a whole, the urban appears as a multifaceted phenomenon, to which the spatial, the cultural, the political, and the economic are all important and defining dimensions.

The spatial dimension of the urban can be traced in the attention given to the locational factors that influence leisure patterns. It is important to note here that this collection covers a very wide range of urban locales, from middle-sized provincial towns (around 100,000 inhabitants) in the contribution of Jansen-Verbeke to capital cities like Brussels, Athens and London and urbanized areas like the Lille conurbation and the Randstad. What at first sight may seem to be national differences may very well be differences that have partly to do with the differences in spatial scale and structure of the urban system.

Most contributions, especially in Sections Two and Three, express a sensitivity to the particular distribution of facilities and/or the population in the city or urbanized area under inquiry, and links are made to the formulation and implementation of leisure policies. The contribution by Jansen-Verbeke criticizes a lack of awareness of the locational particularities in the development of local tourism marketing plans.

The cultural dimension of the urban can be traced in almost all the contributions. The attention paid to this dimension in this collection has several aspects. Culture, that is to say, 'high culture' in the form of large museums, opera houses, art galleries, and so on, is a typical provision or facility that is only thought to flourish in densely populated areas. But what role do these cultural facilities play in the attractiveness of city life in general or in that of a specific city, competing with other cities to attract new industries and well-to-do inhabitants? This question relates to two other aspects of the cultural dimension of the urban. One is the idea of a public culture (Sennett 1979); the other is 'urbanism as a way of life' (Wirth 1938). Although these aspects are not addressed directly, they do produce a backdrop to some of the contributions. For instance, in the papers of Bianchini, Papageorgiou, Hantrais, and Glyptis the theme of leisure is linked in various ways to the stimulation of forms of public life that are accessible to all citizens and not only the privileged. However, the reasons for a policy aimed at stimulating forms of public culture may vary from fears about the disintegration of local or ethnic communities, to the will to provide opportunities for the expression of different cultural identities, including those of disadvantaged groups. A prominent aspect of the urban way of life is the 'footloose' character of the urban population, as is the related process of increasing differentiation of the everyday lives of urbanites. A consequence of this process which now becomes clear and requires policy adjustments is described in the chapter by Rijpma and Meiburg, who note that, for example, there seems to be a shift from team sports to sports that can be practised on a less regular and more individual basis.

A third aspect of the cultural dimension of the urban is the sociocultural heterogeneity of urbanized areas, often closely related to socioeconomic inequality. The larger cities especially have concentrations of ethnic minorities, elderly and/or unemployed, which sometimes result in the existence of ethnic and/or unemployment subcultures. These subcultures form both constraints and opportunities for the development of satisfying leisure patterns, though this topic is not developed in this collection.

Although 'urban as culture' is ubiquitous in the book, it only finds its expression in the public sphere of leisure. This collection lacks any feminist analysis of traditional concepts of leisure or the leisure experiences of women living in the

7

inner city. Although authors touch on class, race, and gender dimensions and their implications for leisure, women remain hidden as elsewhere in history and in leisure. Approaches were made by the editors to potential contributors to secure a feminist contribution. Though these proved unsuccessful, it is important to acknowledge that this is a significant omission. Feminist analysis has and will have a great deal to contribute to a critical analysis of leisure in urban processes.

By convention, the urban can also be seen as a unit of policy. Two aspects of this policy dimension receive most attention. The first is the role of the local authorities in the mediation and implementation of national policies. A typical case is discussed in the chapter by Corijn, Danau, and Bollaert. They consider the significance of divisions in Belgium formed by the existence of two main linguistic communities who are incorporated into the state structure by sports policy in Brussels. They show how a cultural policy, which rests formally on a linguistic division, links with other diverse aspects of social relations in the process of mediation between central state policy and people seeking opportunities to participate in sport. The contribution by Corijn and Theeboom provides another Belgian example of creativity at the margins, when local authorities are left to develop their own forms of leisure policy. They discuss the role of the Antwerp local authority in the setting up of 'Kindervreugd', an organization that provides extra-curricular leisure activities for working-class children.

The second aspect of the policy dimension is the essentially economic role of local authorities concerning the exploitation of leisure provision and the use of the leisure infrastructure in the promotion of a positive city image. The tensions and potentially fruitful connections between the socioeconomic and sociocultural goals of urban leisure policy are discussed by Bianchini, and Mommaas and Van der Poel.

The city is also the location of consumption on a massive scale, both in the more restricted sense of shopping, cinema-going, and dining in luxurious restaurants, as well as in terms of the 'reproduction of labour', implying, amongst other things, the consumption of educational, welfare, and leisure services. Taken together, Sections Two and Three give various examples of how, in the urban context, production and consumption are intertwined. The contributions of Dietvorst and Rijpma and Meiburg focus on

changes in leisure patterns as a consequence of unemployment, which in itself is linked to the restructuring of
the economy. Glyptis and Haywood and Kew explore some of
the policy implications these changes could imply. Glyptis
discusses the programmes of sports provisions for the
unemployed which are premised on the notion that
unemployment is not a temporary phenomenon, and
therefore necessitates some adjustments in existing
provision. The contribution by Haywood and Kew goes one
step further and raises the question of whether leisure
policy should remain oriented toward the simple provision of
leisure opportunities. Behind their contribution lies the
question of whether, if labour ceases to be the main
principle of community organization, leisure could take over
this role. If so, what leisure forms might be conducive to
this end? They focus on the introduction of new types of
sports, instead of forms of organization or management, to
enhance the viability of 'community sports'. However, some
of the contributions in the third section make us aware of
the limited scope of these local policy initiatives, when we
relate them to their national, political, and economic
contexts, as is seen in the contributions of Dewailly and
Spink respectively. Spink makes abundantly clear that
leisure provisions have to compete in economic terms with
alternative allocations of capital and land, which might
secure higher profits. This economic process works
selectively against leisure facilities and activities. For
instance, it makes provision for leisure activities that need
vast areas virtually impossible in the inner city. Of course,
this process works selectively in the leisure patterns of the
urban population, as when certain activities are practised
predominantly by distinct urban groups. Jansen-Verbeke
adds another perspective to this by focusing on the attempts
of city boards to use their consumption opportunities as a
source of economic development, mainly through the
stimulation of tourism. It is now no longer unusual to see the
city as a tourist product, although on the level of local
policy this may still be more an expression of certain
political ideas than a coherent policy with practical
consequences.

In the final chapter, Mommaas and Van der Poel try to
draw together some of the threads spun out in the earlier
chapters and link them with recent debates on the themes of
gentrification, lifestyle, and the restructuring of the urban
landscape.

Introduction

Some may suspect that we are actually sidestepping the problem of conceptualizing the urban by giving the reader an impression of how the urban appears in the different chapters. It must be obvious that some of the approaches to the urban are not consonant with others, or may even be derived from more or less contradictory theoretical perspectives. As we see it, this is all part of the beginning of a debate, a natural starting point for the discussion of an emerging and relevant topic. In the history of the conceptualization of leisure one can trace similar developments which have still not resulted in agreement on the final characterization of leisure. Definitions and conceptual analyses of leisure abound in the literature, stressing features such as 'free time', 'freedom of choice', and 'pleasure in the experience'. However, in general most contributors to this collection would agree that such definitions of leisure are incomplete if they fail to take account of the social context within which leisure is defined, although they might disagree about what constitutes this social context. The notion of the contextuality of leisure none the less implies the recognition that there is no such thing as absolute freedom in leisure. Social and material resources and the prevailing figurations of legitimating and signifying rules to which the individual or group has access will mediate freedom to choose as well as to constrain leisure activities. Caution should therefore be exercised in arguing that those who do not spend time in labour (such as the unemployed, the elderly, the disabled) enjoy more leisure. People live in social relations in which 'legitimating rules' (Giddens 1976) qualify the amount and disposition of a person's or a group's time as free from the claims of relevant others. Obvious examples of this are the labour contracts which regulate the claims of the employer on the employee's time. Equally, however, notions of women's domestic labour in the household are significantly different from those of men working in paid employment. What is free time for men may be defined as committed time for women by the social rules that constitute and are constituted by roles within the household. Leisure for men is founded on and results in work for women. In addition to crucial issues of free time and freedom of choice, there is the matter of how such freedom is exercised and the quality of the experiences sought. In the liberal democracies of the West most people are allowed to choose leisure activities freely according to their wishes. They are not prescribed to do certain things, in certain places, at certain times, with some exceptions such as people in institutions such as prisons and asylums. But however free people feel they are, it is still necessary to see that this freedom is hedged by the prevailing distribution of resources and by rules which qualify activities as admissible or inadmissible pleasures, and which define those activities which may be legitimately pursued in their own right rather than for instrumental purposes, and which specifies by whom they may be pursued (Rojek 1985).

THE COMPOSITION OF THE BOOK

The book consists of three sections. The first incorporates chapters relating to the politics of the state and the development of leisure policies that aim to address urban problems. The purpose of this section is to consider the histories associated with the political espousal of specific leisure policies and to throw into relief the relative roles, influence, and rationales of (groups of actors within) the local and central state in developing specific leisure policies. The second section reviews case studies of particular initiatives, evaluating their rationales and assessing their impact on target populations. The final section focuses on the social, economic, and/or cultural context of leisure in urban environments. In this section leisure is seen both as a product of and a contributory factor in the development of urban processes.

In addition to the three sections, there is a final concluding chapter and a brief introduction to each of the sections which outlines the relationship between the constituent chapters and identifies the key themes of the section. The final chapter will raise some methodological and substantive issues that have arisen while working on this project. They may give some direction to future research.

Any book of this nature will invariably be selective in its treatment, giving scant consideration to some important issues and problems. This selectiveness is certainly not wholly coincidental and in part follows the structure of the leisure studies field as a whole. For instance, an effort has been made to draw on contributions from various national backgrounds in order to create a broader and more balanced geographical distribution. However, interested researchers and writers in the leisure studies field proved difficult to locate in the Mediterranean countries. Even in France and

Germany, where the leisure studies field is further developed, we found difficulty in contacting interested researchers in this field. We wonder how important the language barrier still is in this respect; the exchange between leisure journals of different language groups is also notoriously small.

Other reflections of the structure of the leisure studies field in the composition of this book can be traced in the leisure activities and the sections of the population that get most attention in this collection. Sports, outdoor recreation and tourism are well discussed, but relatively little attention is given to drinking and eating, gambling, fun-shopping, going to the cinema, gardening, do-it-yourself, volunteerism, amateur arts, watching television, and lots of other things people do in their spare time. Furthermore, hardly any consideration is given to the special position of the elderly, women, and children with regard to urban leisure. The fact is that their absence from the agenda of urban leisure policies is reinforced by their absence from analysis in this collection. However, this does not mean that their position does not warrant elucidation, evaluation and greater political commitment.

Although we may explain the selectiveness of this collection by reference to the existing structure of the leisure studies field, to the influence of contract research, and to other factors that are well documented in the literature on leisure, in the end this situation remains unsatisfactory. We do not expect this collection to be the last word on this topic, but rather the beginning of an ongoing and vital debate.

REFERENCES

Dunleavy, P. (1982) 'The scope of urban studies in social science', The Urban Perspective, Milton Keynes: Open University Press.

Giddens, A. (1976) New rules of Sociological Method, London: Hutchinson.

Heidenheimer, A. (1973) Comparative Public Policy, London: Macmillan.

Jones, C. (1985) Patterns of Social Policy, London: Tavistock.

Rodgers, B. (1980) Social Policy: A Comparative Approach, London: George Allen & Unwin.

Rojek, C. (1985) <u>Capitalism and Social Theory</u>, London: Tavistock.

Saunders, P. (1981) <u>Social Theory and the Urban Question</u>, London: Hutchinson.

Sennett, R. (1979) <u>The Fall of Public Man</u>, Cambridge: Cambridge University Press.

Van Moorst, H. (1982) 'Leisure and social theory', <u>Leisure Studies</u> 1 (2) May 1982.

Wirth, L. (1938) 'Urbanism as a way of life', American Journal of Sociology 44 (July).

SECTION ONE:
LEISURE, POLITICS, AND THE CITY

The first section in this collection analyses developments within the field of urban leisure and urban leisure policy, especially in the way both are linked to the changing political landscape of the countries concerned. In doing so, the contributions give an intriguing view of the changing themes and perspectives associated with leisure and leisure programmes within different political-ideological configurations.

What results is at first sight a bricolage of ideological associations in which, on a quite general level, 'leisure' seems to emerge either as part of a discourse on culture or as part of a discourse on welfare.

In the first case leisure is removed from the political agenda because culture is considered to be everyone's business, or, on the contrary, is put back on the political agenda because culture becomes part of the struggle over public representation and public power.

In the second case leisure is put on the political agenda to the extent that the parties concerned feel the state to have some responsibility for the redistribution of social resources. Leisure programmes are developed to give deprived groups of the population equal access to leisure facilities or to generate processes of community development and/or economic revitalization.

However, the dividing lines are not that clear, certainly not when we try to relate the different political labels associated with leisure with the conventional political perspectives as they have developed within the political spectrum of most European countries.

The contribution of Franco Bianchini deals with two cases of what is called a 'post-modern' leftist intervention in urban leisure (the period of the 'estates' policy in Rome under a communist local government during the late 1970s and early 1980s and the period of the 'representation' policy under a socialist local government in London during the early 1980s. Here we see leisure being taken up within a discourse on culture, predominantly taking place as reaction against a more conventional cultural policy of the left which, in practice, favoured highbrow culture and rejected commercially organized mass culture.

A new and younger generation, clearly associating itself with a more radical left policy has tried to tear down the barriers between elite forms of culture and commercially organized mass culture by stimulating popular events. Instead of trying to give disadvantaged groups better access to publicly organized 'high culture' facilities and using leisure as a means of community development, this generation operates through, not against, the private sector, proclaiming that the idea of a unified community is outdated.

In Greece, we learn from the contribution by Fouli Papageorgiou, following the end of the military dictatorship in 1974 and in the context of another socialist government, during the 1980s leisure is conceptually, linguistically, and in terms of policy linked to popular culture. While at the level of central government, interests are predominantly oriented towards projects with a more general cultural appeal, on the local level leisure is predominantly taken up as a means of community development. The rationale of socialist local governments is to see leisure as an important aspect of a more general quality of life, whereas communist-based local governments see leisure primarily as a way to integrate youth. However, there is agreement on the formation of leisure policy, which is seen as a corrective to more commercially organized leisure consumption.

The contribution of Linda Hantrais shows a socialist government coming into power in France during the early 1980s, and putting leisure (or rather free time) explicitly on the political agenda. This was a reaction against a more conservative governmental tradition which, in the ways it dealt with (or ignored) leisure, was considered to be paternalistic, stimulating highbrow culture as part of the 'cultural heritage'. This socialist government proclaimed a programme in which leisure, seen as a public good and a 'citizenship right', was associated predominantly with welfare-oriented policy objectives. During the short socialist honeymoon, urban leisure programmes were developed, either providing better access to facilities or using leisure as a vehicle for the social integration of youth. This policy was also pursued with the intention of preventing the private sector from gaining control over the leisure market.

A quite different picture of the political configuration within which leisure programmes are developed is described by Eric Corijn, Dominique Danau, and Livin Bollaert, who deal with sports policy in Brussels. It seems that leisure is taken up within a more general cultural policy in which conventional class-based political differences intermingle with regional and linguistic differences. This results in leisure programmes in which leisure appears predominantly as a vehicle for the preservation of cultural-linguistic identities. However, as is shown very clearly, it is better to say that existing cultural-linguistic differences are taken up within the realm of policy to sustain vested interests amongst different factions of the Brussels and Belgian state apparatus.

While it is much too soon to draw general conclusions, it might become clear from this section that urban leisure, far from being a politically neutral subject, is inherently connected to a wide range of political tensions and contrasts and to the ways in which these mediate existing socioeconomic differences. These tensions and contrasts concern different views regarding the role of the state in the changing relations between the private and public sectors; between highbrow, popular, and mass culture; between local and central government; and between vanishing and developing class factions.

CULTURAL POLICY AND URBAN SOCIAL MOVEMENTS: THE RESPONSE OF THE 'NEW LEFT' IN ROME (1976-85) AND LONDON (1981-86)

Franco Bianchini

INTRODUCTION

This chapter discusses the use of cultural policy[1] as a strategy of response to the emergence of new urban social movements in the case of two local authorities governed by the 'new left': the first is Rome City Council for the period during which it was controlled by the Italian Communist Party (PCI), from 1976 to 1985; the second is the Labour Greater London Council from 1981 until its abolition in 1986.

Each of the two case-studies is preceded by a discussion of traditional notions of culture and of the relationship between culture and politics prevailing within the PCI and the British Labour party respectively. In the discussion of the Italian case, the focus is on the 'Movement of 1977' and its influence on PCI thinking about cultural policy in Rome. The primary emphasis in the London case-study is on the development of new 'ethnic arts' policies by the Greater London Council, following the black uprisings of the spring and summer of 1981.

The conclusions assess the legacy of the cultural policy experience of the new left in both Rome and London and address the question of its influence on the national cultural policies of the PCI and the Labour party.

CULTURE, THE PCI, AND THE LEGACY OF THE <u>MOVIMENTO</u> OF 1977

In order to understand the significance of the cultural policy of the communist administration in Rome from 1976-85, it is necessary to contrast it with the nature of traditional approaches within the PCI. The attempt to create a socialist culture has been a prominent feature of PCI cultural policy since the war. The party's definition of the contents of socialist culture was based on a particular reading of Gramsci's concept of the 'national-popular', which was used by its author to denote an absence, that is the lack of correspondence between the idea of the 'national' and that of the 'popular' in Italian culture. Gramsci quoted as evidence of this the fact that in Italy 'popular reading habits - sentimental tales, detective stories, historical mysteries and so forth - were mainly catered for by foreign writers' (Chambers and Curti 1984: 101). As Forgacs points out, Gramsci's concept of the national-popular is 'an integral one, whose cultural and political faces overlap and fuse' (1984; 85). Gramsci stressed that a wholesale fusion of the cultural and the political dimensions of party strategy is necessary if the party (which Gramsci, by analogy with Machiavelli, defines as 'the Modern Prince') truly wants to be a 'collective intellectual' and truly wants to proclaim and organize an 'intellectual and moral reform'.

However, in the cultural policy developed by the PCI under the leadership of Palmiro Togliatti during the 1940s and 1950s, when Italy's economy was still predominantly agricultural, the national-popular was reduced to a merely 'cultural concept . . . a sort of slogan for forms of art that were rooted both in the national tradition and in popular life. . . . The concept was seen as involving a double terminological slide - national replaced international and popular replaced proletarian' (Forgacs 1984: 84, emphasis in the original), Gramsci's concept became the combination of two existing realities: the radical elements of national bourgeois high culture and the popular traditions of peasant life.

This approach carried three important implications: the idealization of the 'sturdy authenticity of "organic" rural communities' (Chambers and Curti 1983: 41); a bias against twentieth century popular culture; and a subordination of culture to the priorities decided by the party leadership.

Togliatti's use of the concept of the national-popular was part of the assimilation of Gramsci into the ideological tradition of Leninism. The notions of the party as a 'collective intellectual' and 'the Modern Prince' were reformulated to exclude the 'reciprocal relationship' between the party leaders and the masses that Gramsci had deemed necessary.

Togliatti's intervention against Il Politecnico (a journal founded in 1945 in Milan by novelist Elio Vittorini and other intellectuals who were either members or sympathizers of the PCI and who had tried, in some respects, to develop a national-popular culture in Gramsci's sense) was an example of how the party leadership reasserted its ideological primacy. Togliatti in 1946 condemned Il Politecnico (on whose history see Zancan 1984; Chambers and Curti 1984: 99-100; and Fortini 1973: 59-79) for making 'fundamental mistakes in its ideological orientation' (quoted in Zanotti 1979: 78, italics in original) and finally forced it to close in December 1947.

The changes in communist cultural policy during the 1960s and 1970s - in parallel with the PCI's adoption of a more pluralist political strategy - are embodied in the changing character of the Feste de l'Unita, (FdU), the party festivals launched in 1946 as a 'roughly ritualised, exclusive meeting of devotees' (Ferrara 1984: 122) and now oranized into a network of over 6,000 annual events covering the whole country except parts of the south. In the 1960s the communist microcosm of the FdU was 'opened up to youth groups and the middle classes' (Ferrara 1984: 123). Overtly oppositional practices such as the corteo (a militaristic parade from the festival site through the city) were dropped; by the 1970s 'Westerns and Pasolini films alternated schizophrenically on the screens of the FdUs. Television was everywhere' (Ferrara 1984: 124). Nevertheless, despite these transformations, commentators such as Chambers and Curti (1984: 109-110) were still able to argue that the root attitudes of the 1940s and 1950s towards mass culture, the 'organic community' and the 'primacy of politics' retained much of their force in communist thinking on the eve of the events of 1977.

In 1976, for the first time in 30 years, the PCI co-operated in the establishment of a Christian Democrat (DC) government through the unusual device of abstaining from a no-confidence vote. In July 1977 the party signed a formal 'Programmatic Accord' with the DC and the other parties giving external support to the DC National Solidarity government. Having seen the party's share of the vote rise steadily from 22.7 per cent in 1958 to 34.4 per cent in 1976, the PCI under the leadership of Enrico Berlinguer sought to establish and legitimize its claim to be 'a Party of government'. The party targeted control of inflation rather than reduction of unemployment as the primary goal of economic policy. The PCI and the CGIL (the largest, and communist-dominated, Italian trade union) persuaded the union federation to agree with the employers' organization Confindustria on the abolition of seven public holidays, along with other measures to increase productivity and some form of voluntary incomes policy. This focus on inflation rather than unemployment widened the gulf between the party and large strata of non-unionized youth (the unemployed, casual workers, and workers in the underground economy) that mainstream communist intellectuals like Alberto Asor Rosa (with his famous 'two societies' thesis) defined as 'marginals', as 'something else not only with respect to the official Workers' Movement, but also with respect to society' (Marazzi, in Lotringer and Marazzi 1980: 15).

It is against this background that the Movimento of 1977 developed. The Movimento has been aptly described as 'a confused but authentic expression of the alienation and despair of large masses of Italian youth, a protest against the climate of economic crisis and political conformism that marked the regime of National Solidarity' (Abse 1985: 30). It was profound hostility to the PCI's (and the CGIL's) collaboration with the Christian Democrat government that welded together the Movimento's different components: a unity against rather than for something.

The most significant political actions of the Movimento were acts of defiance against the new communist establishment: the driving away of CGIL leader Luciano Lama from the occupied University of Rome (February 1977), where he was trying to hold a rally; the occupation of the historic centre of Bologna (March 1977), the 'shop window of Italian Communism' (Ruscoe 1982: 103) and the town governed uninterruptedly by the PCI since 1946; the decision to hold in Bologna a 'Congress on Repression in Italy' (September 1977) to protest against the government's attempt (supported by the PCI) to destroy the Movimento by arresting a number of its leaders and activists and by closing down many of its press organs and radio stations.

The amalgamation of groups and movements that constituted the Movimento included student groups (who were suffering from increasing problems of lack of accommodation and who perceived the prospect of unemployment) and movements that found their umbrella organization in the Radical Party (feminists, conscientious objectors, greens, gay and lesbian activists). They acted in peculiar symbiosis with the small but influential Automomia Operaia Organizzata (AOO - also known as 'the armed party'). The Movimento dissolved on 2 December 1977, with

21

the staging of separate marches by the AOO and the nonviolent elements of the coalition. By virtue of the fragmentation of the latter, the well-disciplined AOO had managed until then to control most of the Movimento's assemblies and had used them to legitimize its own strategy of 'mass illegality and violence'. This is why the best-known history of the ten months during which the Movimento was active (February to December 1977) is one of urban guerilla warfare, with loss of life among both the Movimento's supporters and the security forces. (For an outline of the events of 1977 see Bianchini 1987.)

The dismissal of the Movimento as an utterly violent and negative phenomenon is common among communists. Berlinguer described the Bologna Congress on Repression as 'a gathering of plague spreaders' and defined the Movimento activists who drove Lama out of Rome University as '1919-style Neo-Fascists'. Even a communist 'dissident' like Luciana Castellina, when asked whether she thought anything positive came out of the movement, replied: 'Not really. Part of it went into drugs, which started to become a mass phenomenon. . . . In a sense it was the best elements who went into armed struggle' (in New Left Review,151 May-June 1985).

Two responses emerged from the Movimento to the post-1976 ideological crisis of the Italian left (which G. Jervis identifies as 'the crisis of the concept of political vanguard', in Monicelli 1978: 75). The first was certainly the nihilism of diffused terrorism and drug addiction: 'Better a dreadful end than an endless dread' (graffiti in the occupied University of Rome, cited in L'Espresso, 18 January 1987).

The second was a new emphasis on subjectivity, on direct and autonomous action for the satisfaction of individual needs and desires - a response alien to the ideology of austerity, sacrifices, and self-restraint elaborated by Catholic communist intellectuals as a theoretical justification of the PCI's support to the National Solidarity government. This second response embodied a truly subversive feature of the Movimento of 1977: its challenge to the subordination of culture to politics, sanctioned within the PCI by established notions of political organization and leadership. It was this second response that informed the development of cultural policy in Rome during and after the Movimento's career.

The Movimento was preceded by a mushrooming of left-wing youth cultural initiatives during 1976. A series of spring and summer concert festivals were staged, and an extensive network of free radio stations, publications, publishing houses, and workshops were established. On 29 November 1976, during the campaign for the depenalization of abortion, 50,000 women joined a torchlight procession through the streets of Rome, which ended in a giant happening featuring song recitals, dances and theatrical performances. As Chambers and Curti point out (1984: 113), 'others in the Movement consciously appropriated much of the repertoire of feminist public spectacle'. The 'Metropolitan Indians', for example, 'who adopted Red Indian manners of speech, dress and war paint to put across ironic, sarcastic, nihilistic reproofs to the established order' (Ruscoe 1982: 102) seem to have been inspired by the feminists who made up as witches and chanted ironic slogans during demonstrations. The 'Indians' were the most colourful element of the Movimento's nonviolent, 40,000-strong majority which - during the September Congress on Repression in Bologna - never set foot in the sports arena where the main strategic discussions (dominated by the AOO) were held. Instead, they peacefully occupied the city centre, where they conducted non-stop happenings, games, outdoor discussions, or simply smoked, slept, and sat around.

In short, the nonviolent, creative wing of the Movimento saw culture and politics as inextricable. There was no possibility of defining boundaries or priorities between the two. The culture that emerged from this element of the Movimento rejected universalizations, avant-gardes, and organic interpretations of the world. It shamelessly mixed capitalist mass culture (rejected by the radicals of 1968 and, broadly speaking, by the PCI) with concepts, images, and ideas borrowed from the past. It favoured the use of simulation, falsification, pastiche, irony, or downright nonsense and considered them as important political weapons.[2]

COMMUNIST CULTURAL POLICY IN ROME 1976-85

Rome was the city where the Movimento was strongest. It was the main basis of the women's movement, whose largest demonstration was organized in November 1976 by Rome's feminist collectives. It was the main basis of both the AOO and the 'Metropolitan Indians' who recruited especially among the students of the country's most overcrowded university, the unemployed or underemployed youth of the slum suburbs known as borgate, the casual and part-time workers of the city's chaotic public hospitals. It was, finally, the main basis of the Radical Party, which in the Camera elections of June 1976 polled in Rome 12.2 per cent of their entire national vote.

On 20 June 1976, the general election and the local elections took place simultaneously in Rome. In the city council elections the PCI was for the first time the largest party (35.5 per cent and 30 seats). It could form a new administration involving the Socialists (PSI) and the Social Democrats. The DC (33.1 per cent and 27 seats) were for the first time in 30 years in opposition.

Giulio Carlo Argan, an eminent art historian elected as a Left Independent in the PCI lists, became mayor. But the real leader of the PCI group on the council was Luigi Petroselli, under whose leadership the Rome Communist Party had often criticized the lack of internal democracy in the national party organization. Petroselli was unorthodox also in his choice of the assessori, the majority members in charge of the various council departments. For instance, he offered to Renato Nicolini (a 34-year-old Roman architect, one of the youngest and least experienced members of the new administration) a number of portfolios, including tourism, the regulation of bill-posting, parks, public gardens, the zoo, arts, entertainments, museums, and libraries. Nicolini decided to accept only the last four, and formed Rome's first ever assessorato alla cultura.

A PCI member since 1962, Nicolini had, by his own admission, 'the great advantage of not spending too much time in a party environment' (Nicolini 1986). He was, on the other hand, familiar with the culture of the Roman Movimento: the small experimental theatres of Trastevere, the independent cinemas, the free radio stations, the drawings of Andrea Pazienza and Pablo Echaurren, the humour of the new satirical magazine Il Male.

Nicolini shared with the groups working in Rome's alternative arts sector the rejection of the thesis of the centrality of the PCI, seen as the 'Modern Prince', the irreplaceable mediator between culture and society. In Nicolini's words, 'the Prince is obliged to become a vassal, a subject himself, a Prince without a crown who does not think of being a figure outside history' (quoted in Chambers and Curti 1984: 119).

He also shared with them a rejection of the distinction between high culture (e.g. sculpture, painting, theatre, opera, classical music) and low or popular culture (electronic music, television, commercial film, etc.)

One of the theories most often used to buttress this distinction was based on the following passage by Walter Benjamin: 'That which withers in the age of mechanical reproduction is the aura of the work of art . . . its presence in time and space, its unique existence at the place where it happens to be' (Benjamin 1973: 222-3, emphasis added).

Nicolini noticed in the Movimento arts groups a constant flow of communication and cross-fertilization between high and low, past and present, electronic and pre-electronic cultural forms (for instance, a new post-modern theatre had emerged which tried to renew a high art form through the use of revival, electronic media, and the language of low culture). In the wider field of the entertainment industry, he noticed phenomena to which Berlinguer's strategy - with its emphasis on austerity - had paid scant attention: the decline of the political song and the growing popularity - even among the left - of disco music; and the massive consumption of private TV programmes (especially Hollywood movies, pornographic films, American soaps and American-style chat-shows and quizzes) since the 1976 deregulation of broadcasting, and its influence on high forms of cultural production.

When in 1977 Nicolini launched an annual programme of urban animation called Estate romana ('Roman summer'), his intentions were, in PCI terms, 'unorthodox': he had uncompromisingly decided to work within low, popular, cultural forms: 'If we didn't, we would leave all that is fashion, all that is pleasure in the hands of growing private empires like those of Benetton and Berlusconi' (Nicolini 1986). However, by focusing his cultural policy in the summer ('the time of nobody', as novelist Ferdinando Camon has defined it,[3] Nicolini managed not only to obtain an unusually high degree of media coverage but also to present the Estate - both within his own party and to the outside world - in the orthodox language of welfarism: it was being organized by the council as a service provided to residents remaining in town between July and September, who surely were entitled to something better than 'an immobile landscape of closed cinemas and shut restaurants, abandoned to the heat' (Chambers and Curti, 1983: 41).

The general rule followed by the Estate organizers in their attempt at recreating Benjamin's 'aura' was to extend a relationship typical of the theatre to other cultural forms

25

so that the interaction of audience, time, place, situation and 'product' itself could produce a unique unrepeatable event. As G.R. Morteo has explained:

> Theatre, unlike any other . . . form of art, is not a product . . . but a relationship between components . . . it is valid only at a certain time, in a certain place, in a certain situation, in relation to certain actors and a certain audience (quoted in Gallingani 1928: 228, first two emphases added).

Once again, the lesson of the Movimento was important: the feminists and the 'metropolitan Indians' had shown through their happenings, masquerades, and dances how such a relationship could be extended from theatre not only to other cultural forms, but even to forms of political action.

The Estate's main answer to the competition of private television was the outdoor projection on huge screens of non-stop films through the night, in public monuments like the Basilica of Maxentius (1977-79), the Forum (1980), the Coliseum (1981), and the Circus Maximus (1982-84). The same film was never shown twice and the selection was done according to a theme, rather than genre or market criteria: the evening's programme could feature a cult movie followed by a Hollywood great, an Italian farce, and a thriller. The choice of programmes, the extraordinary setting, the enormous audiences, and the freedom of movement between the auditorium, side shows, amenities, and the rest of the city, all contributed to the uniqueness of the experience. Electronic music and television were subjected to a similar treatment: the latest trends in rock co-existed with 'conscientiously demodée styles of dance' (Petrone 1979: 16) in open-air ballrooms, while a 'city of television' invited people to play 'shoot-your-own-soap-opera' games.

The Estate's presence pervaded the whole city centre. 'The squares and streets are transformed into temporary spectacles, populated by theatre happenings, music and acrobatic shows' (Chambers and Curti 1983: 41). Bus services linking various focal points followed routes marked out by illuminated facades. Pedestrian streets, parks, and riverside walks were ingeniously lit. Nicolini, like the majority of the Movimento at the Bologna Congress on Repression of September 1977, preferred to occupy and change the existing city, rather than construct a new and separate one. He rejected, in other words, the model of the Feste de l'Unita (FdU), which usually takes place in a prefabricated city, erected by party volunteers in an enclosed space outside the town centre.

The typical FdU city contained several multi-purpose venues for entertainment; shows were picked up here and there, according to what was available on the market, and were mostly set in generic and decodified spaces. The Estate, on the other hand, featured several 'cities within the City', each of them identified with one precise cultural form (film at the Circus Maximus, dance at Villa Ada, and so on).

' "Putting on your badge" is the rite of entry into the FdU' (Ferrara 1984: 127). The Estate, on the contrary, 'carried no distinctive badge or explicit markers' (Chambers and Curti 1983: 127). The city council devolved the day-to-day organization of events to ad hoc co-ops (formed within Rome's alternative arts sector) and kept for itself only an almost invisible function of overall co-ordination.

There are many reasons for the Estate's popularity. The city centre became a focus of aggregation: this was essential to reconstruct a civic identity encompassing both proletarians from the alienating borgate and the bourgeois residents from districts like Parioli. Rome's night-time economy was revitalized: 'restaurants, pubs, ice cream parlours . . . boutiques, piano bars, jazz, disco and theatre clubs all mushroomed during the summer, employing mostly young people' (Bianchini 1987b: 15). Finally, the Estate was a response to two phenomena embodied in the Movimento of 1977: the rise of culture as an autonomous item on the agenda of politics and the crisis of the left's post-1968 ideology and militancy (the riflusso, 'ebb-tide'). Nicolini's initiative had something to offer to the protagonists of both 1977 and 1968: it was in tune with the cultural demands and language of the first and gave the second the chance, at last, to enjoy a culture previously rejected as capitalist and commercial. As M. Felicori has pointed out, the Estate was 'the public staging of the riflusso. The riflusso is a defeat. By staging it in public, a whole generation (the left protagonists of 1968 and 1968-1976) succeeded in being protagonists . . . even in defeat' (1984: 152).

The Estate's success probably contributed to the consolidation of the PCI's relative majority on 21 June 1981, when the city council of Rome (along with those of Genoa, Bari, Foggia, and Ascoli Piceno, and the regional assembly

27

of Sicily) came up for re-election. The PCI's share of the poll grew by 0.6 per cent in Rome (from 35.5 to 36.1), while it fell by 0.8 per cent in Ascoli Piceno (from 25.6 to 24.8), 7.5 per cent in Foggia (from 22.9 to 15.4) and 8.9 per cent in Bari (from 24.8 to 15.9).

Nicolini's own preference vote rose from 4,000 to 33,000 and was inferior only to that of Petroselli. In June 1983 the assessore alla cultura became an MP. He obtained the third largest number of preferences among PCI candidates in Rome's electoral college, being preceded only by Berlinguer and Pietro Ingrao, the leader of the PCI's new left.

By 1982 all city councils in the 'red belt' (i.e. the regions where the PCI was predominant - Emilia-Romagna, Tuscany, Umbria, and the Marches) had set up their own assessorato alla cultura (Felicori 1984: 179). The expenditure on entry 409 of city councils' budgets (from which the resources to fund programmes of cultural animation are drawn) grew in real terms between 1980 and 1982 by 69 per cent in the red belt, and by 30 and 36 per cent respectively even in DC-dominated areas: the 'white belt' (Trentino-Alto Adige, Friuli-Venezia Giulia, Veneto) and the Mezzogiorno (Latium, the southern regions, Sicily and Sardinia) (Felicori 1984: 174). Most of such increases were used in the organization of Estati based on the Rome model.

Despite these successes, the Estate had obvious limits. It was an imaginative intervention in cultural consumption, but it neglected the aspects of production and distribution. It was dubbed effimero (ephemeral) by supporters of cultural policies aimed at creating permanent structures (libraries, museums, arts centres, etc.) It was finally destroyed by a violent wrangle between the two main partners in the council's ruling coalition, the PCI and the PSI, over the use of historic monuments for mass cultural events. This contributed to the defeat of the left administration at the 1985 local elections and to the return of the DC to power. Its greatest, longer-term importance is likely to be found in the way it succeeded, in at least three respects, in translating into public policy the Movimento's challenge to established notions of the relationship between politics and culture:

1. It widened the notion of culture in which politics could intervene, to include elements of what had until then commonly been written off as low or commercial culture.

2. It raised - temporarily, at any rate - the status of culture on the agenda of politics.
3. It replaced 'an ideal institution ("culture", the "organic community", the political party) by a project that is willing not only to acknowledge how culture is produced but also the accelerated passages of its multifarious consumption' (Chambers and Curti 1983: 41).

CULTURE AND THE BRITISH LABOUR PARTY 1945-1981

The mainstream British Labour Party view of political culture was - unlike the PCI's - based on the analysis of 'general political orientations rather than class consciousness' (Jessop 1974: 49). Perry Anderson exemplifies this attitude as follows:

> There are two prevailing styles of discussion [in the Labour Party] . . . the first is that of the Labour Right, and of percentage psephology generally. In this perspective, the task of the Labour Party is to win over the necessary fraction of votes from the Conservative Party to win each election as it comes up: usually around 3 per cent or 4 per cent. The consequence of this approach is invariably to emphasise the need for prudence and moderation, to win over a floating middle-class vote, which would take alarm at any radicalism. . . . .Counterposed to this is normally a Left Wing approach . . . it calls for a humanist view of people and society, and a radical appeal to their altruism and intelligence as well as their immediate self interest. The two approaches are apparently extreme opposites. But in fact they share a fundamental abstraction. Whether society is seen as a quantum of electors . . . or [as] "common people" versus "the interests" or "the monopolies", its concrete, determinate reality in either case vanishes (Anderson 1965: 259).

Neither the Labour right nor the Labour left, in the period 1945 to 1981, saw the need for elaborating a socialist culture. Raymond Williams could conclude in 1981 that 'through the [Labour] movement's struggles, the working class has made major gains towards its traditional objectives but . . . within a capitalist culture (Williams 1981: 31).
As I have written elsewhere:

Labour became part of a consensus which attributed a civilising, political neutral value to culture, seen as the product of individual genius. The party's policies reflected this notion. They concentrated on pre-electronic, pre-20th century forms, disdained commercialism, were suspicious of technological change (Bianchini 1987a: 59).

The first feature of Labour's relationship with culture in the postwar period - what Pearson (1982: 69) calls the 'erasure of politics' - was embodied in the chief instruments and guidelines of arts policy in Britain: the Arts Council of Great Britain (ACGB) and the 'arm's length principle'. The main thrust behind the creation of both institutions had come from quarters closer to the Liberal Party than to Labour.

The ACGB, set up in 1946, was the institutionalization of a wartime experiment: the Council for the Encouragement of Music and the Arts (CEMA), from which the ACGB took its chairman, Lord Keynes. The 'arm's length principle' was a device that was supposed to insulate the ACGB from political pressure. ACGB members were chosen (until 1965 by the Chancellor of the Exchequer and then by the Arts Minister) 'as persons with a particular knowledge of, or a concern for one or more of the fine arts' (ACGB 1956: 14). The Arts Minister is not accountable to Parliament for the ACGB's decisions about funding.

If the first feature of the consensus described above (the depoliticization of culture) was passively accepted by Labour in power, the second (the bias towards high art forms and against twentieth century commercial culture) was actively constructed by the party's cultural policy (both in power and in opposition) since 1945. This was nowhere more apparent than in Labour's music policy. The only effective interventions by Labour governments in ACGB policy were in support of opera rather than the music traditions of the Labour movement (brass bands, the music hall, folk, and choral music). In the 1945-51 Labour government Chancellors Dalton and Cripps both made 'a special case' for opera by earmarking for the Royal Opera House at Covent Garden part of their grants to the ACGB (10.6 per cent in 1946 and 15.8 per cent in 1948) (Hutchison 1982: 20). In 1959 the party's policy statement Leisure for Living praised them for doing so, and went on to declare that public policy's main concern 'must be with the sort of music that is not usually regarded as "popular" '. In 1962, finally, the music programme of the party's own 'Festival of Labour' included jazz, the Ipswich Co-operative Girls' Choir, and a concert by the Philharmonic, conducted by Giulini. But, as Mulgan and Worpole point out, 'the festival - designed to present Labour's modern image for the 1960's - made no concession to youth culture, skiffle, beat or rock and roll' (Mulgan and Worpole 1986: 63).

Central government cultural policy in postwar Britain was - until the coming to power of Margaret Thatcher's Conservative government in 1979 - fundamentally bi-partisan. The main difference between the two major parties was Labour's higher spending on the arts and greater welfarist emphasis on access to a narrowly defined culture. The average yearly increases in real terms of the parliamentary grant-in-aid to the ACGB were 14.2, 14.7 and 7.3 per cent respectively under the Labour governments of 1945-51, 1964-70 and 1974-79. They compare with 9.5 and 12.6 per cent increases under the Conservative governments of 1951-64 and 1970-74, and with a 1.6 per cent decrease during the first two years of the Thatcher government (1979-81).

There were, however, exceptions to Labour's acceptance of the postwar consensus on cultural policy. The most important were two Arts Ministers coming from Labour's left (Jennie Lee, 1965-70, and Hugh Jenkins, 1974-76) and the party document The Arts and the People (1977), prepared by a left-controlled Arts Study Group of Labour's National Executive (NEC). They seem to be, however, isolated accidents of history rather than part of the Labour left's political strategy.

The cultural policy of Jennie Lee (Britain's first Arts Minister) was, first of all, Labour welfarism at its most radical. Her attempt at widening the audience of culture included a strategy of decentralization (she encouraged the establishment of Regional Arts Associations in England and independent Arts Councils for Scotland and Wales) and the development of a 'Housing the Arts' programme. Her 1965 White Paper (A Policy for the Arts: the First Steps) shows, however, that she had also grasped the need for widening the concept of culture itself:

Diffusion of culture is now so much a part of life that there is no precise point at which it stops. Advertisements, buildings, books, motor cars, radio and tele-

31

vision, magazines, records, all can carry a cultural aspect (Labour Party 1965: paragraph 71).

The ACGB, under the Arts Minister's pressure, admitted in 1967 jazz and photography to the canon of culture worthy of public subsidy. By 1970, when Labour lost power, Jennie Lee had achieved a certain redistribution in the allocation of ACGB resources. An 88.7 per cent increase in real terms in the government's grant to the ACGB allowed the Arts Council to reduce without cuts in absolute terms opera and ballet's share from 48.9 per cent (1963-64) to 28 per cent (1970-71), and to increase the portion for 'Arts Associations, Art, Festivals, Literature, Experimental Projects' (from 4.4 per cent to 11 per cent), for Scotland (from 6.4 per cent to 10.8 per cent), and for Wales (from 5.1 per cent to 6.1 per cent) (ACGB 1971: 20). But it was impossible for Jennie Lee to go further than this without undermining the 'arm's length principle'. Labour Prime Minister Harold Wilson made sure that a provision to safeguard the ACGB's independence was included in the 1965 White Paper: 'The Council will continue to enjoy the same powers as they have exercised hitherto and will in particular retain their freedom to allocate the grant-in-aid made available to them' (Labour Party 1965: paragraph 78).

Arts Minister Hugh Jenkins, appointed by Wilson in 1974, was replaced two years later by new Prime Minister James Callaghan with the moderate Lord Donaldson of Kingsbridge, who in 1981 was to defect to the newly formed Social Democratic Party (SDP). Jenkins' determination to carry out two pledges of Labour's October 1974 manifesto collided with the party leadership's intentions. The first was his campaign not to exempt art property from a wealth tax applicable to all those with incomes exceeding £100,000. By his own admission, Jenkins had not realized that 'the Labour leadership's enthusiasm for the tax itself was vanishing' (Jenkins 1979: 148). By the end of 1975 the ACGB, the art owners' and dealers' lobby, most of the press, his civil servants, some Labour colleagues and Prime Minister Wilson himself were all against him.

His second failed endeavour concerned the October 1974 Labour Party Manifesto pledge 'to make the Arts Council more democratic and representative of people in the arts and in entertainment' (p.16). As a modest starting point, Jenkins proposed to ACGB Chairman Lord Gibson that the council's Drama and Literature Advisory Panels should be invited to elect their own chair, whom the Arts Minister could then appoint to the ACGB itself. This proposal met with total defiance from Gibson, who knew that, after the wealth tax saga, Jenkins' days were numbered.

Lord Donaldson, Jenkins' successor, was a staunch upholder of the 'arm's length principle' and, more generally, of the 'nonpolitical' tradition of arts policy in Britain. His views were in sharp contrast with The Arts and the People, an NEC statement approved at the 1977 Labour Party conference. This was based on a wider document with the same name which - although largely ignoring 'the electronic and commercial forms of culture ... and [confining] ... its arguments to the more traditional notions of "art" ' (Mulgan and Worpole 1986: 29) - had something new (in Labour Party terms) to say on the relationship between politics and culture:

> The arts are politically important. Their funding and administration are as dependent on political decisions as housing, education, defence or any other function of government. ... Politics are inextricably sewn into the fabric of the arts. At present we have an arts policy through which the most heavily subsidised arts are catering for a predominantly middle-class audience. ... The effect of such a policy is political, to favour one area or one type of artistic preference against another (Labour Party 1977: 5-7).

Both Jenkins and The Arts and the People were, in a sense, products of the Labour left which, however, failed as an organized political force to break Jenkins' isolation during the 1974-76 Wilson government or to start an internal party debate on the profound divergence between The Arts and the People and Lord Donaldson's cultural policy. The Arts and the People, for instance, proposed the unification, under a single ministry, of cabinet status of responsibility for the arts (to be taken away from the Department of Education and Science), film (from the Department of Trade and Industry), and broadcasting (from the Home Office) - a reform to which Lord Donaldson was utterly opposed.

The fundamental problem with Labour's left was its economism: most of its energies were absorbed by the economic policy debate. After Wilson's electoral defeat in 1970, the increased control of the party's policymaking by the left led to the elaboration of Labour's Programme 1973, whose most controversial proposals concerned industrial policy. As in the case of the PCI, 'first there were the political and economic questions to be faced, and only later art and ideology' (Chambers and Curti 1984: 100).

LABOUR ETHNIC ARTS POLICY 1981-86

The term ethnic arts was introduced in 1976 by Naseem Khan in The Arts Britain Ignores (1976) to describe the arts of Britain's immigrant communities, both black and white. In its policy document The Arts and the People, the Labour Party espoused Khan's ethnic pluralism by describing 'arts for ethnic minorities' as part of 'community arts' and by stressing their importance 'in building up a unified and harmonious neighbourhood' (Labour Party 1977: 57, emphasis added).

Labour's notion of the role of ethnic arts implied the political neutrality of mainstream British culture, and reflected the abstract view of political culture - common to both left and right within the party - described by Perry Anderson (see p.29). In Stuart Hall's words:

> the [Labour] Party has this notion that the experience of the working class is an undifferentiated one, that there is a kind of automatic unity, in which blacks will love whites . . . everybody will love everybody else, and the Labour Party will be able to speak on behalf of this already united popular set of constituencies (Hall 1985).

A consequence of this attitude was Labour's dislike of blacks' autonomous forms of political and cultural activity. As Raymond Williams has observed, 'the [Labour] movement's political institutions are uneasy about any kind of action to change social conditions which is not regulated by them' (Williams 1981: 29).

By 1982 - after the previous year's uprisings by black youths in London, Bristol, Liverpool, Manchester, and other cities - even Thatcher's conservative government was ready to join the national consensus on community arts and ethnic arts as vehicles of social integration. Environment Secretary Michael Heseltine appointed 'community arts specialists to redevelop those "harmonious neighbourhoods" shattered in the urban riots' (Tomkins 1982: 1).

In April 1986 the Thatcher government abolished the Greater London Council (GLC), the local authority respon-

sible for integrating and co-ordinating the services of the 32
London Borough Councils. Over the previous five years, the
GLC had, according to Stuart Hall, shown 'how a radical left
administration can positively identify itself with popular
cultural life, and feed into itself some of the energy
generated' (Hall 1984: 39).

The Labour Party had taken control of the GLC with
the elections of 7 May 1981, less than a month after police
repeatedly clashed with black youths in the streets of
Brixton, in the London Borough of Lambeth (10-12 April).
The party leader was moderate Andrew McIntosh, who was
replaced immediately after the elections by left-winger Ken
Livingstone as leader of the council.

The new administration created an 18-member cabinet,
the Policy Committee, to 'co-ordinate the work of the other
committees and settle the order of priorities of the various
policies' (GLC 1981: 92). Two-thirds of its membership
consisted of Livingstone's allies on the left of the party,
aged between 25 (Valerie Wise) and 37 (Tony Banks).
Livingstone himself was 36.

Livingstone's GLC broke away from the tradition of
previous Labour administrations in all fields, including
cultural policy. Before 1981, the latter was a remarkably
noncontroversial and unimportant area. The Council lacked
a competent arts staff of its own and its committee in
charge of cultural policy (the Recreation and Community
Services Policy Committee) was a political backwater. Its
role was fundamentally limited to supplementing Arts
Council funding to the 'Big Four' (the National Theatre, the
English National Opera, the London Orchestral Concert
Board, and the London Festival Ballet), maintaining and
managing the Concert Halls on the South Bank (the Arts
complex between Waterloo and Westminster Bridge, on the
south side of the Thames), and providing entertainment in
parks (usually brass bands).

In 1981, the new GLC set up an Arts and Recreation
Committee (ARC). In the words of its first chair, Tony
Banks (1981-83), it was a 'dynamic Committee, with people
who were senior in the [Labour] group, who had some
political muscle' (interview with the author, 29 May 1985).

Cultural policy ceased to be a neutral area of the
Council's activity. The new Labour majority aimed all its
policies (including those on culture) at constructing a
political base no longer centred around the declining
industrial working class.

35

In terms of cultural policy, the central concept was that of representation. Banks' policy advisor Alan Tomkins rejected the mainstream Labour view of community as a 'unified neighbourhood'. He argued that 'major changes [in the post-war period] such as unemployment, continuous inner city redevelopment, immigration and the rise of the nuclear family' (Tomkins 1982: 3) had made it irrelevant and even hypocritical since its 'bourgeois democratic "general interest" . . . masks the true class, race, gender, age, politics'. Instead, he preferred to speak of communities of interest, such as 'black groups, Irish, Greek or Turkish communities, the unemployed, women's groups, etc. (ibid.). His notion of community arts therefore had 'as its central core the production, the celebration of working class, women's, black, youth histories' (ibid., p.5). In other words, he wanted to promote a new 'politics of representation'. 'Representation is not just a matter of parliamentary democracy, it is one of the principal means through which the cultural and political configurations of a social formation are historically produced' (Tomkins 1982: 5).

The GLC's ethnic arts policy was backed at an officers' and members' level respectively by an Ethnic Minorities Unit (EMU, directed by Herman Ouseley) and an Ethnic Minorities Committee, chaired by Livingstone himself.[4] They had both been established (along with a Police Committee chaired by Paul Boateng, the only black Labour councillor) as a first response to the Brixton riots of April 1981. In May 1982 (after new black uprisings in Southall, Hackney, and other London districts in July 1981) Ouseley convened at County Hall (the seat of the GLC) a public consultative conference on ethnic arts, attended by about 250 representatives of mainly Asian and Afro-Caribbean arts groups.

One of the demands of black cultural practitioners arising out of the conference was the institution of independent policy-making and grant-allocating structures. An Ethnic Arts Subcommittee was thus created within the main ARC in September 1982. It consisted of three ARC members and up to 17 advisory members, mostly drawn from participants to the May conference. Majority party members normally voted according to the recommendations of the majority of the advisors. The Subcommittee was endowed with an independent budget of £400,000 (which by 1985-86 had grown to over £2 million) and with a Race Equality Unit (REU), set up at officers' level within the Arts Department.

The REU's principal achievements during its approximately 40 months of activity (September 1982 - March 1986) were:

1. the consolidation and expansion of London's black arts sector (some new groups, particularly in the independent film sector, were established virtually through GLC funding)
2. the launch of various high-profile initiatives (such as a Black Theatre Season, a festival of Third World cinema and The Black Experience, a London-wide programme of exhibitions, seminars, and performances held in February and March 1986)
3. the sponsorship of training courses for black people on arts administration, journalism, film, and video
4. the organization of a spring festival of black culture on the South Bank and the co-ordination of the arts elements of one of the GLC's main campaigns: 'London Against Racism' (1984)

The Ethnic Arts Subcommittee and the REU were innovative in their attempts at forging

> new concepts and new traditions . . . which embrace both the Afro-Caribbean, Asian and other origins of the black experience and its present reality in 20th century Britain. . . . This means developing a new aesthetics which is not 'traditional', 'ethnic', 'folk', 'exotica', but which is appropriate for what needs to be expressed here and now (GLC 1984: 2).

Accordingly, they funded contemporary cultural forms, such as pop music, community radio, video, and photography, traditionally neglected by Labour cultural policy.

The financial strategy they used was, however, an orthodox one: as in the case of the ACGB and of most other Labour local authorities, grants were given on the basis of year-by-year 'deficit funding'. This approach was explicitly rejected by the GLC's Industry and Employment Committee (IEC). Nicholas Garnham, professor of Communications at the Polytechnic of Central London, developed for the IEC a new 'cultural industries' strategy, based on a sharp critique of the deficit-financing model.

His arguments (see Garnham 1983) had a considerable impact on the Economic Policy Group (EPG), a small unit of economists responsible for advising the IEC and elaborating a new industrial strategy for London, whose principal officer wrote in 1984:

> Public sector involvement in cultural activities . . . has tended to be directed towards those activities which can rarely be commercially viable . . . while most people's cultural needs have continued to be met through the market. One result of this is that public policies have tended to have a relatively marginal impact on what cultural commodities and services are actually consumed. . . . For the public sector to have an influence . . . on 'culture' in its broadest sense, intervention musst be directed through and not against the market (GLC 1984a: 1, emphases added).

More specifically, the EPG proposed in 1985

> different forms of finance investment through loans and equity rather than grant-aid and deficit-financing - to break the relationship of dependence which subsidy and grant always imply . . . which tends to make funding bodies appear to serve performers and producers rather than the general public (GLC 1985: 171).

A cultural industries unit was thus created within the Greater London Enterprise Board (GLEB), an agency for strategic intervention in London's industry established by the IEC in 1981. The unit's task was 'to develop projects in such a way that they can be supported as viable enterprises' (GLC 1984: 10). It provided finance and ' "common serices" typical of the commercial sector - management consultancy, marketing, advice on the introduction of new technology' (Bianchini 1987c: 112) to various enterprises, including a black publishing house (Bladestock Publications). This added to previous IEC investments in black cultural industries (the Brent Black Music Co-op, for instance, had received over £259,000 between 1982 and 1984).

The GLC's cultural policies for blacks, as those for other targeted social groups (women, the Irish, gay men and lesbians, 14- to 18-year-olds, the unemployed, elderly, and disabled) were part of the Council's attempt at 'rooting itself in the everyday experience of popular urban life and culture' (Hall 1984: 39).[5] This social targeting was accompanied by a strategy aimed at revitalizing the use of public spaces in the city, in many ways similar to Nicolini's:

> The subsidising of popular entertainment and public occasions on the open access principle: the use of its [the GLC's] sites and hoardings in the city to publicise radical themes and demands, . . . the use of the parks as active centres linked with the general renovation of cultural life, the free concerts, even the diversity of music sponsored . . . classical music, jazz, advanced rock, black gospel music - these and many other examples could be quoted of how cultural life can be reconstructed as a site of politics (Hall 1984).

It is not hard to see how the GLC's initiatives on ethnic arts (and, more generally, on culture) between 1981 and 1986 contradicted the principal assumptions of Labour's postwar cultural policy:

1. Culture, far from being a neutral area, had become an important site of politics.
2. Popular twentieth century cultural forms, far from being considered as marginal or low, were the focus of policy making.
3. commercial culture, instead of being left entirely to the private sector, became - for the Industry and Employment Committee, if not for the Arts and Recreation Committee - a model on which the State could base a major re-thinking of its whole intervention in the cultural sphere.

CONCLUSIONS

As suggested earlier, both the PCI and the Labour Party traditionally tended to conceive culture as a unified body of universal values, which was assumed to possess 'inherent values, of life enhancement or whatever, which are fundamentally opposed to and in danger of damage by commercial forces' (Garnham 1983: 1). As a consequence of this, both parties shared:

1. a certain bias against popular, commercial twentieth century cultural forms (often dismissed as mass or low culture)

2. an idealization of the organic community, namely Labour's 'unified and harmonious neighbourhood' (Labour Party 1977: 57) and the PCI's myth of the authenticity of peasant life

3. a tendency to subordinate culture to political and economic priorities

The new left directing the cultural policies of both the PCI-controlled 1976-85 Rome City Council and the 1981-86 Labour GLC broke away from these traditional notions. Its political and intellectual formation was shaped by the experience of a whole set of post-1968 emancipatory movements (feminism, youth and student movements, community action, environmentalism, pacifism, black and gay liberation, etc.) which broadly rejected the distinction between high and low culture. The cultural and the political were equally important, inseparable dimensions of their action.

The 'integrationalist' leadership of the Labour Party (both in power and in opposition) stressed the autonomy of culture: cultural policy issues were seen as less politically controversial than (and therefore as secondary to) issues around the economy, industrial relations, defence, and so on. Concessions were made to minority cultures in order to achieve their integration into a supposedly neutral national culture.

The 'hegemonic socialist' leadership of the PCI, on the other hand, recognized the importance of culture as a terrain of struggle, but emphasized the need for the primacy of politics, in other words, of the party leadership's ideological and political line. The new urban social movements' cultures embodied in the Movimento of 1977 had to be subordinated to the overall strategic priorities of the Prince-Party, and their requests for autonomy had to be opposed.

The new urban left in power in Rome and London, on the contrary, rejected the view of cultural policy as a vehicle for social integration, welcomed the fragmentation of the myth of universal culture into a plurality of countercultures and acknowledged the parallel crisis of political vanguards and artistic avant gardes. The new left's willingness to devolve power and its receptivity to external demands and ideas enabled it to build a constructive relationship with the new urban social movements. The cultural policies of the new left in Rome and London present, however, two distinct fundamental problems. In the Italian case, the Estate romana could be interpreted as the public staging of a defeat: the strategic and ideological crisis of the PCI in the late 1970s and early 1980s. Culture rose to such prominence in Italy's left politics because nobody believed in politics any longer.

In the British case, the GLC's cultural policy left unresolved the problem of how to create a collective will out of the aspirations and identities of a variegated 'coalition of the dispossessed'.

Rome and London have something to learn from each other: a GLC-style politics of representation and the creation of radical cultural industries could have strengthened the impact of Nicolini's policy; in the same way, the Estate romana's successful attempt to create a civic identity could have helped to weld together the various fragments of the GLC's political constituency and to involve individuals and social groups outside its boundaries.

Despite these shortcomings, the London and Rome experiences have had an important impact on the national cultural policies of their respective parties. Since January 1987, when Labour leader Neil Kinnock replaced Norman Buchan with Mark Fisher as Shadow Arts Minister, the party's cultural policy has had a distinct GLC flavour about it.[6] Tony Banks chairs the Arts Committee of the Parliamentary Labour Party, and Ken Worpole (formerly advisor to the GLC's Community Arts Sub-committee and director of GLEB's Cultural Industries Unit) is Fisher's policy advisor. Voices and Choices, Labour's Policies for the Arts and Media, published in May 1987, clearly shows the influence of the GLC's cultural industries strategy and of Saturday Night or Sunday Morning, written in 1986 by Worpole and his former colleague at GLEB, Geoff Mulgan.

In the case of the PCI, the relative success of the Estate romana has certainly contributed to effect a dramatic change in the party's attitude towards mass culture:

> Old prejudices and value judgements have been swept aside as Communists have sought to come to terms with, and to a certain extent make their own, the images, myths and suggestions that populate the universe of contemporary popular culture. ... This trend may be said to have reached a climax with the publication of Eroi del nostro tempo [Bari 1986], in

41

which a variety of intellectuals either in or close to the PCI explore the possible virtues of such popular media icons as Rambo, Rocky, James Bond and J.R. (Gundle 1987: 15).

Both parties are at present going through a deep identity crisis, in the aftermath of electoral defeats in June 1987. The Labour Party conference of September-October 1987 decided to launch a two-year exercise of thorough review of all the party's policies. It remains to be seen whether the policy review will integrate the radical principles of Fisher's cultural policy into mainstream Labour thinking on major aspects of economic and social policy. Today cultural policy is still a relatively isolated and secondary area. Labour's technically competent but ideologically weak 1987 general election campaign seems to confirm that Kinnock's leadership is readier to take on board the populist style rather than the radical content of the GLC's legacy.

A similar major re-thinking of political and strategic priorities is currently being proposed for the PCI by its deputy leader, Achille Occhetto. Electoral decline - constant since 1976 - and the process of 'secularization' of the party promoted by its leader Alessandro Natta have combined to produce a decline of the party's traditional self-confidence, symbolized by Togliatti and Berlinguer's ideas of the Prince-Party and of the existence of a distinct (and morally superior) 'communist culture'. The mood of uncertainty within the party can perhaps be illustrated with a statement by Fabio Mussi (then in charge of the PCI's Cultural Department) at a 1983 seminar on the Feste de l'Unita: 'The Feste carry with them a certain impulse of hegemony, if one really must quote Gramsci and is not afraid of the dirty word' (Mussi 1984: 11, emphasis added).

In this connection, the PCI's new-found enthusiasm for contemporary mass culture could be interpreted as 'an attempt to exploit the potential of the cultural terrain to compensate for a real and continuing loss of political authority' (Gundle 1987: 17).

In short, both the GLC and Rome City Council used cultural policy to foster values of participatory citizenship: to attempt to build a local alternative to the political culture promoted by the right (which is centred around notions of individual economic agency). Margaret Thatcher's Conservative government (which abolished the GLC in 1986) and the 1983-87 DC-dominated coalition government headed by PSI leader Bettino Craxi (which helped bring about the fall of the PCI-controlled Rome City Council at the 1985 local elections) seem to have realized the potential of such local ideological alternatives better than the national leaderships of both the Labour Party and the PCI.

NOTES

1. I shall use the term 'culture' (and 'cultural policy') to refer to all those social practices which have as their primary purpose the production and transmission of meaning (my definition is adapted from Garnham 1983). This comprises both pre-electronic culture (e.g. painting, sculpture, theatre, opera, classical music) and the forms dominating in contemporary commercial culture, where the boundaries between the moments of production and distribution are often blurred (e.g. design, electronic music, film and video, broadcasting, etc.).

2. Here is, for instance, a selection of 'Indian' slogans: 'After Marx, April'; 'Lama, you are a pipe' (directed at pipe-smoking Luciano Lama, the union leader contested at Rome University on 17 February 1977; Potere dromedario ('Dromedary power': an assonance with serious slogans such as Potere operaio, Workers' power, or Potere proletario); and Cossino assasiga. This last slogan, as M. Torrealta explains, 'attributes the epithet "murderer" (assassino) to [Francesco] Cossiga, the Minister of the Interior [currently the President of the Italian Republic]. Yet what is anathema here is not the insult, but the anagram' (in Lotringer-Marazzi (1980: 10).

3. In Il Giorno, 7 August 1980, quoted in Gallingani (1982; 297).

4. As I have observed elsewhere (Bianchini 1987c: 107), the concept of ethnic arts was 'associated with a philosophy of social integration which the GLC rejected.... The favoured term at the GLC became Black arts, capitalised to stress that it is a specific political and cultural identity that is at issue, rather than a mere colour.'

5. The utopia of the rural revival is also an important part of the ideological traditions of the British Labour Party. It derives from the ideas of William Morris (1834-95) and from Robert Blatchford's Merrie England (1893), one of the most influential books in the early stages of British socialism. For a description of the influence of 'the vision of

"Merrie England" ' on Labour intellectuals and politicians see Wiener (1981).

6. In his draft Charter for the Arts (1986), Buchan proposed the institution of a new Arts and Media Ministry, fully responsible over broadcasting policy, which is now part of the remit of the Home Office. In the ensuing conflict between Buchan and Shadow Home Secretary Gerald Kaufman, the latter prevailed. Neil Kinnock imposed an amendment to Buchan's Charter ('the statutory framework, including the responsibility for the Independent Broadcasting Act and the Licence Charter and Agreement of the BBC would remain with the Home Office') which was approved by Labour's NEC in January 1987. Buchan, who wasn't prepared to accept Kinnock's amendment, was forced to resign. The New Statement (23 January 1987) commented:

> The sacking of Norman Buchan transcended the air-waves. It underscored a conflict between outmoded attitudes and an awareness of new possibilities. . . . Of Mark Fisher it can be said that he looks a more likely candidate to fill the shoes of a new minister of Arts and Media. . . . Fisher and Banks get on well; important if the new shadow minister is to accommodate the populist post-GLC arts lobby within the Parliamentary Labour Party with the largely sedentary majority.

REFERENCES

ACGB (Arts Council of Great Britain) (1956) The First Ten Years: 11th Annual Report of the Arts Council of Great Britain, London: ACGB.
——— (1971) 26th Arts Council Annual Report, London: ACGB.
Abse, Tobias (1985) 'Judging the PCI' New Left Review 153, September-October.
Anderson, Perry (1965) 'Problems of socialist strategy', in P. Anderson et al. (eds), Towards Socialism, Ithaca: Cornell University Press.
Benjamin, Walter (1973) 'The work of art in the age of mechanical reproduction', in W. Benjamin (ed.) Illumin-ations, London: Fontana.
Bianchini, Franco (1987a) 'Review of "Saturday Night or Sunday Morning?" by G. Mulgan and K. Worpole', New Socialist, March.

—— (1987b) 'Living for the City', New Socialist, April.

—— (1987c) 'GLC/RIP cultural policies in London, 1981-1986', New Formations 1.

—— (1987d) 'Cultural policy and changes in urban political culture: the post-modern response of the Left in Rome (1976-85) and London (1981-86)', paper presented to the joint sessions of workshops of the European Consortium for Political Research, Amsterdam, April.

Chambers, Iain, and Curtis, Lidia (1983) 'Italian summers', Marxism Today, July.

—— (1984) 'A volatile alliance: Culture, popular culture and the Italian Left', in Formations of Nation and People, London: Routledge and Kegan Paul.

Felicori, Mauro (1984) 'Feste d'estate: indagine sulla politica culturale dei communi italiani', in A. Parisi (ed), Luoghi e Misure Della Politica, Bologna: Il Mulino.

Ferrara, Fernando (1984) 'The Feste de l'Unita', in Formations of Nation and People, London: Routledge and Kegan Paul.

Forgacs, David (1984) 'National-Popular: Genealogy of a concept', in Formations of Nation and People, London: Routledge and Kegan Paul.

GLC (Greater London Council) (1981) A Socialist Policy for the GLC, Minority party report, 3 March.

—— (1982) Conference on Ethnic Arts, 28 May.

—— (1984a) London Against Racism in Mainstream Arts Policies and Programming, C/AR 258, 16 March.

—— (1984b) Cultural Industries Strategy, IEC 1603, 18 June.

—— (1985) The London Industrial Strategy.

Gallingani, Maria Angiola (1982) 'Il tempo e il denaro: spesa pubblica e politica culturale a Bologna e Venezia', Il Mulino 280, March-April.

Garnham, Nicholas (1983) 'Concepts of culture, public policy and the cultural industries', paper presented at the Cultural Industries and Cultural Policy in London conference, London, Riverside Studios, 12-13 December.

Gundle, Stephen (1987) 'From Apocalittici to Integrati: the PCI and the culture industry in the '70s and 80s', AMSI Newsletter 11.

Hall, Stuart (1984) 'Face the future', New Socialist, September.

—— (1985) 'The gulf between Labour and blacks', Guardian, 15 July.

Hutchison, Robert (1982) The Politics of the Arts Council, London: Sinclair Browne.

Jenkins, Hugh (1979) The Culture Gap, London: Boyars.

Jessop, Bob (1974) Traditionalism, Conservatism and British Political Culture, London: Allen and Unwin.

Labour Party (1965) A Policy for the Arts: The First Steps.

—— (1977) The Arts and the People.

Lotringer, Sylvere and Marazzi, Christian (eds) (1980) 'Italy: Autonomia', Semiotext(e) 3 (3).

Monicelli, Mino (1978) L'ultrasinistra in Italia, 1968-1978, Bari: Laterza.

Mulgan, Geoff and Worpole, Ken (1986) Saturday Night or Sunday Morning? From Arts to Industry: New Forms of Cultural Policy, London: Comedia.

Mussi, F. (1984) Seminario Nazionale sulle Feste de l'Unita, Rome: PCI.

Nicolini, Renato (1986) Interview with author, 5 August.

Pearson, Nicholas (1982) The State and the Visual Arts, Milton Keynes: Open University Press.

Petrone, Francesco M. (1979) 'Tutta la citta ne parla', in Rinascita 27, 13 July.

Ruscoe, James (1982) The Italian Communist Party 1976-81, London: Macmillan.

Tomkins, Alan (1982) Community Arts Revisited, London: GLC C/Ar 4, 18 October.

Wiener, Martin, J. (1981) English Culture and the Decline of The Industrial Spirit, Cambridge: Cambridge University Press.

Williams, Raymond (1981) 'Ideas and the Labour movement', New Socialist, November-December.

Zancan, Marina (1984) Il Progetto 'Politecnico', Venice: Marsilio.

Zanotti, Angela (1979) Impegno e Critica. Gli Intellettuali di Sinistra nel Dopoguerra, Napoli: Liguori.

2

LEISURE POLICY AND THE QUALITY OF LIFE IN ATHENS

Fouli Papageorgiou

This chapter examines leisure policy as a form of intervention which may be vital in improving the quality of life in deprived inner city areas, or, more generally, 'disadvantaged' areas of a large conurbation like Athens. It puts forward the argument that in areas where the quality of the environment, social care, and the opportunities for work and leisure are low, leisure policy may have implications that extend beyond the activities of 'free time'. That is, leisure policy may become the catalyst for environmental improvement, for community development, for identifying and activating neglected and deprived groups, for overcoming perceptual barriers that delineate 'social ghettoes', and for a wider educational and cultural intervention. In particular, the link between leisure policy and environmental improvement is emphasized as the key for an integrated 'quality of life' policy.

In Athens leisure is closely connected with open-air activities, as for almost two-thirds of the year the climate allows, or makes it necessary, to stay out-of-doors for long periods of time. In inner city areas or other areas with poor environmental conditions and overcrowded housing, the lack of open spaces, parks, and playgrounds has a direct effect on leisure. As local open spaces make up the most important recreation resource for the local population, environmental deprivation leads inevitably to leisure deprivation. Thus leisure policy and environmental policy need to be closely connected, addressing as complementary factors the problem of quality of life in deprived areas.

The notion of an integrated leisure/environmental intervention in deprived areas, which can also operate as a catalyst for wider improvement of the living conditions of the local community, is based on certain assumptions. Two basic assumptions are put forward here, which also indicate the necessary conditions for planning such an integrated policy.

The first assumption is that leisure is localized and separated from the model of consumption. This points to two necessary conditions: first, that there is demand for local leisure facilities; and second, that there are non-commercial providers of facilities (i.e. public authorities and the voluntary sector) that are capable and willing to undertake an integrated leisure/environmental intervention in a deprived area.

These necessary conditions of localized demand and supply for leisure must be placed in a dual perspective: the general trends for leisure in a metropolitan area like Athens, and the particular circumstances of the 'micro-cosmos' of deprived urban areas.

Athens, like most major urban centres, has developed a concentration of entertainment and arts facilities in the city centre, while its significant recreation resources are scattered at the periphery of the city, serving the wider conurbation rather than the local communities. This, of course, largely reflects increased car ownership and cheap public transport, which in turn increased the tendency of city dwellers to seek their leisure interests outside their immediate neighbourhood and helped to further commercialize leisure activities.

This model, however, does not apply to areas marked by deprivation, where poverty and lack of access to information have driven people to hold on to more traditional ways of life and more traditional leisure patterns. The results of two surveys in deprived areas of Athens confirm this picture (Papageorgiou et al. 1978; Papageorgiou 1983).

As will be discussed later in this chapter, the local communities of deprived areas tend to restrict their social and cultural activities within the physical boundaries of their area and tend to use local recreation facilities (however poor and unsatisfactory) rather than seek better ones farther away. This tendency often reflects an 'urban village' culture, characteristic of refugee or rural immigrant communities that have settled in the metropolis. However, the size of the demand for local leisure is eventually determined by the interplay of metropolitan trends and the needs and habits of local communities.

An alternative to commercialized leisure is, to a certain extent, provided by public facilities and the voluntary sector. A strong presence of the voluntary sector during the 1970s, and the change from conservative to socialist government policies in the 1980s, raised expectations for a radical move in fostering community leisure and cultural activity. These expectations were never fulfilled, but in the process, local government emerged as the only agent capable of formulating a local leisure policy, of advocating better quality of life for the local communities, and of drawing together voluntary associations and central government resources.

An important issue concerns the content and direction of such policies in relation to political ideologies. A study by the author of nine boroughs in the Greater Athens area, suggested that the interpretation of 'quality of life' and 'leisure' adopted in a borough council's programme of action, as well as the prominence of leisure policies within this programme, varied substantially between boroughs, according to the political affiliation of the council majority.

The second assumption is that the awareness of the local population is raised, concerning quality of life in the area, and their active participation in voluntary and public sector initiatives is ensured. This may be facilitated by strengthening the lines of communication between non-commercial providers and local communities, by reinforcing existing community ties, and by strengthening the feeling of common purpose and identity among the local population.

These three aspects, namely communication, community networks, and identity, emerged as vital factors affecting the appeal of local leisure policies in the Athens boroughs studied. In all three of these factors, the concept of community runs through explicitly or implicitly, although it may receive different interpretations. These interpretations may refer to common place of origin, shared culture or subculture, social cohesiveness, purpose, and shared goals. This last 'community' is the most relevant today in deprived areas. These areas face immediate and pressing problems including housing, infrastructure, or essential facilities for children and youth, which create a sense of common purpose and identity among the local inhabitants. The period between 1976 and 1982 saw a peak of awareness and protest about local problems, and hundreds of public meetings were organized in deprived areas of Athens to draw the attention of government and ask for immediate solutions. The role of the voluntary sector was paramount in spreading this awareness and organizing the protests, assisted in some cases by the local authorities. The importance of communication proved to be vital in these circumstances through use of the local press and public meetings especially to build up a sense of community. However, it is difficult to assess whether in the long term 'communities' created through external sources or on the basis of ad hoc issues can sustain the interest and involvement of the local population in quality of life initiatives.

A simple model of the approach taken in this paper is given in Figure 2.1.

Figure 2.1. A framework for conceptualizing the quality of life and leisure policy

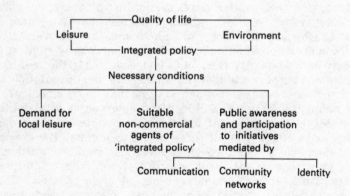

The necessary conditions will be further discussed below in the context of the recent history and the current policies of central and local government in Greece.

THE INNER CITY AND OTHER DEPRIVED AREAS

The city of Athens does not have extensive inner city areas in the sense of a decaying urban core. The decayed areas near the city centre are very small in acreage in relation to the total area of Athens. The character of these areas changed during the 1950s, due to changing land uses in the city centre which limited the residential areas to a minimum. However, the problem of environmental deprivation appears to be very acute in much larger areas, which, strictly speaking, are not part of the inner city. These are the areas of the western section of the Attica Basin, known as the 'degraded Athens'.

Athens is split in two almost equal administrative districts, the West and East Basin of Attica. Not entirely parallel to the administrative line but close enough to it, runs a line of social demarcation, often referred to as the 'class line'. The West Basin contains the poorest and most neglected boroughs of Athens, while the East Basin is mostly formed of middle-class suburbs, well provided, as expected, with social, recreational, and commercial facilities.

The west section of Athens was built almost entirely during the massive urban migration wave of the 1950s and early 1960s. Following the end of the civil war and the victory of the right-wing front, large numbers of the rural population deserted their towns and villages to emigrate to countries of central Europe or to the major urban centres of Greece and especially Athens. The reasons for this massive migration wave were twofold: the economic decline of the country and the intense poverty that followed almost ten years of foreign occupation and fighting (World War II and the civil war); and second, the intimidation of and purges against those who had sided or were suspected to have sided with the left-wing front of the civil war. For those who did not want to emigrate abroad, Athens offered the prospect of an industrial job and the relative security of being one among millions.

The West Basin of Attica offered cheap land and industry situated nearby. Gradually, as the first waves of immigrants established their new settlements, land values soared and consequently, the size of building plots diminished. The total lack of planning or any other type of intervention from the state resulted in a haphazard mode of development, characterized by small private dwellings crammed next to each other along narrow streets, without open spaces or facilities for children and the young. The situation became even worse when these areas were included in the Town Plan, and formal building regulations were issued endorsing a minimal size of building plot (100m^2) and increasing the permitted height of buildings to five or six storeys. The haphazard and often illegal development of these areas was accompanied by a lack of appropriate infrastructure and facilities. It was only during the past ten years that construction of a proper sewage network has begun in many of the boroughs of the West Basin. Social facilities are also scarce. There is no hospital, and only during the past few years have a small number of health centres, day nurseries, and day centres for preschool children and old people been founded.

Another factor responsible for the environmental deprivation in the West Basin is the situation of light and heavy industry in close proximity to, or even within, the housing areas. Significantly, the development of one of the biggest industrial sites of Greece along the coast of the West Basin has blocked entirely the access to the sea of the western boroughs, depriving the inhabitants of one of the most valuable resources for recreation naturally available in the area.

Another type of inner city district, scattered both in the central Athens area and the West Basin, consists of refugee resettlement areas which housed the Greek refugee population who came from Asia Minor in 1922. The 1922-refugee districts have still retained the same type of population (i.e. second and third generations of the original refugees) housed either in small private dwellings built by the resettled families themselves, or in large-scale housing estates built by the state. Most of these districts can be classed as disadvantaged areas, facing problems similar to the West Basin.

The local communities of the deprived areas have a population profile that reflects, to a large extent, their origins. Thus the West Basin has a predominantly young population, while the refugee communities are dominated by an aged population, most of whom are over 60. However, these communities also share some common characteristics typical of deprivation: very low educational level (e.g. in the largest borough of the West Basin, 81 per cent of the adult population finished their education at 12 or younger); an occuptional structure dominated by manual occupations and to a lesser extent unskilled non-manual and self-employed (small businesses); and high unemployment among school leavers.

LEISURE PATTERNS AND DEMAND FOR LOCAL FACILITIES

The word 'leisure' cannot be translated into Greek. The concept of leisure, as analysed by Dumazedier to include 'activities oriented towards self-fulfilment' (Dumazedier 1974) is best rendered in Greek by the word for culture (politismos). Cultural development, in Greek terminology, corresponds closely to those aspects of leisure that refer to personal pleasure and self-actualization through the arts, learning, or recreation. The term 'culture' has come to include most of the pursuits that directly or indirectly result in self-development or attainment of social, political, or artistic development.

Research into Greek leisure activities is almost nonexistent. A recent survey of young people, carried out by the National Centre for Social Research in Athens and a number of provincial cities, included a section on leisure activities and interests. However, it refers only to people under the age of 24 (Kelperis et al, 1985). Previous research at the same Centre has provided some information on single leisure activities, such as cinema-going, participation in clubs and societies, and television-viewing. In 1977 the Technical Chamber of Greece, through its Environmental Committee, commissioned a research team to investigate 'the conditions for establishing Cultural Centres in the deprived areas of Athens'. This study was based on one of the largest boroughs of the West Basin, Peristeri, and included a survey of local residents, with detailed reference to leisure activities and a survey of the local clubs and societies (Papageorgiou et al, 1978).

This study gave a picture of participation in leisure activities that confirmed traditional preferences although, unfortunately, there are no similar data from a wider Athens or national survey with which to compare it. Visiting friends and relations was by far the most popular out-of-home activity (82 per cent) followed by day trips to the countryside or seaside (63 per cent), taverna-eating (60 per cent), theatre-going (48 per cent), cinema-going (46 per cent), and park visits (45 per cent).

As expected, education, occupation, and car ownership affected participation in leisure activities significantly. Tavernas, excursions, sports and theatre were mostly favoured by car owners, white-collar, and skilled manual workers. Visiting friends had a universal appeal, while park visits were predominantly a lower working-class pursuit (unskilled workers). An analysis of location of participation of leisure activities showed a clearer division between the leisure habits of unskilled workers and other occupational categories (skilled, manual, white-collar), and between car owners (34 per cent of the sample) and non-car owners. About 90 per cent of all the leisure activities of unskilled workers were based in the vicinity of their homes. In addition, for the sample as a whole, about half of all leisure activities were pursued locally; some of them (like park visits and going to a cafe) were pursued locally by 90 per cent of the participants.

The picture of largely localized leisure patterns was obtained despite the fact that few facilities were available in the area. There were no sports facilities, only two cinemas, and no theatre for a borough of 200,000 people. There were no proper parks, planned and designed for recreational use; instead, the local authority had acquired a few open spaces which were planted and given to public use.

Although one cannot claim that Peristeri is typical of all deprived areas in Athens, it includes a cross-section of the different types of local communities that are characteristic of deprived areas (e.g. refugee communities, rural immigrants of second or first generation) and also demonstrates a cross-section of the problems of the West Basin, as previously described. In this context, it is interesting to look at the leisure activities people described as their 'favourite' and those they wanted to do more often or take up for the first time. Open-air activities ranked among the most popular in this category (e.g. trips to the seaside, participation in sport). This was also reflected in what people thought their area needed most: sports grounds were ranked first by about half of the sample, and parks by more than one-third. This confirms the importance of open-air activity and open space for people who live in crowded and environmentally poor areas.

AGENTS OF LEISURE POLICY

Central Government

The main channel for policy making in cultural development (and consequently for leisure) is the Ministry of Culture. Until 1985 the Ministry of Culture had rather limited responsibilities, which concerned arts and archaeology (the national heritage). Following the general elections of 1985 and the reform of government structure, the Ministry of Culture was expanded by the addition of three major secretariats for youth, for adult education, and for sport.

The central role of the Ministry is to provide subsidies for the arts, including the financing of the national galleries, the national theatres, and the national opera, as well as grants to various other drama companies and festivals. A small part of its budget goes to local authorities to finance the building of cultural centres or towards festivals or other cultural activities organized locally. The Secretariat of Youth helps local authorities in the creation and maintenance of youth centres, finances recreational or skill training courses for young people, and runs programmes of youth holidays. The Secretariat for Sport finances the building of sport centres, swimming pools, and various other sports grounds, and provides money and personnel to local authorities to run special 'sport for all' programmes, such as 'sport and women', 'children and sport', 'sport and the old', 'dance for teenagers', and so on. The Adult Educational Secretariat organizes social or recreational classes.

Although in principle the Ministry of Culture has great potential for shaping overall policy for leisure, in practice its effect is limited. There are two reasons for this. First, the Ministry operates in separate compartments, rather than formulating an overall policy across its secretariats. Second, the Ministry is heavily centralized and lacks the decentralized mechanisms that would make a regional or local policy relevant to the needs of the periphery. Instead, the Ministry delegates certain responsibilities to local authorities (such as cultural centres or youth centres) by covering part of their cost, or provides subsidies to voluntary associations that can claim cultural goals. The result is a rather haphazard development of leisure and cultural facilities throughout the country, depending on the pressure local bodies can exert on the Ministry and on the enthusiasm and capabilities of these bodies.

Local authorities

As explained above, local authorities are given in principle the opportunity by central government to develop a wide range of leisure facilities through special grants. This special grant system was inaugurated following the 1981 election of the Socialists into government, in accordance with their manifesto promise of wider cultural development at the local level.

However, in practice, these opportunities were hindered by the actual size and the discretionary nature of the grants and by the structure of local government finance. Local authorities levy only 36 per cent, on average, of their total income from local taxation, which can vary from zero to much larger figures; the rest is obtained through various grants from central government. These include a general grant, calculated according to population size, and various special grants for particular projects (such as the Ministry of Culture grants). Given that the income local authorities can generate is small and that their general grant just covers their statutory obligations, they face a very inflexible financial situation and a difficult choice when invited to 'top up' the money offered by the Ministry of Culture for special projects.

Local authorities became closely associated during the second half of the 1970s with the idea of Municipal Cultural Centres (MCCs) independent of central government. Very few authorities actually established cultural centres during that period (only one such centre had been built by 1979). The then Conservative government was not sympathetic to the idea of popular culture and local cultural development. However, the idea of MCCs was seen by the voluntary sector and opposition political parties as a panacea for the quality of life, especially in disadvantaged areas. Following the election of the Socialist government in 1981, funds became available and encouragement was given to local authorities to establish MCCs. By 1984 130 MCCs had been created and today their number has probably doubled. In Athens, most boroughs took advantage of this opportunity and claimed the funds that became available, especially between 1982 and 1984, to establish their own cultural centres.

A cultural centre usually provides an umbrella for art, recreation, and adult education provision (all of which are partly financed by the Ministry of Culture), plus all other activities that a borough council chooses to promote. Examples of such activities include local festivals, sports competitions, art classes, drama performances, or even day trips to the seaside during the summer months. Thus a cultural centre may appear, at least on paper, as the core of leisure policy at borough level.

However, cultural centres did not manage to provide a real alternative to the commercial provision of leisure facilities. They had already come under criticism since their early days because in most cases they did not succeed in playing the role of instigator of cultural and community development that had been expected. Owned and run by the local authorities, without the active involvement of the voluntary sector, they soon became institutionalized and limited their appeal to a small public. In the few cases where local authorities worked closely together with the voluntary sector for the establishment of an MCC, the results were spectacular (e.g. the case of the early days of the cultural centre of the Athens borough of Hymettos); but even such ideal cases were eventually confronted by the question of political ideology and overtaken by the predominance of party politics. Indeed, one of the main drawbacks in the development of successful MCCs was that they became closely associated with party politics.

The voluntary sector

Greece has not had a strong tradition in voluntary associations, compared with other countries such as Britain. However, in the fields of art, folk art and sport, the voluntary sector, although small, has played a leading role, due to the lack of formal policies or adequate resources from central governments. Voluntary associations fall into five broad categories: art, education and science, sport and nature, religious and philanthropic, and 'localistic', i.e. based on place of origin. The last category is the most important numerically. Associations based on place of origin bring together people from a certain village, town, or region, who live elsewhere (mainly in major cities). They represent the effort of the rural immigrant population to maintain contact with members of their old communities, preserve their original culture, and reinforce their identity.

A survey of voluntary associations carried out between 1975 and 1977 by the national Centre for Social Research (Gizelis et al. 1977) found that 46 per cent of all clubs and societies they identified were 'localistic', 19 per cent were art societies, 12 per cent educational, 10 per cent religious, and 7 per cent sports and environmental clubs. However, it was shown that most of these associations had a much wider range of activities than their title implied. The majority of localistic societies and many of the art, educational, and environmental clubs, organized a large number of re-creational activities (excursions, competitions, cultural concerts, and dramas). These societies have become known, irrespective of their title, as 'cultural associations'.

There was a tremendous boom in the number and activities of cultural associations following the end of the military dictatorship in 1974. In Athens this phenomenon was more publicly evident, as some cultural societies were also associated with the publication of journals, confer-ences, lectures and public discussions.

Most of these societies, especially the local ones, were started by young people and were associated with a leftist political outlook. They represented a sudden release of the energy and aspirations that were accumulated and suppressed during the dictatorship. Following the fall of the junta, young people realized that they could think, speak, and act freely, and tried to make up for the lost years of silence and inactivity. Politics and culture became synonymous. The clubs and societies that sprang up everywhere tried to put into practice the message that 'culture is for the people and comes from the people'. Hundreds of amateur or semi-professional drama, dance, or music groups were created during that period, most originating in local cultural societies.

The transitional period of 1974-78 that followed the fall of the junta shaped to a great extent the cultural life of Greece in the 1980s. During this period, the close link between leisure and popular culture was established conceptually, linguistically, and in terms of policy. The theme 'culture from the people' was central to this transformation. Everyday activities that would lead to self-actualization, political consciousness, and a better quality of life were given a new significance as 'cultural' activities.

A small number of local authorities in Athens worked closely with local cultural societies in the context of the cultural movement. The first to undertake such an effort, and the most renowned, was the borough of Hymettus. Situated at the periphery of the urban core, with a population mostly consisting of Asia Minor refugees of second and third generation, it became the symbol of the cultural movement. A local club, set up by the police in 1955 as a social club and operating during the years of the dictatorship as an agent for trips to the seaside, was taken over by a group of young people and transformed into a cultural society. In 1977 they started the 'Open Free University', a series of lectures on art, literature, and politics that attracted audiences from all over Athens. A film club, a drama group, a choir, art classes, and a festival were set up and run with great success. The borough council co-operated with the club and promoted its activities, and it is indeed remarkable that so much was achieved with so little money (the borough of Hymettus is poor by local authority standards).

However, the enthusiasm of the cultural movement did not last long. The reasons for its gradual but marked deflation were several. First, the political excitement that aroused young people after 1974 gradually diminished as the years passed and democratic rule was established in Greece. Second, the 'politics' of these societies became eventually party politics. Once these societies became closely associated with a particular political party, the scope of their appeal narrowed. Third, there was little financial support from central government.

In 1978, of the 2,000 societies that existed all over Greece, only 10 per cent received some financial help from the Ministry of Culture (Pagourelis 1978). As a rule, the most active of the cultural societies were not included in the government's list of subsidies. The lack of funds eventually played a significant role in limiting the number and variety of activities organized by cultural societies, and their membership shrank considerably. A recent survey of young people in Athens, conducted by the national Centre for Social Research, showed that among the 15- to 19-year-olds, 13 per cent were members of cultural societies, while among the 20- to 24-year-olds membership dropped even lower to 12 per cent (Kelperis et al. 1985).

In the deprived areas of Athens, the cultural movement gave rise, as elsewhere in the capital, to a host of cultural societies. Most of these societies gave priority to issues of urgency for the quality of life locally, such as environmental problems (pollution, lack of parks, infrastructure) or social care (facilities for children and young people). A survey of the local associations in Peristeri, the largest borough of the West Basin confirmed the preoccupation of local societies with 'local problems' (Papageorgiou et al. 1978). Of the 23 clubs and societies studied (sports clubs were not included) the main aims of the associations were as follows: ten wanted to improve the local environment, seven wanted solutions to local problems, and six sought support for women and children.

Fifteen of the 23 associations also mentioned 'cultural activity' as a complementary aim. An analysis of all activities and events organized by these clubs during the 24 months prior to the survey is given in Table 2.1.

Table 2.1. A survey of cultural activities of local societies in Peristeri, Athens

Activities	Number organized	Percentage
Petitions for improvement of local conditions	15	15.5
Public meetings to discuss local problems	16	16.5
Club-member meetings	11	11.3
Trips to the countryside	16	16.5
Dinners, parties, fairs, etc.	10	10.3
Talks and lectures	9	9.3
Drama performances	6	6.2
Exhibitions	4	4.1
Other	10	10.3
Total	97	100.0

Source: Papageorgiou et al. 1978.

As Table 2.1 shows, one-third of the activities reflected local problems, one-fourth recreational activities, and only one-fifth referred to art and informal education. Although concern with local problems is only natural in areas that have been termed 'environmental and class ghettos', it is interesting to note that most clubs had a mixed outlook, acting as pressure groups and catalysts for cultural activity, and agents for recreational activity. This lack of specialization, characterized by interlocking or even rotating interests within the same club, had the (perhaps unintended) result of making the local associations agents or mediators of an integrated 'quality of life' intervention in the area.

The relationship between the voluntary sector and local authorities has not always been a happy one. Given that the most active part of the voluntary sector has acquired a political tint, and often has well-known sympathies with political parties, good relationships with the local authorities have depended largely on a coincidence of political allegiance. This limits substantially the scope of local authority provision (as already mentioned in relation to cultural centres) while prohibiting the voluntary sector from maximizing its positive impact on the quality of life in individual areas.

In the survey of the voluntary sector in Peristeri, four types of co-operation and assistance received from the local authorities were identified:

1. setting up public meetings
2. making the facilities of the municipal youth centre available to clubs
3. helping to disseminate information about the clubs and club activities
4. financial assistance (small grants)

This situation has not changed substantially today. The only additional facility offered by local authorities to local clubs is the regular use of the municipal cultural centres, which include large halls for meetings or public performances.

LEISURE POLICY AND QUALITY OF LIFE IN DEPRIVED AREAS

All local authorities in deprived areas of Athens have given some attention to the provision of leisure facilities, as a

61

means of improving the quality of life. Three factors mediated towards this in the 1980s.

First, the pressing problem of infrastructure was solved, thus allowing local authorities to concentrate on other areas of quality of life, in particular, leisure.

Second, subsidies provided by central government to establish certain facilities for recreational, cultural, and social purposes, such as the municipal cultural centres, the youth centres, the day centres for the elderly, the 'sports for all' programmes, and so on, provided an initial core of leisure provision and guided local authorities to show more concern about such issues. However limited the central funds were (and still are), they have acted as catalysts, encouraging local authorities to venture into a new sector of policy.

Third, a special programme introduced by central government in 1983 to relieve unemployment, administered by local authorities, has provided an extra source of finance specifically for environmental improvement. During the past four years a large number of town squares, parks, children's playgrounds, and sports grounds were created or improved in the West Basin and other deprived areas, providing valuable recreation facilities as well as an aesthetic improvement of the environment. Again, this environmental improvement programme, although aimed originally simply at creating jobs, had a very significant side-effect: it stimulated the interest and increased the awareness of local authorities about the quality of the environment and the necessity of open-air facilities for recreation. Most of the local authorities of the West Basin have now a long-term programme of landscaping and turning into recreational use every piece of open space they can acquire.

Some further insights into the role of local authorities in improving quality of life, especially through a local leisure policy, were given by the study of the nine Athens boroughs, as already mentioned. The study was based on interviews with the mayors, analysis of the programmes of action of the local authorities between 1982 and 1986 (between two municipal elections), and content analysis of the minutes of a meeting organized by the local authorities of the West Basin to discuss local problems and quality of life in the area. Three issues will be discussed here as borne out by the results of the study: first, the priority given to leisure policies within a Council's programme of action and the significance attached to leisure as a component of the quality of life; second, the means used by local authorities to raise the citizens' awareness of quality of life and stimulate their interest in initiatives taken by the borough council; and third, the effect of 'quality of life' policies in re-defining the identity of a deprived area.

Leisure policy, as applied by local authorities, includes several levels of activity, which to a certain extent reflects the compartmentalization of central government's policy in this field. Municipal leisure policy differs from central government's model in that it integrates environmental improvement with the provision of basic facilities for leisure. The main 'compartments' of local leisure policy refer to informal recreation, sports facilities, and facilities for cultural activities, complemented by facilities for special groups, such as children and the elderly. The priorities adopted by local authorities concern both the role of leisure policy as a whole within the programme of the council, and the selective development of one or more 'compartments'.

A clear relationship was found to exist between the priority given to leisure policy and the political affiliation of the council majority. Deprived areas in Athens tend to elect either community or socialist councils. Socialist mayors attached considerable importance to leisure facilities, accepting the need for informal recreation, sports, and creative use of free time across all ages. This was confirmed by the council's programme and the weight leisure provision was given in it. In contrast, communist mayors gave leisure a low priority overall, but showed more concern for special groups such as children and young people. These mayors tended to refer to sport and recreation facilities almost exclusively in relation to the young. Within the council's programme, care for the young was given a prominent position.

There was an underlying ideology as well as a particular leisure ethic to justify these priorities. In the former, leisure was seen as independent of work, as a right for everybody, and as a need of equal importance as education or employment. In the latter, leisure was seen as an important part of life, mainly during the formative years of youth. Local leisure provision aimed specifically at keeping youth away from the streets and from major dangers such as drugs or crime.

Political affiliation was also reflected in two other issues: raising citizens' awareness and redefining the identity

63

of the area. Raising the local people's awareness about the quality of their life and the opportunities to improve it was connected with communication and community development. Formal communication through print and broadcasting was favoured by socialist-controlled councils. Some boroughs managed to publish municipal newspapers, some printed the occasional newsletter or review, and a local municipal radio station was planned by a group of West Basin boroughs (this radio station was actually established in December 1987). All these efforts aimed to provide a forum for information, exchange of ideas, and the presentation of problems or achievements by all parts of the community. They also aimed to strengthen a sense of local community by giving the community a voice.

Communist-controlled councils followed a less explicit strategy, based on an effort to strengthen existing community ties. This strategy was more successful in refugee areas, where community ties are still strong. Informal methods of communication were chosen, such as small-scale public meetings in neighbourhoods. The local authorities of these areas also believed that by creating pleasant environmental conditions and opportunities for informal recreation in the neighbourhoods, people would be encouraged to meet one another more often, consolidate existing ties, and develop an attachment and appreciation for their area. The mayor of Tauros, a refugee community, claimed that since the drab open spaces between the state-built blocks of flats were developed into parks and outdoor recreation areas, outward mobility decreased and the borough's population stabilized in terms of size and community relationships.

On the issue of identity, there was a shared concern to reinforce and promote the positive aspects of the area, and gradually remove the ghetto image of the deprived areas. Among the local authorities, there was agreement on the need to create foci of wider attraction in their boroughs, as a means of breaking up the perceptual and psychological barriers that surround deprived areas. Two boroughs, Tauros and Kaisariani, had plans for creating high quality commercial centres. Another two, Haidari and Elefsina, opted for recreation and arts centres. Haidari had proposals for three sites, two open-air recreation and sports complexes and a conversion of an attractive mansion to a cultural centre. Elefsina had proposals for the conversion of disused industrial buildings to a large recreation and arts complex, including an industrial museum, theatre, exhibition halls, and a sports centre.

The philosophy of each local authority was reflected in the formulation of their proposals. The choice of a commercial centre reflected the local authority's concern about employment opportunities and the financial advantages to the community. The proposed commercial centres, including shopping and office accommodation, were seen in close connection with the economic revitalization of the area. This underlined the convictions of communist-controlled councils, who denied the existence of a visual 'ghetto', but admitted its existence in terms of poverty and unemployment. In contrast, socialist-controlled councils, as mentioned previously, attached great significance to leisure, and proposed recreation and arts facilities as a focus of attraction for both local and distant residents of Athens. The assumption behind their proposals was that if the inhabitants of the better-off Eastern and Northern boroughs could be persuaded to visit the West Basin for leisure activities, the cultural isolation of the area would disappear and would act catalytically to gradually lessen its economic and administrative isolation.

One of the main conclusions of the study was that all the borough councils had a clear concept of quality of life, recognized the urgency of the problems relating to it, and had to a lesser or greater extent formulated a strategy to tackle these problems.

There were considerable differences in priorities among councils, especially concerning the role of leisure policy within a strategy that aimed to improve quality of life. There were also great differences among councils concerning the practical aspects of implementing their policies, and especially attracting funds from central government. For example, it was noted that socialist-controlled councils tended, on the whole, to have made quicker and fuller use of the opportunities provided by central government (also socialist), as compared with councils controlled by an opposition party. The different local priorities and different attitudes towards central government, together with the varying financial situations of boroughs, explain the uneven 'map' of services and facilities across Athens, with some boroughs well provided for leisure and others not well provided at all. This uneven distribution has been accentuated by the lack of a central strategy for quality of life and the compartmentalization of central government's leisure policy, which has failed to provide a framework of action for local authorities.

It can be argued that a more substantial change of attitudes is needed in central government, to allow integration at the local level of the various policies linked with leisure, culture, and the environment into a general 'quality of life' strategy. Local authorities would be further helped if, for example, central government set up pilot programmes in a small number of areas, including the deprived areas of Athens, as experiments of an integrated approach to quality of life. Local authorities, on the other hand, need to embark on a more open and systematic co-operation with the voluntary sector in order to avoid the institutionalization of their facilities and services, and to spread the effect of their quality of life policies more widely within the local community.

It must be noted that all the mayors in the study played down the role of the voluntary sector as agents of leisure activity. They tended to refer to voluntary associations mainly as users of facilities or recipients of local authority grants rather than as partners in implementing a policy of common interest. However, as the history of cultural societies in the 1970s has shown, partnerships between local authorities and the voluntary sector can be far more effective than isolated activity from either one alone. In particular, the dynamism of the voluntary sector could help local authorities to overcome major problems of communication and contact with the wider public and broaden the appeal of their policies. As previously discussed, the flexibility of voluntary associations and their ability to combine cultural, recreational, and environmental goals, place them in a unique position as potential agents of an integrated 'quality of life' intervention. This could be usefully exploited by local authorities to overcome their own compartmentalization of leisure and environmental policies, by using the voluntary sector as a mediator for integrated policy implementation.

REFERENCES

Dumazedier, J. (1974) Sociology of Leisure, Amsterdam: Elsevier.
Gizelis, G., Anthonakopoulou, I., Gardiki, O., and Karatza, A. (1977) Practice and Organisation of the Socio-Cultural Activities, Athens: National Centre for Social

Research (in Greek).

Kelperis, C., Mouriki, A., Myzirakis, G., Paradellis, I., Gardiki, O., and Teperoglou, A. (1985) 'Young people: how they spend their time and inter-personal relationships', Social Sciences Review 57: 83.

Pagourelis, V. (1978) 'State cultural policy and private initiatives', To Vima, 16 April; 18-19 April.

Papageorgiou, F. (1983) 'The social survey', in The Town Plan and Redevelopment of Kaisariani, Athens: Public Enterprise for Planning and Housing.

Papageorgiou, F., Pantazis, A., Malouhou, A., Ranou, M., and Sakelariadou, E. (1978) Conditions for Creating Local Cultural Facilities in the Boroughs of the Athens Periphery, Athens: Technical Chamber of Greece.

3

CENTRAL GOVERNMENT POLICY IN FRANCE UNDER THE SOCIALIST ADMINISTRATION 1981-86

Linda Hantrais

LEISURE AND THE SOCIALIST ADMINISTRATION

In May 1981 the presidential elections in France brought to power a socialist president, and the general elections that followed gave the left-wing parties a parliamentary majority. The government formed was a coalition of socialists and communists, until the communists withdrew their support and left the government in 1984. For comparative purposes it is interesting to note that this period of office of the left in France represents a hiatus in an otherwise uninterrupted rule by right-wing and right of centre administrations since the Fifth Republic began in 1958. It therefore provides a useful case-study for analysis of the impact that a change of government and of political ideology can have on leisure policy and its implementation within a given national context. It is also important to remember the pressures exerted by the wider international scene at a time when left-wing governments were the exception in the Western world and the trend was towards less rather than more state control.

The appointment of a Minister for Free Time in France shortly after the 1981 elections can be seen as a symbolic act reflecting the ideological importance of free time and leisure for the left. Many presidential and central government policy statements issued after 1981 placed emphasis on free time, its uses and meaning. They stressed the role that the state could and should play in ensuring greater access to leisure goods and services for a wider cross-section of the public and especially in giving disadvantaged social groups the opportunity to benefit from the nation's cultural heritage, understood in its broadest sense.

Traditionally, administration in France has been characterized by the degree of power exercised by strong central government. Despite moves since the 1950s to devolve power to the regions and to develop stronger regional government and a more balanced economic structure, in comparison with many of the other countries considered in this book, France still emerges as one of the Western post-industrial nations with the most centralized political systems. Under previous postwar governments, cultural policy at national level had tended to favour Paris through prestige projects, which enhanced the centripetal force of the capital. During their term of office, the decentralization policies formulated by the left included moves to give greater control over financial resources to the regions. In the areas relevant to this chapter, regional and local councils were to be empowered to initiate action to provide leisure amenities and to find solutions to the problems of the inner cities, although only in a few cases was an overt link made between the two. As far as social policy is concerned we are therefore talking about a situation in which a predominantly 'corporatist' model of welfare was in the process of shifting towards a more pluralist system, but against a background of centuries of central bureaucratic control.

It is not easy to situate the dividing line between central government directives and local authority initiatives, but the claim is made that leisure policy, like other areas of social welfare, can be more effectively formulated and enacted at local level in response to specific needs, rather than by central government, since local authorities are well placed to identify problems specific to their own urban environment. Where local authorities have different political leanings from those of central government, it is never easy for the two levels of administration to co-operate effectively, and this was particularly problematic during the transitional phase of decentralization. There are examples of local authorities that have been successful in pursuing their own objectives irrespective of the government in power, but the attempts to enact leisure policies targeting particular groups revealed some of the tensions existing between the different levels of government, as will be demonstrated later in this chapter.

In order to gain a better understanding of the impact of the left-wing administration on leisure behaviour, and more especially on that of the disadvantaged social groups within the urban environment, an analysis is made first of the different rationales for state intervention in leisure and of the status attributed to free time and leisure in contemporary French society. The way leisure has been presented in the literature of the left-wing government is then examined in relation to general and specific policy objectives and to changes over their five years in office. The considerations taken into account in the formulation of government policy, the information base underpinning it, and the instruments used by the left-wing government to implement policy decisions are then reviewed. Examples are given of the initiatives launched in response to the special needs of disadvantaged social groups, with particular reference to the problems of the inner cities. The shift towards the decentralization of leisure provision and the role played by regional administration are examined as important factors influencing the way policy was enacted. Finally, an attempt is made to discover how government policy has been perceived by client groups, how it has been monitored and evaluated, how different social categories benefitted from government intervention, and to what extent the government in power can and does influence policy decisions at a local level.

RATIONALES FOR GOVERNMENT INTERVENTION AND THE STATUS OF LEISURE POLICY

Successive British governments have tended to adopt the view that intervention in leisure should be at 'arm's length' (Bramham and Henry 1985:1), as is well illustrated by the Arts and Sports Councils' system of funding and the way the arts and sports are supported in general in the United Kingdom. French governments, on the other hand, and especially those of the left, have not been concerned to avoid what, in the British context, has been interpreted by some groups as an unwarranted intrusion into the private lives of individuals. The policies adopted by the 1936 Popular Front government, introducing the first paid annual holidays in France and reducing weekly working hours to 40, set the tone for postwar French governments and made leisure a legitimate object of concern among policymakers. The most coherent, comprehensive, and purposive leisure policy formulated in France since that time must, however, be attributed to the recent left-wing government, even if doubts were cast at an early stage on its likely effectiveness in achieving the almost utopian aims that were set (Dumazedier 1982).

Although leisure policy is by no means a prerogative of the left in France, it does have a special symbolic meaning for them: the 1936 legislation had been heralded as a landmark in the struggle of workers to assert their right to free time. Their representatives were demanding more than just the right to respite from work; they were also expressing the conviction that leisure should be seen as a social value to which all should have equal access. The Popular Front government responded by creating a Junior Ministry for Sports and Leisure under Léo Lagrange, answerable to the Minister of Health. The need to improve the health of the population was reflected in the stress laid on open-air sport. Attempts to remove the class barriers preventing access to leisure were apparent in the priority given to the provision of leisure facilities, especially in the case of sports, for the working classes. Cheap rail fares were introduced to enable workers to take advantage of their paid annual holidays. Subsequently, ideologically inspired movements such as Peuple et Culture (founded in 1943) were established in order to extend access to groups that had previously considered cultural activities to be beyond their reach. Such movements were concerned with a dual-pronged attack on cultural inequality: their aim was both to gain recognition for popular culture and to make high culture more accessible to everybody.

The governments of the right and centre-right, which enjoyed an almost uninterrupted period of office between 1936 and 1981, were not able to benefit from the same public support for the leisure policies they tried to introduce. In the 1960s, for example, policies focusing on centrally controlled cultural amenities tended to be viewed with suspicion by the working classes. The left (see, for example, Dreyfus 1986) acccused them of focusing on high culture and of concentrating resources on preserving the national heritage - a less politically contentious approach - rather than directing attention to ways of improving access to facilities for disadvantaged social groups. Governments were criticized for paternalism and for their lack of success in breaking down cultural barriers in French society. Whatever their intentions and the outcome of their policies, it is significant that the political parties had become aware of the need to have leisure on their agenda.

Despite the 1936 policies and the sociological interest

shown in leisure in the 1960s (due in no small part to the work of the leading French leisure sociologist, Joffre Dumazedier), it is only in the last ten to fifteen years that the concept of a leisured society has caught the attention of the French public at large and that leisure has come to be seen as an integral part of social welfare. The beginnings of the current public awareness of the leisure ethic can probably best be situated in the early 1970s, in the wake of the 1968 events which provoked widespread questioning of work as a central life interest and resulted in more focused claims for better working conditions. In the 1970s the theme of the quality of life also began to appear in policy documents, and notably in the French economic plans (seventh National Economic Plan for the period 1976-80).

In 1977, under the presidency of Valéry Giscard d'Estaing, in line with the growing interest being shown in leisure as an important aspect of social welfare, a working group was set up to investigate the possible scenarios for leisure within a context in which more people were enjoying more free time. The committee recommended that the state should adopt a more active leisure policy, designed to improve access to leisure for the disadvantaged social groups (Blanc 1977). The problems of the sometimes incompatible functions of leisure policies and of the moral questions involved were raised, and research was generated into the many social problems associated with leisure expectations. There was already considerable debate about the relationship between central government and local providers. As the rapid growth of the postwar economy began to slow down and as the level of unemployment started to rise at an unprecedented rate in the late 1970s, alternative visions of social and economic life were promoted, and policies for reducing work time and restructuring working hours were under discussion with unions and employers in an effort to create more jobs. There was quite widespread public awareness of many of the issues concerned both with worktime organization and the use of free time.

When the group Echange et Projets published its widely quoted proposal for a societal project, La Révolution du temps choisi, in 1980, there was already considerable intellectual and political interest in the idea that individuals shoud be able to reappropriate their time and organize it in such a way as to enhance the quality of their everyday lives. The discussions and debate served as a consciousness-raising exercise and helped to set the scene for the left-wing government. The climate was therefore ripe for the sort of policies the left was committed to pursue. Not only was a coherent leisure or free time policy consistent with the left-wing legacy, it could also be expected to receive wide support because of its perceived positive economic and social effects for the community at large, and more particularly for disadvantaged groups.

THE POLICYMAKING FRAMEWORK AND THE PRESENTATION OF LEISURE AND FREE TIME POLICIES

In addition to a Minister for Culture and Junior Ministries for Youth and Sport and for Tourism, which had existed under previous governments, the left appointed a Minister for Free Time, who held office until the cabinet reshuffle in 1983, when Free Time, Youth, and Sport were amalgamated.

The left-wing government brought to power in 1981 was able to use 1936 as a reference point. In their policy statements President Mitterand and his Minister for Free Time, André Henry, spoke of leisure as a social conquest and a citizenship right: the right to have time to live life to the full (Mitterand at Vieux Boucau, 17 April 1981). They expressed their intention to encourage greater personal control over time (Henry, 10 June 1981), a better balance between work and non-work time (Henry, 19 October 1981), involving the restructuring of time over the day, week, year, and working life (Henry, 20 August 1981), and a more creative, interesting, and adventurous use of time (Henry, 24 June 1981; radio interview, 29 August 1981). Stress was placed on the need to democratize leisure by making it available to the largest possible number of individuals and by creating social conditions that would enable all groups to take advantage of free time by pursuing activities of their own choice. Education for leisure was presented as an urgent necessity and the role to be played by the state was reaffirmed, with the express intention of preventing the private sector from gaining control over the leisure market (Henry, 2 June 1981). Many of the statements issued were couched in the hyperbolic and idealistic terms characteristic of the left, for example: 'Le temps libéré peut devenir le temps fort de la liberté, de l'imagination de de la responsabilité', ('Time freed from constraint can become the best time for expressing freedom, imagination and responsibility', 14 November 1981).

Reference in policy documents is made most often to free time rather than leisure, and the newsletter published jointly by the Ministry of Free Time, the Ministry for Youth and Sports, and the Junior Ministry for Tourism was called Objectifs Temps Libre. This publication, of which the first issue appeared in November 1981, reported statements made in speeches and interviews by the three ministers concerned. It gave information about their actions and schedules and the latest news about policies being discussed and pursued. By the middle of 1983, the title of the newsletter had changed to Objectifs Temps Libre, Jeunesse et Sports, and by November 1984, Temps Libre had been dropped from the title, reflecting the disappearance of Free Time from the Ministry. Any remaining references in the newsletter to free time after that date were concerned with leisure activities for the young, excluding sports, and more particularly with the training of animateurs and the introduction of sport into the school curriculum.

It is interesting to note that throughout the period of office of the left, the Ministry of Culture was kept physically distinct from Free Time, Sport, and Tourism. The Minister responsible, Jack Lang, continued to hold his position when André Henry's Ministry was absorbed into Youth and Sports, under Edwige Avice, and when she was subsequently replaced by Alain Calmat and Free Time disappeared.[1] For many years the Ministry of Culture has produced its own publication, Développement Culturel, uninterruptedly and independently of the government in power or the minister in charge, indicating that it may be a much more widely accepted institution. This publication reports on the results of studies of trends in cultural behaviour, for example in television-viewing, or on the budgets of local authorities for spending on cultural amenities. It does not present a day-to-day account of the Minister's official appointments or policy pronouncements, which may explain why it was able to distance itself from the repercussions of political change.

LEFT-WING OBJECTIVES AND PROPOSALS

The policies announced over the five year period during which the left-wing government was in power were designed to cover both the quantitative and qualitative dimensions of free time.

Policies for restructuring work time, reminiscent of those adopted in 1936, were quickly set in motion. Although the top priority given to resolving the problems of unemployment was an important determining factor, the impact of measures to reduce working hours, extend paid annual leave, and lower retirement age can only be properly understood within the wider context of the government's free-time ideology. The left seized the opportunity to introduce what was, generally speaking, very popular legislation and to justify it both on ideological grounds and as a practical means of reducing unemployment.

By January 1982 the 39-hour working week had been introduced by decree, and the government committed itself to achieving the 35-hour week by 1985. In the private sector employers were left to negotiate salary arrangements with workers, but the public sector set the example by making the reduction without loss of pay. Other forms of restructuring of working hours were introduced through legislation designed to promote part-time work and the reduction of the length of the working life, by lowering the age of retirement and through schemes to encourage early retirement (Grossin, 1986). The fifth week of annual paid leave was extended to all workers from 1 June 1983, with the stipulation that it had to be taken separately from the main holiday. Public holidays no longer had to be 'made up', and statutory overtime was reduced, with the requirement that half of the overtime hours worked should be compensated for by time in lieu. Proposals for sabbatical leave for all workers and the extension of in-service training and retraining schemes became an important feature of the employment scene.[2]

The qualitative aspects of free time were the targets of a wide range of policies, although they less often involved legislation. Advertising campaigns were to be used to promote leisure as a social value and citizenship right, and to inform the public at large about the opportunities available as well as the benefits to be derived, for example, from open-air activities. Popular education was to be encouraged by developing regional cultures, by improving the legal status and financial conditions of associations, and by enhancing the status of animateurs. The leisure of young people, particularly sporting activities, were to be actively promoted by the Minister for Youth and Sports by improving the facilities provided by local authorities and by creating information centres (although these were intended primarily to provide guidance about contraception, and to help young immigrants and the physically handicapped). Holidays and tourism were to be promoted jointly by the Minister for Free Time and the Minister for Tourism by offering financial assistance, by staggering and extending the holiday period and by channelling resources into some of the less popular regions.

CENTRAL, REGIONAL, AND LOCAL ADMINISTRATION OF LEISURE POLICY AND THE DECENTRALIZATION OF LEISURE PROVISION

In leisure as elsewhere, the tradition of central control of funding had resulted in a number of prestigious projects that enhanced the attractiveness, uniqueness, and symbolic value of the capital. In the mid-1970s Paris saw the costly construction of Beaubourg or the Pompidou Centre. Under the left-wing government the Musée des Sciences et de l'Industrie at La Villette was opened, and the conversion of the Gare d'Orsay into the museum of the nineteenth century was completed (opened to the public at the end of 1986). The left did not seek to curtail these building projects, most probably largely due to the fact that they were already so far advanced when it came to power. Nor did President Mitterrand try to distance himself from the policies pursued by Jack Lang, the popular Minister for Culture, since he lent support to the scheme for a costly new opera building, to be constructed symbolically at the Bastille and referred to as one of the chantiers du président (the president's construction sites, according to Dreyfus 1986). All these projects found support from the left on the grounds that Paris is the shopwindow of French culture and that such investment creates jobs on a large scale. The new opera building was justified by the fact that it would bring operatic performances to much wider and less elitist audiences.

If under previous governments resources had been concentrated on the capital, this had not been to the complete exclusion of the regions. Within the context of earlier regionalization policies, in the 1960s multipurpose arts and cultural centres began to be constructed in large and medium-sized towns around the country. However, the prolonged period of cultural deprivation of the regions has had lasting effects on lifestyles and leisure behaviour, with the result that there are marked differences between the leisure patterns of Parisians as compared with people living elsewhere in France (as indicated in studies by Debreu 1973; Ministère de la Culture 1974; 1982). Parisians are much more likely to be active in all areas of leisure and to pursue more activities outside the home. Those living in the heart of the capital have remained the most frequent users of arts and cultural facilities, including theatres, concerts and cinemas, whereas the suburbs have been the greatest beneficiaries of the explosion in home leisure goods. These trends can easily be interpreted in relation to socio-occupational and economic status: the concentration of people employed in the professional and higher administrative grades in central Paris matches the high frequency of elitist cultural pursuits, whereas the outer suburbs are characterized by a younger generation, employed in middle management and the administrative grades, who are less likely to look for cultural interests outside the home (Desrosières 1984). These same factors explain differences within urban areas elsewhere in France, but it is also found that spending per head of population on leisure is greatest in towns at the centre of an agglomeration and lowest in a suburban municipality (Développement Culturel 1984).

The nature of the urban population has been shifting in recent years. As in the other countries covered in this book, recent population censuses in France show that there has been a population drift away from city centres and that the socioeconomic structure of the urban environment has consequently changed. The attractiveness of property ownership and of the house with a garden within commuter distance of a city centre are also increasingly common features of the French environment, but they do not seem to be associated with the same level of inner-city deprivation as elsewhere. The explanation may lie mainly in the fact that industrialization took place later in France than in other North European countries and did not therefore disfigure most of the major cities to the same extent as in Britain, for example.

The politically motivated differences that have been noted in the attitude of central government to leisure and cultural policy are reflected in the commitment to this area of social policy at local level. Within the framework of decentralization, regional and local councils were empowered to initiate action, with help from central government, to provide leisure amenities and to find solutions to the problems of the inner cities. Previously the initiative had come almost exclusively from central administration, or at least projects had to be approved by it in order to secure funding. As in some of the other countries looked at in this study, the uneasy relationship between central and local government, particularly during the transitional phase of decentralization, tended to exacerbate some of the latent conflicts resulting from the ideological differences between right-wing local councils and the left-wing central government.

A study carried out under the direction of Dumazedier (1986) comparing local government spending on cultural services under left- and right-wing councils in 1978 and 1981 provides some evidence about possible differences according to political persuasion. Three measures were used: spending on cultural services as a proportion of the total budget (local authorities were responsible for 46 per cent under this budgetary head, excluding expenditure on education); spending per head of population; and the budgetary head that grew most rapidly during the period under study. In the smaller (10,000-30,000 inhabitants) and larger towns (around 100,000 inhabitants), the right-wing councils devoted a larger proportion of their budget to culture, whereas in the medium-sized towns (30,000-80,000 inhabitants) this was not the case, although the actual amount spent per head of population by the left was lower than that by the right. A higher proportion of the right-wing councils increased their spending under this head by a larger amount. The right tended to devote more funding to creative artistic activities, whereas the left favoured animation and tended to rely more heavily than the right on local associations. The left tended to direct its policies more often than the right towards the underprivileged social groups and to cover a wider range of activities.

Through its control of the training of animateurs, central government is able, albeit indirectly, to influence the development of local projects and associations. Animation has become a recognized and institutionalized public service, and central government continues to contribute to the wage bill for locally employed animateurs, while also playing an important role in recruitment and training and by awarding national qualifications. The animateurs may therefore see themselves as state rather than local employees, like members of the teaching profession.

The left-wing central government did try to offer a solution to some of the problems of regional disparity by providing between 25 and 30 per cent of the funding for the 300 new leisure centres that it promoted and built between 1982 and 1984 in smaller towns in culturally underresourced areas. An attempt was made to encourage the decentralization of culture by allocating 70 per cent of the budget of the Ministry of Culture to projects outside Paris. Grants to local authorities for lending libraries were increased, and 17 new central lending libraries were created.

LEFT-WING POLICY FOR DISADVANTAGED SOCIAL GROUPS: FORMULATION AND IMPLEMENTATION

The policies adopted to meet the needs of particular target groups during the period of office of the left-wing government were explicitly presented as collaborative ventures between central, regional, and local government. They therefore provide a good example of the ways in which the different levels of administration interact and co-operate and of the possible conflicts that may arise. Under previous governments central administration had tended to operate something of a stranglehold on local initiatives through its control of funding. Collaboration and partnership within the framework of decentralization were therefore a relatively new experience and provide some interesting case-studies for assessing the effectiveness of left-wing policies.

In analysing leisure policies and the attempts by a particular administration to implement them, several questions need to be considered: if and why specific groups are selected; how their needs are assessed; how the groups targeted are made aware of what is being provided; if and how they are involved in decisions relating to provision; to what extent their needs have been understood; and what safeguards are in operation to ensure the groups targeted are actually being served.[3] Attention in this section is focused on the criteria for identifying the groups to be targeted, on an analysis of the array of policies formulated, and the ways in which they relate to disadvantaged social groups. In reviewing some of the leisure policies of the left, an attempt is made in the next section to assess how successful particular schemes were in meeting the needs of target groups, and the procedures for monitoring and evaluating the schemes are examined in more detail.

Just as policies to reduce working hours were under discussion when the left-wing government came to power in

France in 1981, the attempt to eliminate inequalities in access to free time and leisure activities was also nothing new, and there was already a sound information base that could be used to identify target groups. Various working parties had been set up under Valéry Giscard d'Estaing's presidency to look into ways of overcoming the social, financial, and cultural barriers preventing a more equitable distribution of leisure opportunities. Reports, such as those by Blanc (1977) and Cotten (1978), had identified differences in the amount of time available for leisure, in the values and expectations associated with leisure, and in access to leisure amenities, all of which tended to reproduce and proliferate social inequalities in leisure.

The studies of trends in leisure behaviour available in the early 1980s (in particular those conducted by the Ministère de la Culture 1974; 1982) suggested that there had been no marked change in patterns since the early 1970s, and that there were easily identifiable culturally privileged and culturally deprived groups in French society. The differences could be attributed to financial, educational, and family circumstances, to age, gender, socio-occupational, and cultural status and regional origins, which remained important discriminators in leisure, producing a cumulative effect of privilege or disadvantage. Perceptions of the quality of the leisure experience had also been found to differ according to various socioeconomic, cultural, and psychological characteristics (as reported, for example, by Grossin 1981; Linhart 1981; Hantrais 1983).

It was demonstrated that use of public facilities since the early 1950s had not increased proportionally with the marked growth in public spending on leisure (Girard 1978). Private sector provision, on the other hand, had undergone significant and sustained growth, which gave rise to a number of questions about whether public subsidy was a democratic way of reaching all sectors of the population. This debate was common to other public services: the objective of compensating underprivileged groups for their social disadvantage had, it was claimed (for instance, by Cotten 1978), often been lost sight of, as the social categories who may need them least were found to have appropriated the services concerned. Use of municipal amenities, such as sports grounds, swimming pools, and family holiday centres was, for example, found to increase with income. All the evidence suggested that if they were to be effective, policies to reduce disparities needed to be selective and designed to introduce an element of positive discrimination.

Despite the claim that they would give priority to the reduction of social inequalities by earmarking resources for disadvantaged social groups, a number of measures introduced between 1981 and 1986 did not correspond to this objective. By being universally applied or aimed at resolving a specific problem rather than compensating a particular group for its social handicaps, several policies were likely to be of most advantage to those best able to manipulate the system. For example, a wide range of measures were designed to relieve the problems of congestion and saturation during holiday periods: attempts were made to stagger holiday dates; publicity campaigns were launched and incentives given to tourist resorts to persuade them to maintain facilities over a longer period; schemes were devised to make holidays more attractive at other times of year; assistance was given to promote less well-known resorts; and attempts were made to encourage people to turn to rail travel by providing entertainment, special facilities for children, cheap fares, and additional services on busy routes. The same problems had been tackled by previous governments using similar methods without much success. In the climate of general economic stringency, which soon followed the left's honeymoon period, the main effect of policies for the geographical and temporal restructuring of holidays was to increase the number of holidays being taken by those who already went away, especially during the winter months. The available statistics suggest that they had little impact on the low-income groups.

Survey data (for example, Ministère de la Culture 1974; 1982) indicated that sport remained a minority activity and that the growth areas, such as jogging and aerobics, were confined to the middle classes. Many of the measures taken to promote sports were aimed at the whole population in the hope that, by casting the net widely enough, all social groups would become involved. A week of sport for all was organized in 1982 throughout France to make people more aware of opportunities and to alert local authorities to potential demand. Sport was to become a legitimate activity in primary and secondary schools, and sports clubs were to be encouraged in schools, universities, and at the workplace. Again, there is little evidence to suggest that these global policies did much to change the socio-occupational distribution of participants.

Subsidies to local lending libraries were increased fivefold by the Minister for Culture in the 1981-86 period; although the number of users doubled, there is no indication whether a wider cross-section of the public was thereby reached.

Other policies did target specific social groups, in particular low-income earners and unemployed youth. An innovative idea was the introduction of 'holiday cheques' for low-income earners to enable them to save up for a holiday, helped by a financial contribution from employers. The number of subsidized holiday villages was increased, again with the purpose of extending access to holidays to a wider cross-section of the population. In the summer of 1983 holiday activities were organized for youngsters, aged between 14 and 19, who were unable to go away from home, and structured social and cultural activities were provided in holiday resorts to occupy young people. In 1982 funds and practical support were earmarked for 16 designated areas in French cities in an attempt to reduce juvenile delinquency by improving both the built environment and opportunities for social life. Priority educational areas were identified to combat social problems among young people, and special programmes of activities were set up under the control of animateurs. Local associations and the training of leaders, particularly for popular education, sports and youth, were given special support.

In 1981 a working party on the social development of local areas was established to look at ways of developing social life in underprivileged areas of towns and cities. The main proposal that emerged was for a scheme to be centred on local primary and junior schools. The Ministries for Education, Social Affairs and National Solidarity, and Youth and Sport collaborated in identifying priority areas on which to concentrate resources. Immigrant children were to be given special attention. Underlying these measures was the conviction that the causes of marginalization had to be acted upon and that primary and junior schools were the ideal place to set in motion constructive group action, which would have long-term effects for the community as a whole. The working party identified 120 areas in 18 different regions (from the 22 administrative regions in France), and the ministries concerned engaged in contracts with local authorities, centred on a team of workers with a co-ordinator supported by additional funds from the state and the regions. The Ministry for Social Affairs and National

Solidarity signed contracts with local authorities that committed themselves to introducing measures designed to help the assimilation of immigrants. In addition to earmarked support intended to help with modernizing teaching methods and renovating the built environment and general facilities, a scheme was prepared for improving the quality of the everyday leisure of young people (known as Loisirs quotidiens des jeunes or LQJ). Leisure projects were to be carried out by the young people themselves with regional and local financial and material support. Other schemes, run in conjunction with the Ministry for Culture, were aimed at assisting the cultural development of socially deprived youngsters. They included special holiday programmes involving workshops, for example on story-telling or the plastic arts, run by animateurs.

Several of the more successful collaborative projects are quoted in publications such as Ecole et quartiers, produced in 1986 by the ministries concerned. Some projects involved the making of films (Cannes and Mougins), or the publication of books (Romans, L'Estaque, in the suburbs of Marseilles) about local life, and the production of local radio programmes (Montauban). 'Intercultural' activities were organized, including, for example, workshops and cultural events (at Belleville, a Paris suburb, and Saint-Quentin, a new town on the outskirts of Paris) in order to improve understanding among different cultures.

MONITORING AND EVALUATION OF LEISURE POLICY

Interest in monitoring the results of worktime policies has focused on attempts to evaluate their effects on unemployment, for one of their main objectives was to release jobs. Their impact on free time is more difficult to assess. Analysts suggest that policies to reduce work time succeeded in limiting dispersion about the mean for hours worked, both within and between different socio-occupational groups (Samuel 1984). Substantial differences do persist in the amount of free time available, and it is clear that any additional freed time is not automatically used for leisure activity. Similarly, early retirement and unemployment have not become synonymous with leisure. Nor did the statutory increase in the length of paid annual holidays suffice to provoke a marked rise in the proportion of the population going away on holiday or to eliminate the privileges of some groups that already had the right to additional leave.[4] The reduction of weekly working hours was accompanied by policies to make work schedules more flexible, and this has undoubtedly resulted in a diversification of working patterns and more personalized worktime organization, but not necessarily to the advantage of the groups most likely to benefit from it (Grossin 1983).

The extent to which leisure behaviour has been affected by changes in worktime organization is difficult to ascertain. The available evidence would seem to suggest that the greater flexibility has been used primarily to match family and work schedules (Bouillarguet-Bernard et al 1985; Linhart and Tourreau 1981) rather than for leisure activities. The efforts to extend part-time work have met with only limited success, and studies (for example, Belloc 1986) suggest that it is seen as a stop-gap measure for people who are looking for full-time employment and are unable to find it, rather than as a means of reducing pressure on organizational schedules and of freeing time for leisure amongst the most time-harried social groups.

The Ministry for Youth and Sports did monitor its schemes and also initiated evaluation studies of specific projects. The Groupe de Recherches en Sciences Sociales of the Service d'Education Permanente at the University of Rennes was commissioned by the Ministry to undertake a study of the 'everyday leisure for the young' projects in five different administrative areas. The scheme was an interesting one to study since it was conceived by central government but implemented locally, leaving each urban area to adapt it to suit local conditions. The intention was to answer the needs of young people between the ages of 11 and 18, living in problem neighbourhoods, who did not make use of existing leisure facilities. In that it was designed to help these groups to learn how to use their free time creatively and productively, the scheme was intended to prevent them from developing delinquent behaviour. The evaluation studies looked at the way local resources were employed in implementing the scheme, how it encouraged the young people concerned to develop their potential, and the extent to which the projects that ensued answered the specific needs for which the scheme had been created.

The authors of the report pinpointed a number of administrative and practical problems, differing in their impact from one area to another, which may have prevented the scheme from being more successful. Its collaborative nature gave rise to major difficulties since a multitude of agencies were involved, each with its own interests and organizational practices, in a situation in which the partnership between central and local government did not allow for the equal sharing of responsibilities and costs.

The participation of the Ministry for Education in a scheme that fell outside its normal remit generated several problems. Representatives of the Ministry felt their members were being exposed to conflicting loyalties, given that the educational profession is structured so as to provide the same service for all and is not meant to concentrate resources on designated groups.[5] The regional offices for Cultural Affairs also had difficulties in accepting any compromise that would divert them from what they considered as their main function. The local Social Security offices could not easily identify the sources of financial support they were expected to provide, since they were in the process of being decentralized. Organizations such as the Family Allowances Funds gave bureaucratic red tape as the main reason for their less than full commitment. The usual problems of the social worker were invoked by individual actors, who felt that the time investment expected of them was too great or that they lacked confidence in the ability of the scheme to have any long-term impact on the youngsters concerned. The involvement of animateurs in what could easily become an interventionist role was also seen as a potential source of difficulties.

The part played by the Ministry of Youth and Sports, on the other hand, was unambivalent, and it emerged as a very positive source of encouragement. The involvement and support of regional councils depended upon a number of factors, not least their political colour. Some claimed they were too preoccupied with the process of decentralization to devote time to the schemes, and others that it focused on urban areas and therefore discounted many of the young people within their administrative remit. Where they were committed to the scheme, they played an important role, serving as a mobilizing force for other agencies. Local councils responded according to whether they felt their borough was likely to benefit from the scheme.

In the event, few of the projects were actually suggested by people in the target group, thereby confirming some of the reservations expressed. Projects that were worked out by the young people themselves generally succeeded because the people were used to operating in a group, as was the case for some young musicians. After a period of induction of about a year, more interest was shown by group members in devising their own projects. A more positive outcome for the different agencies involved was that by being forced to collaborate, a new form of co-operation in problem-solving emerged to the benefit of all concerned.

In terms of the effects on the target group, projects drawing on a small number of young people were evaluated as being the most satisfying. It was felt that in general the scheme did reach the groups identified as being deprived of leisure opportunities. In the areas involved it was claimed that few cases of vandalism had been reported, although the impact may not have been lasting. Not much evidence was available about the effects on character training, but the projects clearly stimulated interest and were enjoyed by the participants. They played an important part in giving the individuals a social identity, in helping them to integrate socially and to accept the institutional environment more readily. Most of the activities in which they engaged were not unlike those pursued by the young people who normally make use of publicly provided leisure facilities. The scheme had the fairly modest objective of creating opportunities for leisure and self-expression among young people who felt excluded from society, and the report concluded that it had been a success on that count.

The results of this example of specific action in favour of a particular target group indicate that positive discrimination can go some way towards solving the social problems of the urban environment. Doubts may need to be cast, however, on the value for money of a scheme involving such a large investment of time and energy by so many different agencies. The problems of collaborating across the many levels of administration may not be untypical of the difficulties to be faced in other areas in the course of the decentralization process.

THE GAP BETWEEN EXPECTATIONS AND REALITY

The left came to power in a wave of euphoria, claiming that it had a mandate to bring about radical social change. Five years later the French, who seemed to have lost their illusions and to believe no longer that social upheaval was either possible or desirable, voted the socialists out of power. In the area of leisure, the early years of the left-wing government gave the impression that new initiatives were being taken and that some major social problems were being tackled, but, as in other areas of social policy, economic realities seem to have curbed the enthusiasm for reform, and it seems unlikely that the left has bequeathed a legacy of social reforms that will have a very marked effect on leisure behaviour.

The policies pursued by the left-wing government in France have to be understood in relation to a particular free-time ideology and what has become an established commitment to leisure as a citizenship right. They should be looked at in relation to a tradition of strong central government and technocratic control, which cannot easily be replaced by collaboration with local authorities. Perhaps too much was expected of the left. Dumazedier's (1982) point that the Minister for Free Time was not to be confused with Father Christmas is well taken. The left can, however, be credited with heightening further the public awareness of free time as a social value and of increasing the visibility of leisure provision within the community. The attention paid to <u>animation</u> may have been justified in that it demonstrated to the public that government, whether central or local, was intervening to answer specific needs and in response often to expressed demand. Certainly, schemes for leisure and culture proliferated, although, as in other areas of welfare policy, many of the ideas launched were perhaps not followed through. The Ministry for Free Time did not outlast the honeymoon period of the left. The Minister for Culture, Jack Lang, although he survived to the end of the left's term of office, gained a reputation for what were called <u>opérations-charme</u>, or policies to woo the electorate, and it may be that the left believed that leisure policy was a particularly appropriate and useful tool for achieving such an aim.

NOTES

1. The disappearance of the Ministry in 1983, which faded away rather than being publicly dismissed, can perhaps be attributed to the general shift away from social and economic policies in the face of a rapidly increasing budgetary deficit. Idealism, it would seem, was forced to yield to economic necessity, as the price to be paid for social welfare was found to be unacceptably high.

2. A tax of 1 per cent of the wage bill of firms is used to subsidize training, and regular release for attendance on courses has become a standard practice for most employees.

3. Some of these points are covered in Long's (1987) study of the Glaswegian context.

4. Workers on the national railways have eight days leave over and above the statutory level, banks customarily offer extra days for leave taken outside the main holiday period, and members of the teaching profession have nearly 80 days official leave.

5. The teaching profession has traditionally been tightly controlled by central government, and its members, who are highly unionized, tend to react strongly to any scheme that might change their status or the nature of their work. The conflictual situation illustrated here could therefore be interpreted as an attempt by a professional body to undermine government policy.

REFERENCES

Belloc, B. (1986) 'De plus en plus de salariés à temps partiel', Economie et Statistique, 43-50, 193-4.

Blanc, J. (1977) Choisir ses Loisirs, Paris: La Documentation Française.

Bouillarguet-Bernard, P., Boisard, P., and Letablier, M-T (1985) 'Le partage du travail: une politique asexuée', Nouvelles Questions Féministes, 14-15, 31-51.

Bramham, P. and Henry, I. (1985) 'Political ideology and leisure policy in the United Kingdom', Leisure Studies 4: 1-19.

Cotten, M (1978) Les Equipements Publics de Quartiers: Etude RCB sur les Services Collectifs de Voisinage en Milieu Urbain, Paris: La Documentation Française.

Debreu, P. (1983) Les Comportements de Loisirs des Français: Enquête de 1967, Résults Détaillés, Collections de l'INSEE, no. 102, Paris: INSEE.

Desrosières, A. (1984) 'Les pratiques culturelles', Données Sociales, Paris: INSEE pp. 509-12.

Dreyfus, F. (1986) 'La politique culturelle à Paris depuis Mitterand', paper presented at the conference on 'La Politique Culturelle sous Mitterand', Roehampton Institute, London.

Dumazedier, J. (1982) 'Le ministre du temps libre n'est pas le père Noël!' Les Cahiers de l'Animation 35: 1-15.

―――― (1986) 'Problèmes de la planification économique et

sociale du développment culturel. Réflexions sociologiques sur l'expérience française de A. Malraux à J. Lang (1959-1985)', paper presented at the Colloque International, Economie de la Culture, Avignon.

Echange et Projets (1980) La Révolution du temps choisi, Paris: Albin Michel.

Girard, A. (1978) 'Industries culturelles', Futuribles 17: 597-605.

Grossin, W. (1981) Des Résignés aux Gagnants, Nancy: Université de Nancy.

—— (1983) 'Le temps de travail des salariés: vers une diversification des statuts', Le Travail humain 46: 297-311.

—— (1986) 'The relationship between work time and free time and the meaning of retirement', Leisure Studies 5: 91-101.

Hantrais, L. (1983) 'Leisure and the family in contemporary France: a research report based on an empirical study of the family-leisure interface in a small French town in the Paris Basin', Papers in Leisure Studies 7.

Linhart, D. (1981) L'Appel de la Sirène ou l'Accoutumance au Travail, Paris: Sycomore.

Linhart, D. and Tourreau, R. (1981) 'Mon vendredi . . . !' Revue Française des Affaires Sociales 18: 139-57.

Long, J. (1987) 'Planning for success', Leisure Management 7 (2): 33-34.

Ministère de la Culture et de la Communication: Service des Etudes et de la Recherche (1974) Pratiques culturelles des Français, Paris: La Documentation Française.

—— (1982) Pratiques culturelles des Français, Description socio-démographique, évolution 1973-1981, Paris: Dalloz.

Ministère de la Jeunesse et des Sports (1985) Loisirs quotidiens des jeunes: Etude évaluative sur quatre départements, Charente-Maritime, Finistère, Hauts-de-Seine, Pas-de-Calais. Report prepared by the Groupe de Recherches en Sciences Sociales, Service d'Education Permanente, Université de Rennes 1.

Samuel, N. with Romer, M. (1984) Le Temps libre: Un Temps Social, Librairie des Méridiens, Paris: Klincksieck.

4

CULTURAL POLICY AND SPORTS POLICY IN BRUSSELS

Eric Corijn, Dominique Danau, and Livin Bollaert

In Brussels you either 'swim in French' or 'in Flemish'. The same is true for nearly every leisure activity imaginable, at least for those organized or subsidized by governments of any type. Leisure policy is part of the overall cultural policy, and thus in Belgium it is related to the national question of linguistic divisions; as such it is framed by the semi-federal state.

The independent Belgian state, founded in 1830, is the outcome of both the struggle of the industrial bourgeoisie against Dutch trade-capitalism and international diplomacy in the era of the Vienna Conference. It was a multi-national state, with the Flemish in the north and the Walloon in the south. The ruling class spoke French, thus introducing in the north a class and language barrier between itself and the people. This formed the early base for a Flemish national (cultural) liberation movement.

Brussels grew into a large urban centre as the capital of the unified Belgian state. At the beginning of the nineteenth century the city walls contained some 75,000 inhabitants.[1] As a result of the construction of the new state apparatus, the population doubled by 1846 to 123,874 within the city and 33,239 in the suburbs, a total of 157,113. A century later, in 1947, the metropolitan area had grown to 955,929 inhabitants.

Brussels never developed into a megalopolis. The exponential increase of the population came to an end and the metropolitan area stabilized at around one million inhabitants (1,014,032 in 1950; 1,015,710 in 1979; 976,536 in 1986). The main reasons for this development lay in the fact that the city continued to be dominated by tertiary sector activities and that an important industrial infrastructure was never formed. The workforce for administration and services largely commutes daily by train and private car (about one million commuters each day from nearly every corner in Belgium). The city centre has suffered from an unresponsive urban policy oriented towards large-scale building projects like the World Trade Centre towers and the development of urban motorways leading right to the heart of the city. The attractive areas around the centre became slums, predominantly populated by an immigrant population of approximately 250,000, who were brought into the country in the 1960s from the Mediterranean as cheap labour. The earlier indigenous population was driven out to new suburbs in as many as 20 rural municipalities forming a belt around the urban centre.

The growth of Brussels is not the result of natural expansion, but of constant immigration into the capital. The capitalist ruling class concentrated in the city from 1830 onwards. The town contains a large concentration of petty bourgeoisie, in particular, professions such as lawyers, doctors, accountants, and all sorts of administrators. As in all big cities, commercial and distribution activities are well developed. The industrial working class forms only a minor part of the population. Since industrial activity is underdeveloped, Brussels, unlike other capitals such as Paris or London, has no large belt of working-class municipalities. The basic industries of Belgium have remained, as far as their production units are concerned, concentrated in other cities like Antwerp, Ghent, Liège, or Charleroi, no farther than 100 km from their administrative headquarters in the capital. The working class in Brussels is predominantly white-collar. This 'abnormal' social composition in Brussels forms one of the bases of the specific provincial atmosphere in the capital of Europe. The cultural and ideological climate is dominated by petty-bourgeois layers, imitating the dominant standards of a bourgeoisie importing its culture from abroad. This is the basis of the city.

At the beginning of the nineteenth century Brussels was a Flemish town, containing, like every other Flemish town, a 5 per cent minority of French-speaking aristocrats and administrators. After independence, in 1846, the number of French-speaking people in Brussels formed almost a third (32 per cent) of the population, and by 1910 this proportion had increased to 48.7 per cent. Thus, during the whole of the nineteenth century the Dutch-speaking population constituted the majority in the city, but grew less rapidly than the French-speaking groups. None the less, the city was dominated by French culture as this was the culture of the elite, and French the official state language. The ruling elite spoke French and was oriented towards Paris. All official documents were written in French, and orders in the army and in factories were delivered in French.

At the beginning of the twentieth century a new phenomenon added to the growth in population: the lower classes changed their language to French as a result of cultural pressure from above. In 1920 58.7 per cent of the population described itself as French-speaking. The figures for 1930 and 1947 are 62.7 per cent and 70.6 per cent respectively.

This process contrasts with the trend in Flanders where, during the first half of the century and particularly in the interwar years, the Flemish popular movement developed into a force that obtained official recognition of the Dutch language and culture in Flanders, thus introducing a bilingual state. In the 1930s both secondary education and universities in Flanders were transformed into Flemish institutes. For the first time, higher education was delivered in the people's language. New elites, the new Flemish bourgeoisie, formed the most dynamic faction of the ruling class. This found a parallel in the defensive reaction of the French-speaking petty bourgeoisie in Brussels.

At the end of the economic boom of the 1960s the Belgian state was under pressure from these centrifugal forces. The political landscape was altered by the rise of regional parties and the economic crisis began to make a significant impact on large-scale capital. A reform of the state structure was inevitable if it was to survive.

On some of the principles of structural reform of the state there was complete agreement among the ruling powers. They all wanted the maintenance of a strong central state apparatus and government, fearing above all a possible socialist 'experiment' in the south. As a result, only a small percentage of the national budget has been regionalized. On some other principles no consensus existed at all. Compromise led to a very complicated semi-federal state structure. The dominant faction on the Flemish side pressed for maximum autonomy, with top priority given to cultural policy and territorial matters. The divided nature of the French-speaking movement became clear. On the one hand there was the demand for cultural autonomy and a proper French cultural policy. Here Francophone interests in Wallonia and Brussels were in accord. However, in respect of economic and territorial issues there was no consensus. Given the domination of the Brussels French-speaking population by bourgeoisie and petty-bourgeoisie groups whose economic interests were linked to the ruling class and to the central administration and services, such dissention was perhaps inevitable. Wallonia was populated by a majority of working-class organizations looking for new industrial initiatives and fighting against that same bourgeoisie.

As a result the Belgian state was divided into two cultural communities and three socio-economic regions. The five parts have a legislative body and a government. In Flanders the community and the region fused into one Flemish state apparatus. In Wallonia the regional structure is independent from Francophone interests in Brussels, while cultural policy is linked with the French-speaking community in Brussels. The Brussels region is thus culturally divided, being linked to both the Flemish and the French-speaking institutions, but socio-economically homogeneous as it waits for the implementation of an autonomous regional government.

The other two regions (Flanders and Wallonia) have continued to oppose economic autonomy for the Brussels region, which has no independent economic infrastructure. Brussels receives a great deal of income from taxes levied on the headquarters of firms situated there while producing in another part of the country. A cultural rift exists because the Flemish minority in Brussels wants guarantees against oppression, while the French-speaking majority takes a defensive stand against the cultural shift towards a new revival of the Flemish language. This has led to demands for autonomy for Brussels under the supervision of the national government, for the establishment of a council for the city-region (which has not been elected for the last 15 years), and for independent cultural commissions supported respectively by the Flemish and French-speaking communities.

In these circumstances it is not difficult to understand why a homogeneous cultural and leisure policy does not exist; nor is it surprising that there should be a significant difference between official government leisure policy on the one hand, and the leisure behaviour of the Francophone and Flemish populations on the other. While the government groups people together for the purposes of leisure policy in linguistic communities, civil society tends to subdivide into interest groups on the basis not of cultural linguistic communities, but of shared interests in activities and leisure forms. Nevertheless, for administrative convenience such groups conform to government policy by declaring themselves to be Flemish- or French-speaking.

We will illustrate this by one example, which relates specifically to sports policy in Brussels, of a study of the functioning of Flemish-speaking sports associations in the city (Bollaert and Danau 1986). In this study we selected 279 Flemish sports-associations, of which 124 agreed to participate in the research. These associations were registered as part of the Flemish culture in Brussels, serving the Flemish minority in the city. A questionnaire was distributed among the organizations, and this aspect of the research was supplemented by interviews with key individuals.

Seventy per cent of the clubs had come into existence after 1970. This probably reflects a general growth in interest in fitness and sporting activities, but it is also a result of the foundation of the Dutch (i.e., Flemish) Commission for Culture and its changed subsidy policy. These new clubs were scattered all over the Brussels region, with no specific concentration in areas of higher levels of Flemish-speaking people. The kinds of activities practised in these clubs were (in decreasing order of importance) gymnastics, volleyball, football, walking, and indoor football. In comparing these findings with similar research (UNIOP-INUSOP 1987) we found a difference between our sample and that of the Brussels population as a whole for whom the order of preference for activities was: tennis, swimming, football, jogging, walking, and gymnastics. Our sample was, however, drawn solely from Flemish organizations, while the other data reflect preferences in French-speaking associations and in activities undertaken by individuals.

A more significant difference is shown in comparing activity preferences in Flanders and Wallonia with those in Brussels. In Flanders and Wallonia swimming and tennis are rated first and second, followed by football and walking. In Brussels tennis is the activity with the highest participation, followed by swimming, with jogging in fourth place. This is consistent with the social composition of the city, which is dominated by petty-bourgeois interests. Tennis and jogging are typical of the lifestyles associated with the petty bourgeoisie, whereas swimming and walking are less distinctive features (Featherstone 1987b).

Most of the Flemish associations served the whole population. More than half (51 per cent) made no restrictions on membership at all. Others were restricted only in setting a minimum and maximum age. In total more than 90 per cent of the clubs were open. Only 3 per cent were explicitly restricted to the use of Flemish-speakers. This highlights an explicit departure from the 'official' language-based policy.

This situation exists for all types of associations. Over half (56 per cent) were oriented towards recreational activities; only 21 per cent were strictly competitive and 23 per cent were mixed. Most of the associations had members of both linguistic cultures, but for rules of subsidy they had to declare one or the other language as 'official'. The majority (102) of the 124 clubs declared that their members only spoke Flemish, while only 56 per cent seemed to be actually composed of Flemish membership.

Cultural-linguistic affiliation was in most cases not 'advertised' by the club. Most of the clubs' leadership did not think that language played an important role in sports and 43 per cent of the clubs had an explicitly mixed membership.

Language was not a decisive factor in the choice of the club by the membership; the most important factor was, of course, the kind of activity presented by the club. Furthermore, distance from home and introduction by friends and relatives were decisive factors in selecting a club.

It should be noted that there is no separate sports policy oriented towards the ethnic minorities in the city. No separate provision is made for such groups, nor do any separate voluntary leisure organizations seem to exist. In this area official policy is oriented towards integration of other ethnic groups within both the officially recognized Flemish and French culture. Furthermore, immigrants have no political rights in Belgium, which makes them an electorally ineffectual group with no power position in state structures.

The sports clubs in Brussels show a patchwork pattern that cannot be classified by one criterion only. Nevertheless, all these clubs are listed as Flemish- or French-speaking. How has such a state of affairs come about? The most important factor would seem to be the rules of public subsidy. Equal treatment of linguistic communities can only be achieved if such a classification exists. None the less, we should note that subsidy contributes only one-third of the clubs' finances. The contribution of members is the most important source of income (44 per cent), followed by charges for activities (26 per cent); only 23 per cent is gained through state subsidy or grant aid from the Netherlands Commission for Culture (NCC). However, it should also be pointed out that the most important element of expenditure is that for rent (40 per cent of the total expenditure). This expense constitutes an important form of repayment to the state, as owner of premises and other leisure infrastructure.

At first sight, then, the notion of an autonomous Flemish cultural policy seems to be misleading in so far as sports policy is concerned. It seems that associations are primarily oriented towards a type of activity in a certain area of the city and that the cultural identity of the association is in many cases a formal construct developed in order to comply with state regulations. In fact, the reality of the situation is more complex. It is true as far as the activity is concerned that associations make no distinctions as to the national origin of the participant. Moreover, there is also a clear trend in favour of individual sports at flexible times, thus expressing the trend towards individualization and commodification of sports practices.

However, the superstructure of the clubs does integrate into the culturally segregated city superstructure. Sixty per cent of the clubs do organize other activities, mostly dinner parties and dances. Increasing social contact is one of the aims of the clubs' leadership, and reflects a major motivation of participants in sports activity. But there is also a financial rationale for these kinds of activities: 71 per cent of the associations in our sample were affiliated to their local sociocultural Flemish council, and thus were formally integrated in the Flemish community in the municipality. By this the multi-national reality of Brussels is reduced to reflect the bi-national state-structure. Only Flemish and Francophone cultures are recognized and therefore organized. The many other cultures, one-third of the city's population, are invisible in the organizational framework for leisure because their members do not have political rights and the cultures do not form part of the state structure.

Thus, through organizational and financial constraints, cultural policy attempts to adapt social reality to reflect the relationship of forces in the state apparatus. Through a superstructural integration and formal acceptance of subsidy rules, the individual associations attempt to maintain some flexibility that will reflect the desires of members to obtain local access to specific activities, with only a secondary concern for the cultural affiliation of the organization.

Our data did not include the individual activities of participants and the context of participation in sports clubs in Brussels. This is of major significance since sports play a big part in the Belgian lifestyle (Featherstone 1987a; 1987b). It has been argued that leisure preferences, like other lifestyle preferences can be related to class structure. Choice and practice of sports then become elements of taste reflecting social stratification. One 'can talk about a universe of sporting bodies which can also be mapped onto the social space' (Featherstone 1987b: 129). Further research in Brussels could show a difference in tastes between the French-speaking and the Flemish communities. This may be linked to the upward social mobility of the Flemish in contrast to the defensive and somewhat conservative status of the French-speaking petty bourgeoisie. It may also be the case that the 'new-style' sports, being better developed in the Flemish sector, do attract a fraction of the French-speaking public.

Whatever the results of further research, the study on which this chapter is based closely illustrates that the language-based cultural policy of the Belgian state does not square with the organization of sporting life in Brussels. Policy and rules are the result of a long-running power-struggle within the state apparatus. Developments in sports practice and organization can attract subsidies as long as they formally adapt to the institutionalization that legitimizes the power of the federalized state, which tends to reduce culture to language. The management of the clubs therefore serves as an intermediary between state power and policy and the individual club member.

NOTE

1. These and subsequent figures are taken from Senelle 1978; Corijn 1978; and Roosens 1981. The figures are updated with the latest data of the Nationaal Instituut voor Statistiek (Brussels).

REFERENCES

Bollaert, L. and Danau, D. (1986) Het Brussels Sportbeleid - Doorlichting van de nederlandstalige sportverenigingen in de Brusselse agglomeratie, Brussels: V.U.B., Centrum voor Navorsing van de Vrijetijdsbestedingsproblematiek.

Corijn, E. (1978) 'La question flamande', L'Actuel 3 (2): 18-53.

Featherstone, M. (1987a) 'Lifestyle and consumer culture', in E. Meyer (ed.) Alledaags Leven, Vrijetijd en Cultuur, Tilburg: Centrum voor Vrijetijdskunde.

Featherstone, M. (1987b) 'Leisure, symbolic power and the life course', in J. Horne, D. Jary and A. Tomlinson, Sport, Leisure and Social Relations, London: Routledge & Kegan.

Roosens, A. (1981) De Vlaamse Kwestie, "Pamflet" over een onbegrepen probleem, Kritak: Leuven.

Senelle, R. (1978) 'The reform of the Belgian State', in Memo from Belgium: Views and Surveys, no. 179, Brussels: Ministry of Foreign Affairs.

UNIOP-INUSOP (1987) Sportuitgaven van Sportbeoefenaars in Vlaanderen, Brussels: VUB-ULB.

SECTION TWO:
URBAN INITIATIVES IN LEISURE AND SPORT

In Section One authors discussed urban leisure and urban leisure policy more generally in terms of the way these are taken up within different political configurations in various European countries.

This section deals with urban leisure initiatives organized within the framework of a welfare or community-oriented local policy. In doing so, the contributions concentrate on the level of the planners, providers, managers, and users involved in the initiatives: what is the rationale behind the planning and production of these initiatives; how are initiatives actually planned, financed, produced and run; what kind of use do specific target groups make of leisure initiatives; what is the relation between the one and the other; how do initiatives relate to more general urban problems and to more general urban planning; and what is their historical background? These are the questions addressed in the contributions that follow.

First, we are confronted with an analysis of a unique leisure initiative, organized by the Antwerp municipal school system in 1937. In their contribution to this section, Eric Corijn and Marc Theeboom analyse the historical, political, and pedagogical background of what is typified carefully as an 'extracurricular leisure programme': a programme offered to deprived working-class children of the municipal primary schools in Antwerp during their free Wednesday afternoons and their holidays. This programme is organized on a voluntary basis by the teachers involved and very firmly rooted within more traditional social-democratic welfare objectives. It combines aspects of social integration and the maintenance of social order, with care for the well-being and development of working-class children.

The contribution of Adri Dietvorst focuses on the way groups of unemployed people in Nijmegen, a city near the eastern border of the Netherlands, use different private and public urban leisure facilities. The city can be seen as an example for all those cities in Europe which, during the 1960s and 1970s, were confronted with a declining labour-intensive industrial sector. Since the late 1970s and early 1980s, due to demographic changes and the related growth of the labour force, these cities have experienced a rapid growth of unemployment. As is shown, unemployment increases existing socioeconomical differences in the use of leisure facilities. However, most important of all seems to be the observation that unemployment does not so much lead to a more intensified use of sociocultural public facilities, but to a more intensified and informal use of general public space like markets and the woods just outside Nijmegen. The unemployment policy in Nijmegen does not seem to be in line with this trend, and arguments are put forward for more research into the 'informal sector'.

Another city in the Netherlands, Rotterdam, is the setting of an analysis by Sjoerd Rijpma and Hank Meiburg of sports initiatives, organized especially for ethnic minorities and 'marginal' youth. Here we are presented with an interesting overall view of the different contexts against which these initiatives operate: the urban distribution of different factions of the population and the resulting production of problem areas; the policy culture with its mixture of social and bureaucratic motives, a culture within which decisions are made about what are to be considered as target groups and what kinds of initiatives are to be set up for them to meet the chosen objectives; the strategies developed by social workers to meet the often contradictory cultures of officials and users; the way the selected target groups are approached and the use they make of facilities; and finally, the marginalized cultures in terms of which we have to understand the use that is made of such facilities. Their contribution also shows clearly the way these initiatives depend on political fads and fashions. In the context of a more market-oriented municipal revitalization policy, priorities have changed and parts of programmes in question are discontinued.

A similar analysis is delivered by Sue Glyptis, but on a broader national scale. Results are presented from a review of sports provisions for the unemployed in the UK, of which virtually all operate in urban contexts. Here also a mixture of social (or need-oriented) and more specific rationalizations for the programmes have developed. Rationales vary from a genuine concern to help the unemployed through a deviancy-control perspective to 'keeping up with the Joneses' (i.e. neighbouring authorities) or political window-dressing. The unemployed are to be presented with a new identity and a related structure of relevancy: 'some sort of active interest', 'becoming involved', 'developing a sense of belonging'. Although getting a job remains the first priority for the unemployed, the programmes involved do give them some spare moments with more relaxing activities, diverting their thoughts from their troublesome position. The projects deliver an opportunity for a temporary imaginary escape from unemployment, which can become something to look forward to.

The last contribution challenges an issue present in all the contributions to this section and even in some contributions in other sections of the book: the shift from a facility- and provider-oriented approach to one that is community- and target group-oriented in the planning of public urban leisure facilities. In the context of case-studies of urban community-based recreation provisions in Bradford and Sheffield (UK), Les Haywood and Frank Kew come to the conclusion that the shift towards the local community in sport programmes is manifest solely in a new type of management process and not in new types of activities. Community sport per se remains untheorized and unproblematic. On the basis of a structural analysis of the forms of sport and physical recreation, they construct a classification system of sport activities and make recommendations for its utilization in the planning of future sport provisions.

In all of these contributions, aspects of the policing of public urban leisure provisions pass in review, providing the ground for a broader analysis and discussion of the possibilities and pretensions associated with public provisions in a welfare approach to leisure. Can public leisure provisions organized for specific disadvantaged target groups actually counterweigh deprivation? If we say that these provisions meet the local needs of people living in deprived areas, what kind of needs do we mean? Is 'community development' still a realistic objective in light of the multi-ethnic and multicultural character of many European urban areas? And if so, can leisure provisions actually help in regenerating informal social networks, giving communities not only some common identity, but more potential for economic survival?

These questions may sound provocative but they nevertheless address the issues involved in attempts not just to replace conventional integrating mechanisms that are now becoming obsolete, but also to counteract forms of urban decay through the organizing of public facilities.

5

LEISURE EDUCATION AND THE ANTWERP SCHOOL SYSTEM

Eric Corijn and Marc Theeboom

Antwerp, a port with almost half a million inhabitants, has had for more than 60 years a so-called 'labourist' local government, with a coalition formed by the social-democratic and Christian-democratic parties. When the socialists became part of the Antwerp local government in 1921, they took control of one of the most important departments - education. Since then, for more than 50 years, the situation has remained unchanged.

At the moment the Antwerp municipal education system has 215 schools and over 36,000 pupils between the ages of 3 and 22. This municipal system is bigger than both the free (Catholic) system and the state-organized system in Antwerp.

Undoubtedly, one of the most remarkable characteristics of the Antwerp municipal education system is the provision of organized leisure activities. For over 50 years teachers in Antwerp have voluntarily engaged in organizing extracurricular leisure activities within an organization called 'Children's Joy' (Kindervreugd).

An account of the work and evolution of this organization is given in this chapter by means of documentary study utilizing archival resources as well as through oral history. Explanations for the different developments that characterize this unique model of an extracurricular leisure organization are sought and an attempt is made to analyse its specific relation with the local leisure policy of the Antwerp education department. This chapter also incorporates a comparison of this initiative with other existing leisure education models as part of an evaluation of the role and function of leisure in relation to the school system.

THE ANTWERP MUNICIPAL EDUCATION SYSTEM

The independence of Belgium (1830) was based on a compromise between landed nobility and traditional village leaders on the one hand, who were organized and unified in a Catholic party, and a new liberal industrial bourgeoisie. Within this compromise, education was controlled by private initiative. In Belgium the Catholic free educational system remains the largest school system. Public education, organized by the state or local authorities, can be seen as merely supplementary and its introduction has always been fiercely contested. Each time industrial development in Belgium required a certain level of education, a struggle ensued between these competing interests to gain control over this newly defined educational domain. This happened in 1879, for the first time, when the liberal Van Humbeek introduced universal primary education. It recurred during the 1950s when secondary education was democratized.

Since the end of the nineteenth century socialists and liberals have united on this issue. Before the existence of a strong socialist movement (the last third of the nineteenth century) the liberals opposed the clerical private school system. Later, social-democrats became the advocate of public state education.

Thus the history of Belgian education has been characterized by an ongoing struggle between philosophical and ideological groups to gain control over education in order to control the transmission of ideology. When industrial labour for children under 12 was prohibited by law at the end of the nineteenth century, socialists began to insist on the introduction of compulsory education. In working-class neighbourhoods especially, young children were often left alone by their parents who themselves were forced to work long hours. Therefore, these children were often compelled to spend most of the day untended on the city streets. Gradually this situation was changed by the introduction of free public education.

The Antwerp municipal education system has been motivated from its inception by concerns for social welfare. Since the beginning of the nineteenth century, the Antwerp liberals were keen advocates of an introduction of a public (free) education. As a result the first Antwerp municipal school was founded in 1819. It provided free education for boys whose parents could not afford to send their children to private (proprietary) schools. This innovation occurred more than 20 years before municipalities were oblige by law to provide free education to needy children. From that moment on, more and more children stayed in school during the daytime hours, thereby reducing the problem of looking after them. However, the original problem remained during school holidays. At the turn of the century, those involved in the educational system began to see the necessity of taking care of children during these free days. As a direct result of this concern, the first 'vacation colonies' were founded. A Swiss educator, Bion, is credited by many as the pioneer in the formation of these colonies. Groups of children, accompanied by their teachers, could stay for a few weeks in homes outside the cities during school holidays. Priority was given to needy working-class children with poor health who were selected by school doctors. Later, as the number of vacation colonies increased, other children were also sent there. Although a stay in the fresh air for several weeks was beneficial to the poor health of these children coming from large cities, it was usually insufficient to remedy the health problems of the weakest among them. The need for the organization of permanent school colonies, where children could be taken care of during the entire school year, was therefore recognized. The Antwerp municipal education system has played a leading role in this evolution. With the Diesterweg Open Air School (Openluchtschool Diesterweg) Antwerp founded in 1903 the world's first permanent school colony.

In 1914, in response to pressure from 'anti-clerics', the municipality of Antwerp decided to organize vacation classes, where children could visit schools during their vacations to play under the supervision of teachers. As with the introduction of the law on compulsory education for six- to fourteen-year-old children during that same period, these plans for organizing vacation classes had to be postponed until after World War I. This initiative was finally implemented in 1919, but according to the municipal reports, it was not repeated because of its 'lack of success'. However, it is not clear what was meant by this: it was not possible to discover whether or not this was a matter of low participation by children. What is apparent, however, is that most of the teachers involved had great difficulties in supervising and handling these working-class children in a non-school context.

CHILDREN'S JOY

The 1930s were characterized by huge social movements (strikes in 1932, and a general strike in 1936) of which one of the outcomes was the introduction of the annual paid holidays. The idea of a vacation for everybody spread. In the mid-1930s the Antwerp municipal educational system started organizing holiday trips, which gave schoolchildren the opportunity to make short trips in and out of the city during holidays accompanied by their teachers. This initiative, started by several enthusiastic teachers, soon won the approval and support of the municipal authorities because of the continuing concern for the care of children not only during vacations, but also during time away from school in the school week. In 1929 the free Thursday afternoon was replaced by free afternoons on Wednesday and Saturday. This reorganization of the school week enabled several Antwerp teachers to organize on free Wednesday afternoons activities outside the classroom. These activities, such as guided walks around the town, choir and theatre afternoons, visiting museums, football games, and so on, were the result of personal initiatives taken by teachers and were soon approved and supported by the Antwerp school inspection authorities. In 1937 an organization called 'Children's Joy' (Kindervreugd) was founded to co-ordinate and develop these initiatives. Initially, the most important work of Children's Joy consisted of organizing and supervising leisure activities on free Wednesday afternoons, which took place in schools or at different public locations (parks, squares, etc.). The extension of the organization soon found favour among Antwerp socialists. An increasingly large proportion of personnel (educators and administrators) within the Antwerp municipal education system volunteered to work after hours for Children's Joy. Ten years later another important feature of the work of the organization was initiated, namely the 'vacation programme'.

Currently, Children's Joy has developed into an organization with more than 14,000 members (children, parents, teachers, and supporters). For several years at least one-third of the total school population of the Antwerp municipal educational system has participated regularly in the activities of the organization (see Figure 5.1).

In reviewing Figure 5.1 one should take into consideration that from the mid-1970s onwards an important change took place in the composition of the school

105

Figure 5.1. Participation in activities of Children's Joy among the total Antwerp municipal school population

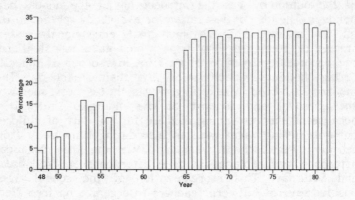

population of the Antwerp system. Since that time there has been a rapid annual increase in the number of children of Moroccan and Turkish immigrants in the municipal schools, although for the schools in the Catholic (fee-paying) educational system, the ethnic make-up of pupils has not changed significantly. In 1986 25 per cent of the school population of the Antwerp municipal primary schools consisted of immigrant children, while in some primary schools immigrant children constitute the majority of pupils. Although exact figures are not available, it is clear that only a very small percentage of these children participate in the activities organized by Children's Joy. The only exceptions to this are some sporting activities organized during Wednesday afternoons that are popular with some boys from the immigrant population. Since the costs to participants of the holiday activities of Children's Joy are relatively low compared with other organizations, and since activities on Wednesdays have been free of charge for some years now, it seems unlikely that the low participation rates of immigrant children can be seen as a result of financial difficulties. A more likely explanation for this phenomenon can be found in the lack of effort of Children's Joy to provide information to the parents of these children. The information brochures and subscription forms of the Children's Joy activities that are handed out to children at their own schools are all written in Dutch, and one might therefore anticipate that parents who have difficulties in understanding this language will be unlikely to respond to this offer.

The distinct yearly increase in participation that occurred during the 1960s can partially be explained by the expansion of the number of activities organized by Children's Joy and by the expansion of the different age groups for which it catered. Apart from the various activities for children from primary schools, during this period Children's Joy started several initiatives for children from infant school and secondary schools, as well as for mentally retarded children, thereby increasing the total number of potential participants. However, primary school children have always remained the most important group, for the majority of activities were specifically organized for them. In addition to activities mentioned earlier (Wednesday afternoon and vacation programmes), Children's Joy also organizes other large sporting and cultural events for Antwerp children during the school year.

ACTIVITIES ORGANIZED BY CHILDREN'S JOY

As previously indicated, the organization of activities during Wednesday afternoons were initially the major element in the work of Children's Joy. The supervision of the different activities was always conducted by teachers, who participated voluntarily from the outset with great enthusiasm. Such a voluntary contribution of time and energy by professionally trained education personnel is unique, and this remains one of the outstanding features of Children's Joy. Although activities take place after school, there is constant integration with the school programme itself, not only because several activities are organized and take place within the school facilities, but also because the promotion and subscription of participating children take place in school during school hours. Thus the relationship that has always existed with the Antwerp municipal system makes it possible to describe Children's Joy as an extracurricular organization.

The different leisure activities organized by Children's Joy on Wednesday afternoons may be divided into sporting and cultural categories. The sports groups are characterized by a more recreation-oriented approach, where the competitive elements are subordinate to the pleasure of the game or play. The cultural groups (singing, theatre, drawing, etc.), are often asked to participate in the displays and festivals that are organized every year by the municipal educational system. At the moment over 5,000 Antwerp schoolchildren between 8 and 18, involved in more than 100 groups, participate in the leisure activities organized during these free Wednesday afternoons.

The other important part of the work of Children's Joy, which occurs during the school vacations, started immediately after the second world war. Previously, there had only been financial support from the organization for initiating holiday trips. However, from 1947 Children's Joy began organizing vacations for children. Every year Antwerp children were offered several possible time periods during which they could go for one or two weeks to either the Belgian coast or to the Ardennes. In later years several other destinations were added to the holiday programme, together with alternative ways of spending vacations, such as 'day residences', where children were based during the day but were taken home in the evening.

Children's Joy has always tried to reach those children who had not the opportunity of going away during school vacations. Therefore, the organization constantly evaluated its existing holiday programme to ensure that it was open to all potential participants. This social concern was the major motivation for initiating day residences. For several years this particular scheme has been the most popular way of going on vacation with Children's Joy. As with the activities on free Wednesday afternoons, teachers also voluntarily supervised children during the vacations. Because of the increasing success of the work during the school holidays, Children's Joy was forced to rely also on senior students in secondary schools and on students who were in their final year of a teacher-training programme. These students received brief preparatory training on how to work with children during their leisure time. As in the case of activities on Wednesday afternoons, there is a close relationship with the school in recruitment for activities during vacations. Children are informed during the school day about the nature of the holiday programme on offer, and they may also enrol through their school. In 1986 almost 7,500 children went on vacation during one of the 39 Children's Joy holidays offered.

DEVELOPMENTS IN THE WORK

Over the years there have been a number of remarkable developments in the work of Children's Joy with regard to both the Wednesday afternoons and school holiday programmes. The evolution of these developments will be described and some explanations for these developments suggested. For a period of 15 years following the end of World War II, the annual participation rate stood at some 4,000 children for activities organized during free Wednesday afternoons (See Figure 5.2).

Figure 5.2. Participation in activities on Wednesday afternoons between 1935 and 1983

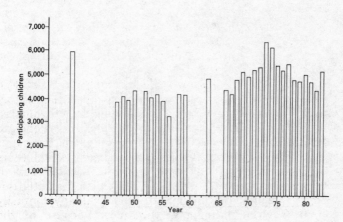

Data are missing from this Figure for two reasons. The first is the inactivity of Children's Joy throughout World War II, during which only a few small-scale initiatives took place. For the other periods, especially during the 1960s, no data were available in the municipal archives. Nevertheless, some trends may be identified from this Figure. From the 1960s to the mid-1970s there was a steady increase in the number of participating children. The absolute number of

109

participating children and the proportion participating from the whole Antwerp municipal school population reached a peak in the mid-1970s. Since then, there has been a slight decrease which seems to correspond with the general decrease in the birth rate. The increase in participation in 1983 can be explained by the fusion of the city of Antwerp that year with several surrounding muncipalities to become 'Greater Antwerp'. This has resulted in an increase in participating children, although this effect will be more apparent in Figure 5.3 when we discuss the activities during the holidays, where data were available up until 1986.

Figure 5.3. Participation in organized vacations

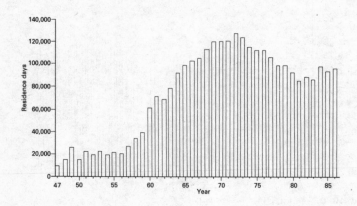

Note: Residence days represent the number of children multiplied by the number of days they spend on the organized holiday.

From the very beginning, participation in sporting activities has been considerably more popular than participation in the cultural groups. This situation has not changed over time; in fact the difference has become more pronounced. In 1986 more than two-thirds of the children who participated in the activities on Wednesday afternoons were to be found in the sports groups.

During this period there have been some changes in the organization of leisure activities during free Wednesday afternoons. The teachers' enthusiasm for taking care of working-class children during the time they were free from school is based primarily on the socialist tradition of the Antwerp municipal educational system. Over the years, the Wednesday afternoon programme has been characterized by this concern for social welfare. However, during the mid-1970s this social policy rationale seems to have been replaced by a desire to offer children a wide variety of meaningful recreational leisure activities. Increasing emphasis was placed on the learning of various leisure activities, which led to an increasing level of specialization within the different groups. Whether or not this represents a real shift in rationale for this kind of work is difficult to establish. It may be that, due to changing circumstances, such as the increasing influence of television and the growing number of commercial alternatives, Children's Joy simply altered its strategy in order to remain attractive as a leisure organization, without losing its original social welfare motives.

In the evolution of the work of Children's Joy during school vacations, one can see an almost similar pattern in the different changes over the years. However, the development of this programme is characterized by three very distinct periods.

These periods are associated with different phases in the development of Belgian postwar history, and the changes that took place in the evolution of the work with children during school vacations can be situated within a broad social context. This suggests explanations for some changes and developments during this evolution of their holiday programme.

The first phase to be considered is located between the beginning of this holiday work in 1947 and the end of the 1950s. It is characterized not only by the creation of new types of vacations, but also by the disappearance of various activities. This phase provided the foundation of the work during the vacation periods, not only from an organizational point of view, but also for the emphasis on a specific child-leisure approach. At the end of this period there was a distinct increase in the number of children who went on vacation with Children's Joy. This happened at a point when, for the second time in 80 years, a major struggle between political factions in Belgium over education was taking place.

After World War II the reconstruction of Belgium developed in a context of national consensus and class reconciliation. By the early 1950s Belgian social democracy had developed a new strategy of severing the educational system from the church in order to facilitate the formation of a new electorate. This strategy became the foundation upon which the expansion of a democratized secondary educational system unfolded during that period. For eight years (1950-58) a fierce struggle ensued between the public non-denominational educational system and the free (Catholic) system. This struggle to gain control over the organization of the educational system between the most important philosophical and ideological groups was also represented in an escalating confrontation between the two major political camps for control of the organization of leisure activities for this large segment of Antwerp schoolchildren. The municipal educational system represents a staunch socialist tradition and an important aspect of the vacation periods is the continuity of influence exerted on the children by the municipal educational system. It would be remiss to neglect the importance and probable ideological impact on socialization of these children during their leisure activities.

The second phase is clearly situated in the 1960s. It is in this period that the number of possible types of vacations as well as the number of participating children increased very rapidly, reaching a peak in the early 1970s. From that point onwards, the holiday periods became the most important segment of the work of Children's Joy as a whole. This constantly increasing number of children participating in the organized vacations can be seen in the light of the increasing economic prosperity during this period. The 'Golden Sixties' gave a higher living standard to a greater part of the population, which made it possible to expand the consumption of consumer durables. For many this situation led to the formulation of some very optimistic ideas about an evolution towards a 'leisure society'. Leisure was to become the central value in human life at the cost of the traditional work ethic. During those years various leisure activities (hobbies, travelling, and so on) became very popular. The rapid increase in the number of participating children for organized holidays must therefore be seen in the light of this developing perspective. It provided the possibility for all children to go on organized holiday. Furthermore, it also created the leisure for the parents of these children to go on vacation.

The third phase, extending from the early 1970s to the present, can be described as a period of decreasing popularity for the organized vacation programme. Particularly during the first half of this period, one can see an annual decrease in the number of participating children. Some explanations may be suggested for this decline. First, the decreasing birth rate reduced the number of children available for participating in the vacation programme. Indeed, it has been demonstrated that, proportionately, the percentage of Antwerp schoolchildren who went on vacation with Children's Joy has not diminished over the years. What is remarkable is that the non-residential holiday programmes have lost a great deal of their popularity. Although several explanations can be suggested, it would seem to be mainly due to the fact that the thinking related to this type of programme has become dated. Looking at other types of organized vacations, in which children stay several days or longer away from home, one can see an explicit change in concept which took place during the last decade. There has been an increasing number of 'theme-' or 'product-oriented' type of organized vacations, in which emphasis is put on a central theme such as sports, music, creativity, exploration, and so on. Parents who send their children to these kinds of organized vacations know exactly what they can expect to happen to their children. On the other hand, the more traditional type of organized vacation also remains popular among Antwerp schoolchildren. This type is best described as 'process-oriented' and is characterized by a far less explicit activity programme. Here emphasis is put on the spontaneity created through several group dynamic processes; being together is more important than the activity as such. This trend in the organization of vacations by Children's Joy must be seen in the light of an increasing individualization of society and the emphasis put on a more 'market-oriented' way of thinking which replaces the ideology of a welfare state as known in the 1960s. This explains the decline of the process-oriented concerns of the non-residential programmes with their strong social character.

A related and important factor to bear in mind is the constantly increasing number of youth organizations that operate similar vacations for children, and therefore put Children's Joy in a kind of competitive position.

As described in Figure 5.2, the increase in participation that has occurred in recent years can for the most part be explained by the formation of Greater Antwerp which brought with it a larger pool of available children.

MAJOR ORGANIZING PRINCIPLES OF THE LEISURE PROGRAMME

The social function of the work of Children's Joy

The social objectives of the work of Children's Joy on Wednesday afternoons and during school holidays has already been mentioned. As an extracurricular leisure organization of the Antwerp municipal educational system, Children's Joy has always tried to be open for all children of this school system, across the entire age range and social class spectrum. Within the various activities no distinction was made with regard to gender or social class. Although from the early 1970s onwards the activities of Children's Joy were open to children from other educational systems (schools from the national state-organized educational system as well as Catholic schools), it was mainly children from the municipal school system who participated in the various activities.

With its predominantly socialist teaching staff, the work of Children's Joy was primarily aimed at working-class children who were unlikely to go on vacation or to spend their free Wednesday afternoons under supervision. Children's Joy took care of these children during vacations at a minimal cost, often for free, on Wednesday afternoons. Surveys were held among the Antwerp municipal school population to establish the numbers of children who would not have the opportunity to go on vacation.

We have already noted non-residential programmes as a good example of the social welfare character of the work of Children's Joy. Children are brought back home every day after spending several hours on one of the municipal playgrounds that are often located in the suburban areas.

Especially in the 1960s it was evident that there was a great need for these programmes, for they were extremely popular at that time (see Figure 5.4).

Figure 5.4. Comparison between day and long-term residences

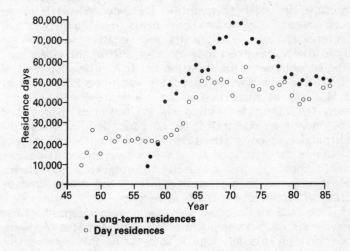

- Long-term residences
- Day residences

Thus one of the more important motives for the work of Children's Joy has been social work, which had a rather paternalistic character with relatively rigid conceptions of discipline, especially during its early period.

The relationship with the Antwerp municipal educational system

As mentioned, Children's Joy grew out of the Antwerp municipal educational system. From the very beginning this organization largely consisted of people involved in the educational system, with the alderman of education as its chairman and several school inspectors as members of the board. The work of Children's Joy has always been based on personal initiatives taken by Antwerp teachers who were stimulated and supported by the board.

The ideological importance of the work of Children's Joy, especially during school holidays, has also been noted. On several occasions during the school year children are informed about the forthcoming holiday programme, and given the opportunity to register at the same time. Although the organization has always tried to use the municipal infrastructure for its activities, during its first years it was often obliged to rent more appropriate accommodation, especially for activities during vacations. Therefore, in order to maintain its independence, it was forced over the years to create its own facility infrastructure. During vacations its own centres were always fully utilized. However, they were vacant for the larger part of the school year. This situation led to the development of an initiative which only years later was to be introduced by the Ministry of Education in all Flemish school systems, namely the 'integrated work periods'. These can be described as a kind of extramural form of education in which the traditional school structure with compartmentalized subjects is transformed in an environment outside the formal school programme into an integrated educational process in which problems are formulated and solved by dealing with concrete real-life situations.

If we take into account the special relationship that has always existed between Children's Joy and the Antwerp school system, it is only logical to describe this organization as the extracurricular leisure organization of the municipal educational system, rather than as an independent and separate body.

SCHOOL AND LEISURE

At this point it is necessary to look more closely at this exceptional relationship between school and leisure. Studying the historical evolution of Children's Joy, the relationship beteween this organization and the educational politics of the different socialist aldermen of education became very clear. The development of the public education system is based on democratic and social goals. Children's Joy, as an extracurricular leisure organization, was therefore promoted on the basis of a similar desire for social integration. This raises the question of what might be learned from Children's Joy as a model for leisure education.

There is a clear etymological link between the conceptions of school and leisure. The Greek notion of skole was central to the lives of free Athenian citizens who, unlike slaves, were not submitted to the necessity of work. According to Greek ideals, skole was a necessary condition of complete human development and an essential feature of practice in the arts, sciences, or politics.

It is from this notion that our word 'school' has derived (Shivers 1981; Murphy 1981). 'Of course, reasoned the Greek, given leisure, a man will employ it in thinking and finding out about things. Leisure and pursuit of knowledge, the connection was inevitable - to a Greek' (Shivers 1981: 41).

However, this relationship changed completely during the nineteenth century. Leisure essentially remained a characteristic of the upper class (Veblen 1899). Education became more widely available because of the need to train and discipline the growing industrial proletariat. With the introduction of compulsory school attendance, the word "school" became associated with forced labour (a-skole) rather than leisure (skole).

Nahrstedt et al. (1979) state that the first context in which the word Freizeit was used was in relation to the school system, when Pestalozzi, Frobel, and Schmeller first employed the term 'leisure' at the beginning of the nineteenth century. More than 50 years later it was introduced in a labour context. This use of the term indicates a separation of the school day into lessons and moments of free time, which hints at the function such a concept of leisure performs.

It is only with ongoing industrialization and the widening of opportunities for education that the school educational system became oriented towards the preparation of pupils for a working life, with scant or little attention paid to non-working time. In the literature, education which is primarily aimed at non-working time is described as 'leisure education' (Freizeitpadagogik). However, there is considerable disagreement about how to develop leisure education. Children's Joy provides a useful example of leisure education for evaluation and analysis.

We have discussed elsewhere the problems of analysing leisure education in terms of principles of pedagogy (Corijn et al. 1986; Corijn 1988; Theeboom et al. 1988). Some authors place an emphasis on 'leisure for education', leisure time or disposable time being available for normal educational activities. In contrast 'education for leisure' sees leisure as an explicit learning goal. This educational activity can be categorized by reference to the attitude taken to prevailing labour relations. An adaptive approach sees leisure education merely as a complementary education for consumer society, whereas an emancipatory or critical approach regards leisure education as a way of opposing integration into the system. Some authors such as Langeveld (1963) therefore reject any notion of educating people for leisure. Others plead for active compensatory programmes (Dumazedier 1962; Friedman 1963) or alternative learning (Nahrstedt 1974; Opaschowski 1977a).

There is no evidence for any explicit educational rationale behind Children's Joy. As the activities are run by teachers, there is of course some educational practice, mostly in the form of an extension of school-based education. Children's Joy, then, has to be seen as a complementary leisure education, incorporating an attempt to compensate for the consequences of social inequality. It promotes social integration and therefore defuses oppositional practices. As such it is a programme wholly consistent with a social-democratic reformist policy based on integration into the state apparatus.

LEISURE EDUCATION AND THE SCHOOL

Even without a separate and explicit education rationale, there must be some educational significance in the programme of Children's Joy given that it is clearly linked to the school system. It is thus seen as a process of 'continuing' education.

'Although the entire responsibility for leisure education cannot be vested in any single agency, it seems obvious that the school system has a major role to play' (Mundy and Odum 1979: 117). However, some authors believe that the education in schools is not suitable for leisure education and that, instead, other sources such as social-cultural organizations, the family, and mass media are more suited for this purpose (Gattas 1981). As has already been suggested, advocates of a critical leisure education, such as Nahrstedt and Opaschowski, believe that this kind of education does not belong in schools. According to these authors, the emancipatory learning goals that they attempt to realize through leisure education are not feasible within the tight structures of the present school system.

As for the present day, there is general consensus in the literature that little attention is given to leisure education in schools. Several studies (Weber 1963; Kelly 1977; Kranzhoff and Schmitz-Scherzer 1978) have pointed out that schools have very little impact on the leisure behaviour of youngsters or adults. Iso-Ahola does not find these findings very surprising and states that 'educators continue to ignore education for leisure and persist in stressing work-related skills' (Iso-Ahola 1980: 149). This underlines one of the most fundamental criticisms of the school system, namely the emphasis that is placed on career-orientation and selection. This work-orientation is also reflected in the educational models used in the school system, and the absence of any attempt to integrate leisure education into the normal curriculum.

In order to situate the organizational model of Children's Joy in relation to alternative models present in the leisure educational literature, we must make a distinction between the two most important kinds of work of Children's Joy: that undertaken during free Wednesday afternoons, and the activities during school holidays. The first kind of activity forms part of a programme aimed at offering choice in extracurricular leisure activities. Here there is a strong resemblance with the German <u>Freizeitgemeinschaften</u>. On the other hand, the work of Children's Joy during vacations does not seem to correspond to any of the models or examples identified. Children's Joy appears to be almost unique in that the relationship between the school and the organizers of initiatives during school vacations is so clearly apparent. The voluntary co-operation of teachers in these kinds of activities during vacations and the fact that the holiday programmes are promoted in schools is atypical of practices in other leisure education schemes. It has always been one of the identifying features of the work of Children's Joy to have the organization of different activities and initiatives carried out by people who are involved in the mainstream educational system. However, it is important to point out that this work has never had a specific educational function; rather, it was inspired by an explicit social welfare rationale. The emphasis has always been on taking care of children who could not afford to go on vacation and to supervise them during time free from school, rather than on developing educational potential. Apart from some very general information, the teachers in Children's Joy have never received specific educational directives with regard to this programme of leisure activities for children. The nature and organization of the

119

activities always derived from the personal contribution of participating individuals, rather than from any educational goals.

CONCLUSION

For more than 65 years the Antwerp education department has been governed by socialists. Compared with other big Flemish urban centres, the continuity of the Antwerp situation is rather unique. There is no other similar long-term initiative in Flanders which is related in the same way to local educational policy as Children's Joy. Undoubtedly the most important contributory factor in this context is the unchanged political configuration within the Antwerp education department. Children's Joy therefore represents a unique initiative for the organization of leisure activities for children within an urban leisure policy. Children's Joy is linked in its policymaking, infrastructure, staff, and management to the municipal school system. At first sight it might seem surprising that no specific educational objectives have been or are being developed. There has been no attempt to develop a programme of leisure education; rather, the central motivation for the activities of the organization is one of social welfare. Children's Joy is seen as a means of promoting social integration and social order. It therefore represents primarily the result of the social-democratic concepts of social management through (local) state power (Miliband 1972; Fejtö 1980; Buci-Glucksmann and Therborn 1981; Ross 1982). Children's Joy has not promoted radical leisure education, nor was such an outcome ever feasible. The range of activities Children's Joy undertakes is limited by the rules of the local state and the school system. Thus there are no specifically 'socialist' or 'anti-capitalist' features of the activities of the organization: its programme is much more determined by systemic characteristics than by ideology.

REFERENCES

Buci-Glucksmann, C. and Therborn, G. (1981) Le Défi Social-democrate, Paris: Maspero.
Corijn, E. (1988) 'Leisure education and emancipation in today's context', European Journal of Education (in print).

Corijn, E., Theeboom, M. and Bollaert, L (1986) 'Vrijetijdsopvoeding is een diskussie waard', Vorming Vlaanderen 2 (1): 41-53.

Dumazedier, J. (1962) Vers une Civilisation du Loisir? Paris: Editions du Seuil.

Fejtö, F. (1980) La Social-démocratie Quand-même, Paris: Laffont.

Friedman, G. (1963) Où Va le Travail Humain? Paris: Gallimard.

Gattas, J. (1981) 'Leisure education, media and participation', in T.J Kamphorst and A.P. Spruijt (eds) Vrijetijdsgedrag in het Perspektier van Socialisatie, Utrecht: Rijksuniversiteit.

Gittenaer, M. and Theeboom, M. (1987) 'Kindervreugd: een historische reconstructie en verklarende analyse van een parascolaire vrijetijdsorganisatie', Persoon en Gemeenschap (in print).

Iso-Ahola, S.E. (1980) The Social Psychology of Leisure and Recreation, Dubuque: William C. Brown.

Kelly, J.R. (1977) 'Leisure socialisation, replication and extension', Journal of Leisure Research 9 (2): 121-32.

Kranzhoff, U.E. and Schmitz-Scherzer, R. (1978) Jugendliche in ihrer Freizeit (Psychologische Praxis no. 52), Basel: Karger.

Langeveld, M.J. (1963) 'Die Schule als Weg des Kindes', in H.W. Opaschowski (ed.) Freizeitpädagogik in der Schule. Aktives Lernen durch Animative Didaktik, Bad Heilbrunn: Verlag Julius Klinkhardt.

Loesch, L.C. and Wheeler, P.T. (1982) Principles of Leisure Counseling, Minneapolis: Educational Media Corporation.

Miliband, R. (1972) Parliamentary Socialism - A Study in the Politics of Labour, London: Merlin Press.

Mundy, J. and Odum, L. (1979) Leisure Education. Theory and Practice, New York: John Wiley & Sons.

Murphy, J.F. (1981) Concepts of Leisure, Englewood Cliffs: Prentice-Hall.

Narhstedt, W. (1974) Freizeitpädagogik in der nach-industrieller Gesellschaft, vols. 1 and 2, Neuwied und Darmstadt: Herman Luchterhand Verlag.

—— (1979) Freizeit als Thema in Schulen. Entwicklungsstand in Wissenschaft, Richtlinien, Unterrichtshilfen, Schuladministration und Schulpraxis (Bielefelder Hochschulschriften, Band 51), Bielefeld: Pfeffer.

Opaschowski, H.W. (ed.) (1977a) Freizeitpädagogik in der Leistungsgesellschaft (Klinkhardts Pädagogische Quellentexte), Bad Heilbrunn: Verlag Julius Klinkhardt.
—— (1977b) Freizeitpädagogik in der Schule. Aktives Lernen durch Animative Didaktik, Bad Heilbrunn: Verlag Julius Klinkhardt.
Ross, J. (ed.) (1982) Profils de la Social-démocratie Européenne, Paris: PEC-La Breche.
Shivers, J.S. (1981) Leisure and Recreation: A Critical Analysis, Boston: Allyn and Bacon.
Theeboom, M. and Bollaert, L. (1988) 'Leisure education and the school', European Journal of Education, special issue on Education for Leisure.
Veblen, T. (1899) Theory of the Leisure Class, London: Macmillan.
Weber, M. (1963) 'Das Freizeitproblem. Anthropologisch-pädagogische Untersuchung', in H.W. Opaschowski (ed.), Freizeitpädagogik in der Schule. Aktives Lernen durch Animative Didaktik, Bad Heilbrunn: Verlag Julius Klinkhardt.

6

UNEMPLOYMENT AND LEISURE: A CASE-STUDY OF NIJMEGEN

Adri Dietvorst

INTRODUCTION

The Dutch urban system consists of a large proportion of medium-sized cities and a relatively small number of primary cities (Amsterdam, Den Haag, Rotterdam, Utrecht). As a consequence of functional specialization between cities, there has not been a single dominant urban centre in the Netherlands. Indeed, it seems more appropriate to consider the country as a whole as one urban field divided into three concentric zones; the Randstad core area, the transition or intermediate zone, and the border or peripheral zone (Buursink 1986). The Nijmegen region, where this case-study took place, is usually seen as belonging to the intermediate zone. However, in respect of its poor employment record Nijmegen would seem to have more in common with cities of the peripheral zone. Nijmegen is a middle-sized town in the eastern part of the Netherlands with nearly 150,000 inhabitants, surrounded by river, lowlands, woodlands, and hills.

Since the 1960s the industrial sector has played a declining role in the Dutch economy in terms of the provision of employment. Between 1963 and 1978 the number of industrial jobs decreased by 21.5 per cent, and between 1976 and 1983 by 12.5 per cent. There appears to have been a disproportionate reduction in industrial employment in the Randstad and certain peripheral areas (Atzema 1986). Furthermore, by the end of the 1970s the growth in jobs in the service sector had stopped as the Dutch economy moved into a phase of stagnation. With a labour force of increasing size, this led to high unemployment rates. Many were forced to make use of the social security system with as a consequence, diminishing potential for private consumption.[1] At the end of the 1970s and the beginning of the 1980s unemployment in the Nijmegen region had increased to 25 per cent (1983). Therefore this region could be characterized as going through a severe economic crisis (the Dutch average at that time was 16.8 per cent). The loss of jobs in the industrial sector was, however, not the only factor responsible for the dramatic fall in employment; reduced government spending also reduced job opportunities in the public services and educational sector. Although in 1987 unemployment in the Netherlands as a whole had slightly decreased, the Nijmegen region was still among those regions with the highest unemployment rates.

LOCAL UNEMPLOYMENT POLICIES

Confronted with these rapidly growing unemployment figures, local authorities and other public and private organizations have developed several types of initiative (Van Gestel 1985). First, there are a number of public and private organizations very actively promoting employment growth. According to Van Gestel, some of these organizations promote different political strategies to cope with the unemployment problem. Some organizations aim at strengthening the market sector and are not primarily concerned with expanding employment. Others, however, do have a primary focus on the expansion of employment and improvement of labour conditions. The former group (heavily funded by national government) is concerned to stimulate investment in industrial development. Van Gestel holds the view, however, that these initiatives, especially the Regional Economy Action Programme, do not contribute significantly to the solution of regional unemployment problems. Among the latter group of initiatives are some operating from an explicitly feminist viewpoint. They aim to promote economic independence of women by means of paid labour, attempting to erode traditional gender role-patterns. These types of development seem to have met with only limited success. The next category of initiative is that of local authority unemployment policy in Nijmegen itself. The main objective here has been to create conditions for the expansion of jobs in traditional industries and also to stimulate investment in new areas of economic potential. In the period from October 1977 to July 1985 the economic policy of the local authority succeeded in attracting 16 companies with 800 jobs. Most of these new posts were occupied by men (86 per cent). The official policy of 'gender neutrality' in job creation has done little to improve the disadvantaged position of women in the labour market. Furthermore, the long-term policy aim of achieving a healthy regional economic structure presupposes a highly qualified labour force. A substantial number of the unemployed, however, have few educational qualifications and/or little training. The characteristics of the unemployed labour force are not consonant with existing employment policy and for those who have been without a job for more than two years, the chances of obtaining employment are minimal. Furthermore, it is feared that the younger long-term unemployed may become a 'lost generation'.

This brings us to the third type of initiative. More or less independent of its economic policy, the local authority has attempted to improve the situation of the unemployed by making it one of the foci of its welfare policy, and in particular by promoting leisure provision for this group. In 1983 the 'Social Cultural Plan 1983-1986' was announced and in 1986 this was superseded by a further plan for the period 1987-90. The central objective of these plans was the maintenance of the quality of life in the city. Priority was given to young people with low levels of education, to the long-term unemployed, to women, and to ethnic minorities. The local authority intended to create a climate that would allow these deprived groups the resources to improve their own position within the city. Unlike national welfare policy which has been under pressure in the form of severe cuts, the city of Nijmegen has been very concerned to preserve the existing framework of sociocultural facilities, even though national government cuts have undoubtedly limited the city's ability to sustain the level and quality of these forms of provision. As a consequence, there has been heavy emphasis on efficient use of scarce resources. To this end, the local authority developed a new classification of districts in accordance with the objectives of the Social Cultural Plan 1987-1990. This classification of districts was based upon a 'welfare needs' score. By a statistical analysis of ten indicators of living and working conditions, education, gender, ethnic divisions, and so on, each district was ranked on a 'deprivation scale'. Districts high on this scale would get high priority in municipal welfare policy, and among these districts were De Biezen and Hengstdal which are included in the case-study reported in this chapter. By contrast, Neerbosch and Brakkenstein, which were also included in the case-study, had relatively low scores on this scale.

Among the measures announced by the local authority in the Social Cultural Plan was financial aid for various projects in constituent districts. Examples of the titles of some of these projects include: the Foundation of Alternative Activities, the Foundation Workshop for Odd-jobs, the Centre for Unemployed, and a number of district workshops for young unqualified unemployed people, and for the older unemployed. Many of these projects started as local initiatives and some of them would seem to have been successful. However, there are severe problems in developing projects to which unemployed people will relate, and to which they are therefore likely to respond. This is a point to which we will return.

THE CASE-STUDY

Against this background of a stagnating economy, rising unemployment, cutbacks in the funding of sociocultural facilities, welfare, and unemployment benefits, and the new local employment initiatives cited, a case-study was carried out in the Nijmegen region in 1983 that focused on the effects of unemployment on participation in leisure activities. In modern industrial societies leisure has normally been structured and given meaning (at least for men) by contrast with paid employment. Unemployment therefore raises the question of just how leisure should be perceived and structured in a non-work situation. In formal terms the unemployed have plenty of free time, but do they use this free time as if it were leisure? What use do they make of the leisure opportunities provided by various public and private facilities? How do they cope with their decreased buying-power? These kinds of question were central to the concerns of the case-study.

The research project had the characteristic elements of traditional survey design. It was presumed that free-time activities would not be influenced solely by unemployment but also by other factors. The different aspects of unemployment interact with the personal and situational characteristics of the individual in bringing about changes in leisure activity patterns. Some of these factors are: life cycle phase, socioeconomic position, duration of unemployment, and the living situation in an urban setting.

Accordingly, hypotheses were formulated and a questionnaire was constructed which contained questions concerning personal characteristics, leisure activities, the use of facilities, holiday and day-trip participation, and daily pursuits.

In 1983, the Regional Labour Exchange Office in the region of Nijmegen registered some 20,000 people (that is 25 per cent of the labour force) as unemployed. A sample of 1,063 unemployed people was selected from four districts of Nijmegen (and from Wijchen and Druten). The latter are localities close to the city of Nijmegen. A total of 434 people (40.8 per cent) were willing to take part in the study. For practical reasons the sample did not contain unemployed belonging to a specific ethnic minority, since interviewing would have required linguistic skills unavailable to the research team. Of the people interviewed, 250 lived in the city of Nijmegen, and it is this group that concerns us here. The group consisted of 66.1 per cent men and 33.9 per cent women. This ratio roughly equals the ratio for the total labour force in the region of Nijmegen. Approximately 50 per cent were younger than 29 years and 39 per cent were between 30- and 49-years-old. A quarter of the people investigated had been without a job for a period of 1-2 years and some 50 per cent for a period of one year or less. One-fifth had had no job for a period of more than two years. One can conclude from these figures that for many in the sample there was also a relationship between long-term unemployment and low socioeconomic status; and in addition, respondents with few educational qualifications seemed to have been more likely to have been made redundant earlier than those with a better education and/or training background.

A BRIEF DESCRIPTION OF THE FOUR DISTRICTS REVIEWED IN THE CASE-STUDY

For the city of Nijmegen the sample was selected from registered unemployed people in four districts (see Figure 6.1). The restriction to four districts was designed to test the assumption that the living situation, the location of the home, would have an influence on daily activity patterns. As we have already noted, two pairs of districts with more or less comparable socioeconomic characteristics were selected: districts with a relative low socioeconomic status, De Biezen and Hengstdal, and those with higher socio-economic status, Neerbosch and Brakkenstein.

127

Unemployment in Nijmegen

Figure 6.1. The survey area: Nijmegen unemployment study

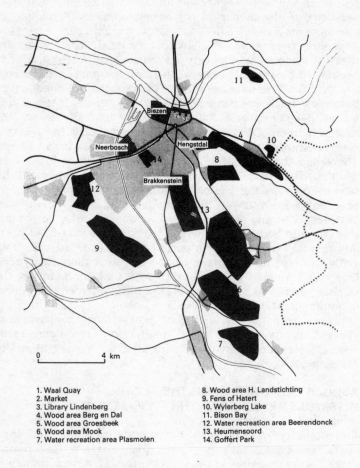

1. Waal Quay
2. Market
3. Library Lindenberg
4. Wood area Berg en Dal
5. Wood area Groesbeek
6. Wood area Mook
7. Water recreation area Plasmolen
8. Wood area H. Landstichting
9. Fens of Hatert
10. Wylerberg Lake
11. Bison Bay
12. Water recreation area Beerendonck
13. Heumensoord
14. Goffert Park

De Biezen is one of the older urban districts in Nijmegen, located west of the city centre. In 1983 it had a population of 6,067, including a disproportionate number of elderly people. This district still bears an industrial character. The ageing of its population, its generally poor housing conditions and large industrial wastelands do not constitute a pleasant living environment. Only 1 per cent of the total area can be characterized as green space, so the potential for outdoor recreation within the district is minimal. However, there is a sports complex just outside De Biezen. Hengstdal is a similar old urban district, southeast of the city centre. In 1983 its population numbered 7,592, of whom many (17 per cent) were over 65. Some parts of the district have been subject to urban renewal. Unlike De Biezen, this district is favourably located, close to green space to the east of Nijmegen.

Brakkenstein, with a population of 4,325, is located in the southern part of Nijmegen. Just north of this district lies the university complex, while its southern boundary borders on the vast natural areas of Heumensoord. Brakkenstein is fairly well equipped with sociocultural facilities. Neerbosch was constructed in the 1960s. In spatial terms, it is in an isolated position, surrounded by motorways and a canal. In 1983 its population was 6,718. The population is younger than those of the other three districts. In the 1970s many young high-income families migrated from this district to the suburbs and since then the district has become something of a problem area.

THE LEISURE ACTIVITIES OF THE UNEMPLOYED

Respondents were asked to cite their most significant leisure activities. The time spent doing each activity was registered, together with details of whether there had been any change with regard to participation when compared with leisure during periods of employment. A distinction was made between activities taking place in and around the home (including gardening) and outdoor activities. Figure 6.2 summarizes the participation percentages for each of these activities. Activities in which participation was highest among the unemployed were watching television (and video), reading, paying visits to friends and/or relatives, walking and/or cycling. Certain activities became more popular during unemployment (see Figure 6.3). People spent more time on activities such as doing odd-jobs in and around the

Figure 6.2. Participation percentages for each of the leisure activities

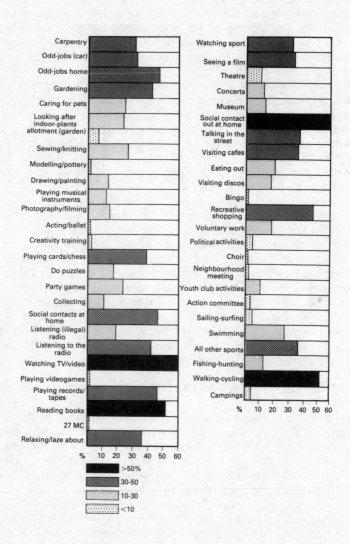

Figure 6.3. Percentages of respondents spending more time on certain activities after unemployment

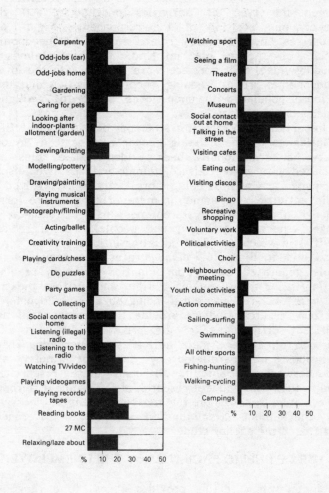

home, gardening, shopping, walking, cycling, and watching television. Thus it would seem that the unemployed spend more time participating in many types of leisure activities than they did when in employment. This is consistent with the results of other studies. There is a weak relationship between the type of activities undertaken and the socioeconomic position of the respondents. Figure 6.4 summarizes how activities relate to the socioeconomic position of the people involved. Watching television (including video) and sport are more popular with the lower socioeconomic groups; reading, shopping, visiting museums are more popular with unemployed people of a higher socioeconomic position.

In participation rates for a number of leisure activities, the influence of the existing gender role patterns in our society has traditionally been evident. Male roles are associated with active leisure, female with passive leisure forms; men are seen as being more likely to be involved in 'public' activities and women in more 'private' leisure forms (although these gender stereotypes may be subject to change, especially among young people). Yet there are activities in which the differentiating influence of gender is not so evident. Figure 6.5 demonstrates that women in the sample generated higher participation rates in reading, relaxing/lazing about, seeing a film, and visiting theatre. Men were over-represented in doing puzzles and sports. In fact, our research findings provide little evidence of any significant differences on the private/public axis with regard to female and male activities respectively. These conclusions are paralleled by those of Knulst and Schoonderwoerd (1983: 30). Although these researchers found in their time-budget research of 1975 some difference between men and women for the time spent outdoors, in 1980 they found a diminution of gender differences identified in the earlier study.

THE USE OF PUBLIC FACILITIES BY THE UNEMPLOYED

Life in an urban setting provides access to a range of commercial and public facilities. Our analysis focused on public facilities such as libraries, markets, the woods, and recreation projects in the immediate surroundings of Nijmegen and their use by the unemployed. Generally, relatively few unemployed people used the public facilities available in the urban districts with the exception of the

Figure 6.4. Participation percentages related to socio-economic position

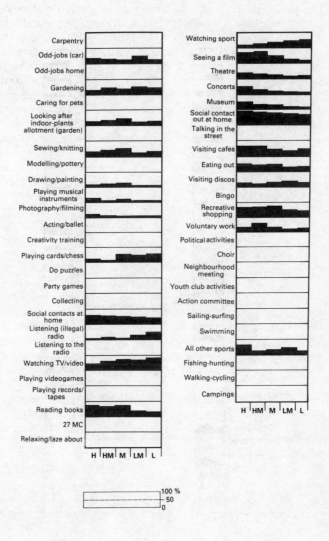

Figure 6.5. Participation percentages and gender

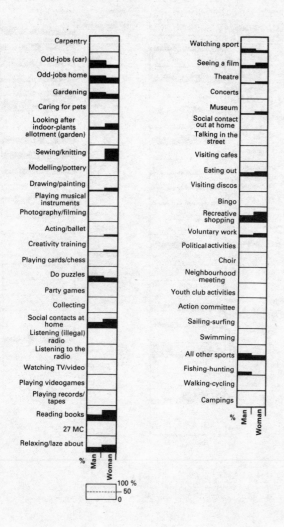

public library (where there was one). The community centres in the four urban districts surveyed were rarely visited (e.g. only three out of the 108 respondents in Hengstdal used this facility). In fact, the absolute figures in this respect were so small that a more detailed analysis of the use of public facilities on the local level is not possible. Analysis is therefore restricted to the use of facilities on an urban and/or regional level.

In sharp contrast to the low level of use of local public sector facilities was the popularity of the regular markets in the districts and the city centre. For a significant number of unemployed people, these markets play a prominent role in the way they spend their time. It is not simply a matter of a cheap commercial attraction; the market place is also visited in order to meet other people or to break the routine of daily life. Also striking was the frequency with which visits to the Nijmegen waterfront alongside the river Waal were mentioned. (It should be noted, however, that the waterfront was of unusual interest at the time of the survey because of the annual flooding of the river, and work on the replacement of a major railway bridge across the river). Compared with activities during periods of employment, the use of the different urban facilities had not intensified. There was a slight decline in the use of facilities for which payment was necessary but differences in respect of free facilities were not great. If, however, the use of urban facilities is compared with the use of non-urban facilities for outdoor recreation such as woods and recreation projects, significant differences can be identified. A remarkable increase in visits to non-urban facilities as compared with periods of employment was evident. Taken together with the almost total lack of use of local urban facilities, an impression is obtained of a 'countryside bias' in recreational activities. A similar conclusion is reached by Woldringh and van Rossum (1983) in their research among social security clients. Thus, of all recreation facilities, the free outdoor facilities within easy reach are those used most frequently by the unemployed.

THE RELATIONSHIP BETWEEN USE OF PUBLIC FACILITIES AND SOCIOECONOMIC POSITION

The phenomenon of social inequality even in leisure participation is well known (Christiansen and Lehmann 1976; Knulst 1977; de Vink 1983). Generally, those with relatively high socioeconomic status exhibit higher participation rates and have a more varied pattern of leisure activity than those with low socioeconomic status. The question addressed here is that of the extent to which socioeconomic position affects the level of participation in leisure activities of the unemployed. In order to answer this question the research population was categorized according to socioeconomic position by a mixture of professional and educational characteristics. The sample was split into five socioeconomic classes: high, high-middle, middle, lower-middle, and lower (respectively H, HM, M, LM, and L in Figure 6.6). The corresponding percentages are 8.5 per cent, 12.4 per cent, 15.9 per cent, 50 per cent and 10.1 per cent. In Figure 6.6 the participation percentages for different leisure facilities in relation to the socioeconomic position are set out. The results confirm the anticipated relationship. With the exception of visits to the market, a lower socioeconomic position generally implies lower participation rates. Especially siginificant are the low participation rates for the lower-middle socioeconomic group when one considers the size of this group.

There may be a complicating factor here. For one facility (the woods area of Berg and Dal) the home location of the respondent seems to be an important factor, since this area is adjacent to Hengstdal, a district in which unemployed people of high socioeconomic status (former university students) are over-represented. However, for the other districts the distance of respondents from outdoor recreational facilities was not a significant factor in explaining the different leisure activity patterns: here socioeconomic position would seem to have been an important contributory factor.

CONCLUSIONS

Notwithstanding the exploratory character of this case study a number of conclusions can be, drawn from the research results. Despite local efforts to preserve a variety of sociocultural facilities, few of the unemployed used the public facilities available in the urban districts, with the sole exception of the public libraries. This is surprising because one would have assumed there to be an intensification of visits to free public facilities as a consequence of the fall in income and the necessity to break out of the restrictions of daily routines. Possibly the

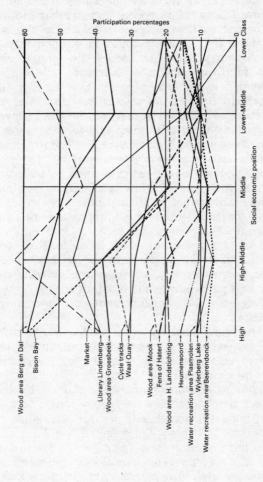

Figure 6.6. Participation percentages for different facilities in the Nijmegen area related to socioeconomic position

character of the facilities offered is not consonant with the lifestyles of the majority of the unemployed. A number of sociocultural facilities, often heavily subsidized, seem only to appeal to the higher, more educated socioeconomic groups. Fortunately, some measures proposed in the Social Cultural Plan 1987-90 appear to be rather more promising in this respect. These proposals relate to the subsidizing of workshops for the unemployed in the districts. This type of provision may serve to reduce the gap between existing local facilities and the interests of the unemployed. However, our research suggests that funding might be more effectively directed not primarily at facilities, but rather at activities of direct interest to the unemployed. Here the widespread interest in doing odd-jobs on an informal basis might be seen as significant. The informal sector of the economy can provide a starting point for work with the unemployed since it gives relevance to their activities, and much of this type of work is readily accessible because it requires no formal qualifications. For social and psychological reasons, one should therefore be aware of the potential of the informal sector. Unfortunately, however, some of the measures that form part of unemployment policy seem to fit better into the framework of an implicit strategy of control, to preserve the existing socioeconomic order or to legitimate the existing economic system, than a strategy of the enhancement of unemployed people's interests.

The importance of Nijmegen's markets in the pattern of activities which emerged from the time-budgets of the unemployed people in the study is remarkable. The marketplace appears to offer variety and distraction. It also functions as an important meeting place. Furthermore, it is a factor that structures time, since visits to the market can be anticipated, scheduled, provide a regular commitment, and so on. For many unemployed the lack of paid labour means the loss of an important source for the structuring of time. Many respondents mentioned the need for a certain 'rhythm of life' with planned activities to look forward to. The market, with its regular weekly schedule, functions as just such a structuring factor.

Unemployment was not the most important factor by which to explain a given leisure pattern. This study found a clear relationship between levels of participation in certain activities and the socioeconomic position of respondents. The conclusion reached was that existing socioeconomic inequalities in leisure are reinforced by unemployment, despite the efforts of local authorities to provide sociocultural facilities for deprived groups. Indeed, many unemployed respondents appeared to compensate for their non-use of public facilities by undertaking many 'housebound' activities, but nearly 25 per cent of the low socioeconomic groups mentioned problems in spending their time meaningfully. This is also the group that seemed to spend most of its time in the home. Members of this group tended not to go on holiday but remained within their neighbourhood. For them the world had become very small; its boundaries had in a sense been shrunk by the experience of unemployment.

NOTE

1. The following information concerning the Dutch social security system may be helpful in understanding the financial position of the unemployed in the Netherlands. In 1987 all existing regulations were incorporated into a New Unemployment Act. With the exception of civil servants (who have their own specific arrangements) and the self-employed, all employees are insured. The right to unemployment benefit presupposes a working period before discharge of at least 26 weeks. Initially the unemployed obtain a benefit of 70 per cent of the original wage (with a fixed maximum) for a specific period. The length of this period depends on the length of employment (i.e. for 10-15 years employment, one year of unemployment benefit; and for 35-40 years service, four years benefit). When the period of eligibility for unemployment benefit has come to an end, the unemployed are subject to the benefits of the General Social Security Act. Social security benefits are deduced from the fixed minimum wage level (the minimum wage of a 23-year-old person). In 1987 this social security benefit amounted to 1,488.50 guilders per month for a (married) couple. Under certain conditions this amount can be raised by rent subsidies and allowances for children.

REFERENCES

Atzema, O.A.L.C. (1986) 'Deconcentration, mobility and urban planning in the Netherlands', paper presented at the symposium on spatial mobility and urban change, Utrecht.

Buursink, J. (1986) 'Economic urbanization and de-urbanization within the Dutch settlement continuum', in J.G. Borchert et al. (eds), Urban Systems in Transition, Amsterdam/Utrecht: Nederlandse Geografische Studies.

Christiansen, G. and Lehman, K.P. (1976) Chancenungleichkeit in der Freizeit, Berlin: Technische Universität Berlin.

Dietvorst, A.G.J. (1984) 'Werkloosheid en voorzieningengebriuk in Nijmegen', in K. Bower, P. Ekkers, P. Hendriks, and E. Wever (eds), Wonen en Werken in het Nijmeegse. Assen: Geografisch en Planologisch Instituut van de Katholieke Universiteit, pp. 135-48.

——— (1986) 'Werkloosheid en [vrije]tijdsbesteding', Werkgroep Recreatie en Toerisme, Nijmegen: Geografisch en Planologisch Instituut KU.

Dietvorst, A.G.J. and Slevin, J. (1985) 'Unemployment and free-time projects: Some theoretical and methodological considerations', paper presented at the conference Alledaags leven, Vrijetijd en Cultuur, Tilburg.

Dings, M. (1983) 'De wereld is helemaal kapot, Tijd-special, De stille dagen van de St. Jozephstraat', De Tijd, 15 October.

van Gestel, N. (1985) 'Vrouwen werkgelegenheid en politiek in de region Nijmegen. Een onderzoek naar de effekten van vcht lokale werkgelegenheidsinitiatieven en het beleid van de gemeente Nijmegen ter bestrijding van de regionale werkgelegenheidsproblemen, in het bijzonder van vrouwen', unpublished doctoral thesis, Nijmegen: Geografisch en Planologisch Instituut Katholieke Universiteit.

Knulst, W. (1977) 'Een week tijd', Den Haag.

Knulst, W. and Schoonderwoerd, L. (1983) 'Waar blijft de tijd', Den Haag.

de Vink, G. (1983) 'Vrijetijd en de economische crisis', Recreatie 1: 5-10.

Woldringh, Cl. and van Rossum, G.M.J.M. (1983) Bijstandskli nten, hun levensomstandigheden en ervaringen. Een longitudinaal onderzoek, Nijmegen: Katholieke Universiteit.

7

SPORTS POLICY INITIATIVES IN ROTTERDAM: TARGETING DISADVANTAGED GROUPS

Sjoerd Rijpma and Henk Meiburg

ROTTERDAM: THE POLICY CONTEXT

Rotterdam, like many other Western European cities, has lost almost a quarter of its population to surrounding suburban areas over the last two decades. In the 1960s Rotterdam had a population of 750,000 but by the beginning of 1987 this number had dropped to 572,000. This reduction is in part the result of a deliberate state policy of urban deconcentration, which was fuelled by a fear of over-crowding of the Randstad. It included the building of attractive new towns in the vicinity of the four big cities (Amsterdam, the Hague, Rotterdam, and Utrecht) that are the nuclei of the Randstad (the 'rim-city'), and which were intended to provide for the anticipated overspill from these cities. In the 1960s it was projected that the Dutch population would grow to approximately 20 million by the year 2000. The beginning of the 1970s, however, witnessed a dramatic fall in birth rates and it became apparent that the population figures would probably stabilize at somewhere around 16 million. However, before the new town development plans were revised in line with the new population projections, significant demographic changes had already taken place in the composition of the city populations concerned.

Migrants to the suburbs largely consisted of middle-class families. They were attracted by (and could afford) the single-family dwellings, in green and quiet environments with facilities for children's play. However, at the same time there was a substantial immigration, particularly into the inner city of people from former Dutch colonies (Surinam and Indonesia) and from Mediterranean countries such as Morocco and Turkey. By 1987 Rotterdam had about

78,000 inhabitants who belonged to one of these ethnic minority groups (14 per cent of the total population), most of them living in the inner city neighbourhoods (24 to 32 per cent). In many of these districts more than 50 per cent of the children belong to one of the ethnic minorities. Besides the composition of the city population at large, the composition of households has also changed considerably. By the end of 1985 single-person households formed 34 per cent of all households, two-person households (i.e. married couples, unmarried couples, or one parent with a child) formed 34 per cent, and households with three or more persons 32 per cent. In 65 per cent of the households there were no children. Rotterdam has also been shown to have relatively high percentages of pre-adults, elderly, ethnic minority groups, and unemployed people (van Wijngaarden 1986).

In the inner city, the surrounding nineteenth century districts, and the older parts of the harbour many jobs, especially semi- and unskilled ones, have been lost. This was initially mainly as a consequence of urban renewal projects in which small factories and workshops were removed to more appropriate settings in industrial zones at the edge of the town; later, jobs were also lost because of the general economic crisis. New jobs have been created within the public sector, often requiring relatively high-level qualifications. Most of the people who work in these jobs, however, prefer to live outside the city: the commuter traffic into Rotterdam has doubled within a few years. In 1983 out of the 280,000 or so jobs in Rotterdam, 130,000 were occupied by people who lived in the suburbs! Thus Rotterdam has changed from a prosperous city with little unemployment to a city which is still fairly prosperous but now has a high level of unemployment among its resident population, the unemployment rate at the beginning of 1987 representing a little more than 20 per cent of the working population. This situation has, of course, undermined the attractiveness of the city as a place to live.

Confronted with the sharp decline in population, city renewal became one of the highest priorities in local policy of the 1970s. Since then, 36,000 houses have been either renovated (19,000) or rebuilt (17,000), and about 44,000 new houses have been built on new estates within the city boundaries. In 1985, for the first time for many years, the population of Rotterdam grew. The Rotterdam philosophy of the 'compact city' fosters high population densities. In fact, a high population density is seen as an important condition for a viable commercial and cultural city life, which in turn is necessary to make the city attractive to high-income groups as a place to live. The local authorities are now trying to reshape the city's image, which has been that of a rather dull industrial city, dominated by the harbour and the petrochemical industries in the Botlek area. The new image for which Rotterdam is now striving incorporates the idea of a modern city centre, an attractive place, with restaurants, pubs, museums, shops, and an agreeable street life. Private enterprise is being encouraged to build expensive tennis halls and dazzling subtropical swimming pools (Center Parcs). Museums are being renewed and new ones, like the National Museum for Architecture, are being developed. Many initiatives are aimed at giving the impression that something is happening in Rotterdam: the Rotterdam marathon, World Tennis Tournament, Worldport Baseball Tournament, World Championship Gymnastics, Jazz Festival, Film International, David Bowie in the Feijenoord stadium, and so on. These huge cultural and sports events are designed to put Rotterdam on the 'leisure map'. Rotterdam is striving to attract the tourist market, but these leisure events and facilities are also part of the policy of improving the quality of life in Rotterdam, which is seen as an important factor in attracting new industries and commercial services, especially those operating in the growth areas of high-tech, biotechnology, information services, and the like.

All these developments have had an impact on leisure policies in general and sports policy (which is the primary focus of this chapter) in particular. However, local authorities have also had to deal with the effects of cutbacks by national government in the fields of outdoor recreation, sociocultural facilities, and other forms of leisure provision. Most authorities simply do not have the resources to compensate for this reduction in central government support. Thus there are dual tensions to use leisure to promote a new image for the city, and to deal with financial cutbacks.

The city redevelopment policies we have cited will only begin to affect the local economy in the longer term. In the meantime, economic and social problems are building up, concentrated in the areas adjacent to the 'revitalizing' city centre. These are the areas in which most of the elderly, unemployed, and the ethnic minorities live. The few available sports facilities in these areas therefore are under pressure because of both economic and demographic factors. The new or renovated houses are on the whole bigger than the older ones they replaced, which has resulted in a diminution of the total number of houses in these areas. The combination of this with the growth in small households has meant a declining population in these areas. On the other hand, this has been to some extent offset by an influx of ethnic minorities in which, on average, households are bigger and sports participation rates lower. These changes have led to a declining market for existing sports facilities in such areas. Ironically, in some areas obsolete sports facilities have been turned over for use as construction sites for new houses in an attempt simply to redress the population effects we have described. Sports provision has suffered further problems in terms of their management. Traditionally a lot of the work in sports facilities has been done by volunteers. These volunteers have tended to be drawn predominantly from the middle-class population, but as we have seen, it was predominantly the middle class who moved out from these areas.

To accommodate some of these problems, Rotterdam sports policy has gradually moved in the direction of a 'target-group' approach. Two such initiatives will be discussed below: sports policies aimed at ethnic minorities and policies directed at 'marginal youth'. However, first we should consider some information relating to general trends in sports participation.

TRENDS IN SPORTS PARTICIPATION

In the Netherlands sports participation has experienced explosive growth since the Second World War. Nowadays 80 per cent of all young people participate in one or more sports. In the 1970s two important changes appeared in the big cities: the absolute number of young people decreased (a reflection of an ageing population), and preferences for different types of sport became more and more diverse. Together this led to a declining popularity of 'old', mostly team sports such as soccer, handball, korfball, and gymnastics, while 'new' sports, most of which can be practised on a more individual basis, such as surfing, golf, martial arts, aerobics, tennis, badminton, running, and cycling came into favour. Demographic changes and shifting sports preferences have had a severe impact on the existing sports structures, especially in the older areas of the big cities where many of these developments coincided. This is illustrated in Table 7.1 by the developments in organized soccer in Rotterdam.

Table 7.1. Population changes in Rotterdam 1976-86

	1976	1981	1984	1986
Total population in Rotterdam	585,500	570,500	561,500	572,000[*]
5 - 39 years-old (in %)	49.5%	48.8%	48.2%	46.1%
Expected number of soccer teams following demographic developments (base 1976)	2,087	2,002	1,950	1,844
Real number of teams	2,087	1,957	1,602	1,447

Source: Compiled by the author.

[*] including 17,000 as result of boundary shift.

Demographic developments alone would have led to a diminution of soccer teams of 12 per cent in 1986. In fact, their number declined by some 31 per cent. Other sports which traditionally had a smiliar attraction, especially for youth, show comparable figures.

The changes in sports preference are consistent with change in the traditional 'sports career', with more individually based choices in leisure, diminishing club loyalty (people changing more readily from one club to another), and an enormous growth of opportunities in sport. Young people may often still start their sporting career playing soccer or gymnastics but change to other sports earlier and more often than had formerly been the case (Uphus 1984; Rijpma 1986). Participating in sports has now become the norm, but just which sports are practised has become more subject to fashion (Giljam and Rijpma 1987).

It is perhaps fairly obvious that these changes relate to the lifestyles of the young and well-to-do. Their lifestyle, with its small households, flexible time-schedules, mobility, and orientation towards hedonism, has become more prominent in city life, and this certainly is one of the factors that has fostered changes in sports participation. Furthermore, as we have indicated, these developments resonate with aspects of Rotterdam's sport policy. However, it is recognized that many groups do not enjoy this type of lifestyle, and two of these underprivileged groups have been made the subject of experimental target group sports policies.

TWO TARGET GROUPS

In general, the scale of these experiments has been small. One cannot compare it with large-scale campaigns such as 'Sport for All' in the United Kingdom. The rationale behind these experiments is only indirectly related to an ideal of equal opportunities or of health care. This becomes apparent when one notes that not all underprivileged groups are subject to these policy initiatives. Most attention is directed at potentially 'troublesome' (mostly unemployed) youth, and ethnic minorities. The reasons for the selection of these two target groups seem to be a mixture of political, social, and financial considerations. With regard to the ethnic minorities, the City Board of Rotterdam has expressed concern about their isolation from the local community and has sought ways of integrating them. Although in the end this policy failed, it had been a policy aim to avoid concentrations of ethnic minority groups by dividing them up and locating them in different neighbourhoods so that they could be easily integrated within the neighbourhood communities. Sport has also been seen as a possible way to strengthen relations between ethnic minorities and the rest of the population. The experiments described below were meant to establish how this could be accomplished, and had, as an important aim, to generate some applied knowledge about the integrating processes involved.

The policy focus on the young unemployed resulted from a slightly different set of circumstances. The Ministry of Welfare, Health, and Culture (WHC, which incorporates responsibility for sport) started a national experimental scheme in the four big cities of the Randstad, aimed at the more problematic segment of the young unemployed (the randgroepjongeren or marginal youth). This scheme was also intended to generate more knowledge about the sports preferences of these young people. This kind of knowledge was thought to be potentially helpful in developing activities to provide experiences to facilitate the unemployed's re-entry into the labour market.

In addition to the factors already listed there are two further reasons for the special attention paid to these two groups. The first is the suspicion that isolation and disintegration may prove a fertile breeding ground for vandalism, aggression in public, drug addiction, and other forms of deviant behaviour. The second is that special programmes for the unemployed and ethnic minorities are of political significance. They allow the Social Democrats who dominate the Rotterdam City Council to display well-intentioned public policy which is partly financed by central government and which obscures the cuts that have been implemented in almost all local government spending programmes, including expenditure on sport.

ROTTERDAM'S ETHNIC MINORITIES

By 1987 approximately 160,000 Turks, 120,000 Moroccans, and 150,000 Surinamese were living in the Netherlands. Together with other smaller groups, the ethnic minority population totalled more than 550,000, much of it disproportionately concentrated in the inner-city districts of major cities. Rotterdam's population incorporates a significant proportion of the Dutch ethnic minorities with 28,000 Surinamese, 22,000 Turks, 11,500 Moroccans, 12,500 people of other Mediterranean groups, and 4000 Dutch Antilleans.

Reports by Brasse (1985) and the Ministry of WHC (1986a) conclude that older members of ethnic minority groups hardly participate in sport at all. In respect of young people, however, boys participate as much as non-ethnic Dutch boys of comparable school level, while girls, once they have left school, participate in sport very little. Brasse concludes that 70 per cent of the Turkish boys are active sports participants, whereas in the case of girls of Turkish extraction, the figure is only 5 per cent. The Ministry of WHC calculated that 45 per cent of Turkish boys and 40 per cent of Moroccan boys participate actively in sport.

However, only half of this number were active in Dutch (non-ethnic) sports clubs or private sports schools, the remainder playing sport in their own informal way in streets, parks, or sociocultural centres in their own neighbourhood.

Favourite sports of boys from these ethnic groups appear to be soccer, various martial arts, and weight training. Some of the best players in the Dutch soccer league and the best karateka are of Surinamese origin, whereas the best boxers traditionally originate from Mediterranean countries. Many women belonging to ethnic minorities have expressed an interest in swimming. This is true also of Muslim women, when a female-only environment can be provided. There is an increasing interest shown by women in sports such as volleyball and gymnastics and in table tennis by men. The participation of women from ethnic minorities in cycling courses is also surprisingly high. Cycling is a most common and, of course, a relatively cheap way of transportation in the Netherlands, but many members of the ethnic communities have had little experience of cycling. Many women from various ethnic communities seem eager to learn, while the men probably look upon it as a 'harmless' and 'useful' thing to do and therefore raise few objections. This activity is considered to be an example of cultural integration (WHC 1986b).

Policy experiments in Rotterdam were introduced in 1980, when two advisors were added to the Rotterdam Service for Sport and Recreation. Initially the Surinamese and Turkish worker were paid by national government, but after the experimental phase they were employed by the Rotterdam municipality on a regular basis. The general approach this scheme has adopted is to work towards goals on a step-by-step basis. The first goal was to get people playing sport, subsequently to get them playing in competitions of their own, and finally to attempt to integrate clubs and/or competitions into the Dutch leagues (Gemeente Rotterdam 1982). The advisors do not therefore try to create as many clubs as possible, but attempt to develop existing clubs, to help informal groups to enter regular competitions, and to create ethnic cadre. They show interested groups what is involved in financial and organizational terms in running a club of their own. However, it requires a lot of time and energy to help an informal group achieve independent club status and participate in a regular league. There are only one or two such groups each year which transform themselves into regular clubs. Difficulties that arise are mostly related to financial and organizational matters, such as the payments required to compete in national leagues, organizing competitions effectively, arranging annual meetings, organizing matches outside Rotterdam, and so on. People from these clubs are encouraged to participate in the Recreation Sports Leaders Course (which is roughly equivalent to the UK A-level) and in courses that prepare people for roles such as chairman or treasurer of a sports club. These courses are brief, very practical, and avoid the didactic approach of a formal school education. Nevertheless, relatively few (10 to 20) members of ethnic minority groups take part in the RSLA-courses each year.

Some examples of specific initiatives are included in the following. The Surinamese advisor arranged a very successful summertime soccer competition. Such out-of-season arrangements are very unusual in the Netherlands and he had to overcome many sceptics within the Sport and Recreation Service before he could start the competition. The Surinamese 'soccer festivals', however, are very popular now, even in other cities. Teams gather from all over the country bringing large bands of supporters with them who play music, socialize, and hold picnics. Every summer the competition is played on a huge sports complex near Rotterdam Airport, where many grounds are now more or less redundant because of the outmigration of previous residents.

Swimming has been promoted specifically for women. Creches, all-female spaces and female instructors have been provided. Groups of 20 to 30 women participate, and it seems that although most of the older women experience problems with the skills required to participate fully, they remain enthusiastic about the activity, partly because of the opportunities it provides for social contacts. After this scheme had got underway some of the husbands announced that they also wanted to learn to swim, though unlike the female group, the males were more serious about the activity itself and were more clearly motivated to follow a formal diploma-based course of instruction (Gemeente Rotterdam 1982).

Some centres for weight training and martial arts have also been set up that are intended to be easily accessible in social and financial terms. Besides some small-scale centres there are two larger ones, one on each side of the river.

Most centre users are of Surinamese or Mediterranean origin.

Finally, in order to reinforce the reciprocal cultural exchange between ethnic minorities and the rest of the Dutch population, the advisors have tried to introduce ethnic sports such as the Turkish 'tric-trac' to Dutch people (Gemeente Rotterdam 1985).

The experiment is considered to have been successful and working with and for immigrants is now incorporated in many activities. Further improvements could be made by integrating the initiatives of the sports sector with policy initiatives of the special Sub-department for Immigrants. Up to the present these sectors have developed their own plans and organized their separate activities for the same target group. Other groups of immigrants should also be approached. So far the primary focus has been on the Surinamese and the Turks because of their size relative to other minorities. One can expect more attention to be paid to the Moroccan group in the next few years. However, other groups in Rotterdam (Chinese, Cape Verdians, and others from African countries) might not be sufficiently numerous to justify special attention, while other European immigrants (Italians, Greek) have also tended to be discounted.

'MARGINAL YOUTH'

The term 'marginal youth' refers to people between 15 and 25 years old, who are confronted by an accumulation of problems such as unemployment, low levels of education, poor health, and poor living conditions, and those who have had 'contact' with the police and the judiciary. They are deemed to have problems spending their spare time usefully (Ministries of Social Affairs and Employment and WHC 1984). Depending on how strictly the boundaries are drawn, there are some thousands to tens of thousands of marginal youth in the Netherlands.

Marginal youth receive considerable attention in educational, welfare, and judicial policies. Sport is regularly cited as an important medium through which to communicate with and '(re)activate' marginal youth. For this reason in 1983 the Ministry of WHC started an experimental sports scheme aimed at this target group in the four major Dutch cities, including Rotterdam. Two advisors were recruited to set up 49, mostly small-scale, projects. During the four years for which the programme lasted they worked with a small budget of 25,000 guilders per city per year. The experiment was charged with providing an answer to the question of ways in which sport could be used as a means to 'motivate' marginal youth and to 'integrate them into wider society'.

From the beginning the advisors worked within the existing organizational infrastructure. In their approach to young people they employed sports organizations, street corner work, youth centres, and regular (lower level) forms of education. The results of these efforts were intended to inform the work of existing organizations, rather than being aimed at any new form of organization to be founded specifically for marginal youth. In their final report (Landelijke Contactraad 1987) the advisors conclude that existing sports clubs are not a suitable organizational framework for working with marginal youth. The problems of these youths are too wide-ranging and deeply rooted to be dealt with by organizations that are mainly run by volunteers. The report therefore advises against the use of existing clubs for implementation of schemes aimed at marginal youth. It promotes the establishment of clubs which are based on already existing informal groups among the target youth group. As is the case with the work with ethnic minorities, helping to establish groups that have a realistic chance of survival is costly in terms of time and effort.[1]

Street corner work proved to be a better starting point for sports projects with these young people. Two of the projects that operated in Rotterdam indicated that there was a lot of interest in sport among youth who, because of their circumstances, also require help with basic problems such as housing, welfare benefits, drug addiction problems, and so on. When approached and given the opportunity many of these young people were likely to spend five to ten hours on sports every week. The most popular sports were soccer, circuit training, boxing, and weight training. Furthermore, some members of this group also expressed an interest in some kind of formal sports education.[2]

Open youth centres (neighbourhood centres without formal membership) provided another useful channel through which to reach this target group. In a number of these centres small-scale facilities for weight training were installed. These centres were open all day and it is possible to use the facilities for a few hours a day in small groups (five to ten persons). The centres attract marginal youth for various reasons: they are cheaper than the well-equipped sports schools, any lack of skills on the part of participants is not conspicuous in such settings, and the young people concerned are likely to be surrounded by friends.

Out of these different small-scale initiatives, a scheme called the 'Sports Platform' was developed which currently involves work with some 25 centres. The Platform was formed to guarantee greater continuity for sports initiatives within sociocultural organizations. The centres are also able to develop a broader range of sports opportunities and a more effective use of materials, workers, courses, and so on. The Platform organizes courses specifically tailored to the needs of young people with few educational qualifications. These courses are designed to train supervisors of weight training and conditioning, organizers of soccer tournaments and the like, and provide information about regular sports initiatives in Rotterdam that are aimed at young people. Young people obtain some basic training in exercise physiology, equipment, and constructing recreation programmes, but it has been the aim of the Platform to link this instruction with official courses for sports school workers. In the first year of operation 30 young males with low levels of educational experience took part in this type of course, and this group met with considerable success. This was an important initiative because entry into these courses had in the past been available only to those with some academic qualifications. Subsequently, in Rotterdam one sports school has developed an education programme specifically for young people 15 to 17 years old, who do not possess the normal educational requirements. This programme includes considerable practical involvement in sport, and relates academic subjects on the curriculum (such as Dutch language, biology, etc.) directly to practical sporting concerns. All the lessons are designed to accommodate the shorter attention span associated with this group. Following this success, a similar initiative has now been taken at another school aimed at youths of 17 and older who have also had little educational experience.

However, girls and young women living in difficult situations are seldom attracted to the sports projects. They stay at home, marry at an early age and in this way partly avoid being officially labelled as unemployed (when the definition of being unemployed is restricted to 'paid jobs', see Naber 1985). There have been small-scale recreation projects in some schools for secondary education, which are called 'home economics schools' (and which are almost entirely female), and also in some neighbourhood centres. Females from 13 to 20 years of age took part in these recreation projects and appeared to be motivated more because of the social contacts the projects provided than because of interest in the sports activities. However, it also became clear that these young females with few educational qualifications hardly ever participated in sport under normal circumstances, and that this kind of project (based at a location with which they are familiar) did for some provide a stimulus to participation.

Other research has indicated that the number of young females becoming involved in sport is growing. A research study in Amsterdam (Gerlof 1987), for example, reported that of the females interviewed, all between the ages of 14 and 18, 66 per cent participated in sport, and that females were beginning to enter typical 'male sports' like soccer, weight training and conditioning, more often.

One can conclude therefore that these sports projects have proved to be useful, generating valuable insights into ways in which to reach marginal youth through sport. Despite this success, however, funding for these projects has only been provided in Amsterdam and the Hague. In Amsterdam 60,000 guilders per year has been earmarked for these types of sports projects, while in the Hague the sum is 25,000 guilders. In Amsterdam there is one advisor primarily concerned with coordinating the work of the neighbourhood centres and that of the Amsterdam Sports Service. A similar approach is to be taken in the Hague, although here there will be a particular focus on support for informal groups among marginal youth.

At the national level very little remains in terms of support for a specific sports policy directed at marginal youth. In the cities local authorities are confronted with an ever worsening financial situation which has meant that hardly any new projects have been initiated in the sphere of welfare policy. Furthermore, there appears to have been a growing feeling that these 'delinquents' do not deserve to be supported. There are also growing doubts about the connection between hooliganism and marginal youth, so that the problem(s) of marginal youth are perhaps felt to be less urgent. In Rotterdam this has led to the present situation, in which there is no specific budget to support expenditure on sports provision for marginal youth. Provision for this group of young people is now part of the general local youth policy and integrated within larger generic youth projects, which are predominantly financed by national government.

In the sports sector in particular, there is no specific focus on the needs of this group. Major concern is reserved for restructuring the supply of all kinds of sports facilities to accommodate changes in demand and to strengthen the tourist/leisure image of Rotterdam. Difficult target groups are now increasingly neglected in city policies, or in more appropriate sports terms, such groups have been relegated to the sidelines.

NOTES

1. In the Hague one of the advisors was instrumental in the establishment of the soccer club 'Exception'. The membership of this club consists of former drug addicts. Within its first year of existence the club was playing regular, competitive indoor soccer. This simple form of organization acted as a kind of training period for the second year, when Exception evolved into a fully fledged soccer club, playing outdoors. There were many internal and external problems in getting the club going (aggression among the members, financial problems, prejudices in the outside world, and so on). Nevertheless, at the time of writing Exception was continuing to operate successfully.

2. The street corner project in the centre of Rotterdam at the time of writing had run RSLA courses twice. One of the advisors was involved in the teaching of these courses and reported that it had proved impossible to succeed in working with young people still addicted to heroin. However, some success had been experienced in working with those who were already using methadon. This special RSLA course took twice as long as normal, was very practical in design and supervised very heavily.

REFERENCES

Brasse, P. (1985) Jonge Immigranten en Hun Vrije Tijd, Amsterdam: Universiteit van Amsterdam.

Gemeente Rotterdam (1982) Sport Bevordert Integratie, Rotterdam.

Gemeente Rotterdam (1985) Migranten op weg naar Sport en Recreatie, Rotterdam.

Sports Policy in Rotterdam

Gerlof, T. (1987) Redenen van Sportuitval bij Meisjes, Amsterdam: Universiteit van Amsterdam.
Giljam, M. and Rijpma, S. (1987) 'Stimulering sportdeelname onder de loep', Sport en Spel 1: 15-22.
Landelijke Contactraad (1987) Bloed, Zweet en ... te Weinig Banen, Dordrecht.
Ministries van SoZaWe/WVC (1984) Nota Jeugdbeleid, Den Haag: Staatsuitgeverij.
Ministerie van WVC (1986a) Minderheden in Perspectief, Rijswijk: Ministerie van WVC.
—— (1986b) Projecten Sport en Minderheden, Rijswijk: Ministerie van WVC.
Naber, P. (1985) Vriendinnen, Amsterdam: Vrije Universiteit.
Rijpma, S. (1986) 'Sportdeelneming in ontwikkeling', Sportintermedium 6: 29-36.
Uphus, M. (1984) Sportloopbaan, Breda: NWIT.
Wijngaarden, M. van (1986) Openluchtrecreatie onderzoek Rotterdam/Rijnmond 1985, Rotterdam.

8

PUBLIC SECTOR SPORT AND RECREATION INITIATIVES FOR THE UNEMPLOYED IN BRITAIN'S INNER CITIES

Sue Glyptis

Unemployment in the United Kingdom in the 1980s is dramatically higher than at any time in the preceding half century. Concurrent with the onset of high unemployment has been a change of emphasis in public sector leisure policies. This chapter briefly charts recent trends in unemployment in the UK and examines, using sport as an illustration, the nature and extent of special leisure policies for the unemployed and the effectiveness of special provisions.

BACKGROUND: UNEMPLOYMENT IN THE UK

From the start of the 1980s it was clear that unemployment was set to become one of the defining features of the decade. Until the mid-1970s, even with extra people entering the labour market, unemployment stayed below one million. In August 1975 it crept up to 1,151,000; then, after a further steady rise, it doubled within two years, from 1,390,500 in 1979 to 2,733,800 in 1981. Since September 1982 unemployment has exceeded 3 million, the official figure for January 1987 was 3,297,000, representing 11.9 per cent of the workforce. However, to these must be added around three-quarters of a million people who are out of work but engaged in various government training schemes.

The prospects of re-employment are reducing. Forty-five per cent of unemployed men in the UK have been out of work for over a year, 21 per cent for over three years, and 10 per cent for over five years. In the 55-59 age group, 63 per cent of those unemployed have been without a job for at least a year, and 17 per cent for over five years.

There are few signs to suggest that unemployment is merely a passing phase: it is rooted in structural changes in the economy, and exacerbated by worldwide depression, the rapid adoption of labour-saving technologies both in the manufacturing and service sectors, and the deflationary economic policies pursued by UK governments in the past decade.

Unemployment is unequal in its impact, geographically, socially, and occupationally. The inner cities, and in particular their semi-skilled and unskilled manual work-forces, have been particularly hard hit, especially those with a traditional dependence on a specialized (and therefore narrow) manufacturing base. The Archbishop of Canterbury's Commission on Urban Priority Areas (1986) described 'a vicious circle of causes and effects' in the inner cities, with economic decline compounded by physical decay and social disintegration. Data for the Inner City Priority Areas (Table 8.1) illustrate the extent of inner-city unemployment and the persistence of a north-south divide. The three London boroughs shown, despite their high absolute volume of unemployment, have a lower unemployment rate than their counterparts in the Midlands and the North. Figures for particular neighbourhoods can be high still, as the Archbishop's Commission confirmed: 'We have been confronted with the human consequences of unemployment, which in some urban areas may be over 50 per cent of the labour force and which occasionally reaches a level as high as 80 per cent' (Archbishop's Commission 1986: xiv).

There are further concentrations by age and ethnic origin. In spring 1985, with an overall unemployment rate for Britain of 10 per cent, the burden of unemployment was carried disproportionately by young people and ethnic minorities: within the 16-24 age group, 16 per cent of whites were out of work, 24 per cent of the Indian population, 34 per cent of West Indians, and 48 per cent of Pakistanis/Bangladeshis (Employment Gazette, January 1987). It should also be noted that a substantial proportion of female unemployment is 'invisible', due to the ineligibility of many married women to register, and the decision of others not to do so.

THE CONTEXT OF LEISURE POLICY

Against this changing social and economic scene must be set a changing policy approach to leisure services. Faced with the realities of under-used facilities, under-involvement in recreation by certain social groups, and underprivilege in

157

Table 8.1. Unemployment in inner-city priority areas, 1981

	Employers/ managers (%)	Professional workers (%)	Skilled manual (%)	Semi-skilled manual (%)	Unskilled manual (%)	Total (%)	Long-term[a] unemployed (%)	Age[b] 16-19 (%)	Age[b] 60-64 (%)
Birmingham	6.5	4.2	17.8	18.3	20.0	21.8	49	36	21
Gateshead	7.7	2.6	17.5	18.4	22.4	16.8	46	25	22
L.B. Hackney[c]	5.7	5.9	15.0	12.6	14.5	15.4	43	27	12
L.B. Islington[c]	5.5	4.8	13.0	11.2	13.4	12.9	38	24	9
L.B. Lambeth[c]	5.6	5.3	14.3	12.0	10.6	14.4	40	28	10
Liverpool	9.3	3.7	19.8	16.9	22.8	22.1	51	37	21
Manchester	8.8	3.4	19.1	17.9	22.5	20.3	45	32	17
Newcastle upon Tyne	4.7	2.5	18.0	21.1	21.7	17.7	44	30	19
Salford	7.1	14.3	21.4	18.9	23.5	20.8	47	30	18
Average	6.8	5.2	17.3	16.4	19.0	18.0			
Great Britain	3.4	2.5	9.8	10.8	14.3	9.4	37	18	12

Source: Faith in the City (1986) based on Manpower Services Commission data and 1981 Census of Population

a Per cent of unemployed people in 1984 out of work for over a year.
b Unemployment rate among the 16-19 and 60-64 age groups.
c L.B. = London Borough.

terms of access to housing, employment, and community resources, a new policy thrust emerged. The 1970s fashion for facility provision was supplemented - and in places supplanted - by 'community recreation', concerned with meeting the needs of various target groups within society whom recreation provisions had hitherto failed to attract. This new emphasis was evident, for example, in the work of the Sports Council. In the late 1970s the Council created a special category of grant-aid to assist projects in 'areas of special need', and initiatives were launched under special programmes concerned with 'Urban Deprivation' and 'Football and the Community'. These were aimed at a range of target groups, including school leavers, the elderly, women, the disabled, the unemployed, and the 'socially deprived'.

The 1980s brought stronger support and a stronger call for the community approach. By now there was surging unemployment, and the economic recession was deepening the divide between the 'haves' and the 'have-nots' in society. For community recreation providers, the unemployed became the dominant target group, both at the discussion table and in terms of the number of new schemes set up. The Sports Council launched three national demonstration schemes of sport for the unemployed in Derwentside, Leicester and Birmingham (Glyptis, Kay, and Donkin 1986), and the unemployed were the prime target group in the Council's 'Action Sport' programmes, established initially in Greater London and the West Midlands, and recently adopted in other regions (Rigg 1986). Owing to the acuteness of the unemployment problem, there was further impetus to initiate schemes at local level; lessons might be learned in due course from the national demonstration projects, but many local authorities, especially in inner urban areas, felt there was a need for more immediate action. A great many programmes of recreation for the unemployed thus developed, often in the form of deed before full diagnosis.

LOCAL AUTHORITY SPORTS PROVISION FOR THE UNEMPLOYED: THE CONTEMPORARY SCENE

The extent of local authority sports provision for the unemployed has been reviewed twice in the 1980s, first for England and Wales only (Glyptis and Riddington 1983) then, more substantively, for the UK as a whole (Glyptis and Pack 1987 forthcoming). Both appraisals involved a postal census of all district councils and metropolitan boroughs. The later review also involved extensive interviews with local authority officers developing and running schemes, and with unemployed users. Both enquiries sought details of sports provision specifically for the unemployed or from which they could benefit. The reviews were not confined to urban areas, though virtually all schemes of provision currently operating are urban-based. For the purposes of this chapter the general nature and development of schemes will be discussed with reference to the national scene; the operation of schemes and the response by the unemployed will be discussed using illustrative examples from urban areas.

At the time of the first review (1982) 53 per cent of authorities were making special provisions for the unemployed, and a further 7 per cent were offering more general price concessions available to the unemployed and others. Their schemes are categorized in Table 8.2.

Table 8.2. Local authority sports provision for the unemployed

	Per cent of local authorities		
	England 1982	England 1985	UK 1985
No provision	40	30	29
Price concessions for all users	7	8	7
Price concessions for unemployed	42	33	33
Organized sessions	-	4	5
Concession cards	5	16	14
Sports leadership	5	8	9
Other	1	-	3
Base (% of all local authorities)	316 (79%)	334 (90%)	454 (90%)

Source: Glyptis and Riddington (1983); Glyptis and Pack (1987)

By 1985 both the extent of provision nationally and its scale within particular authorities had increased, reflecting the increasing scale of unemployment, its continuing prominence as a leisure policy issue, and the increasing feeling among councillors and officers that local authorities should be seen to be responding. In the UK as a whole 64 per cent of local authorities were operating special schemes for the unemployed, and a further 7 per cent gave general price concessions; corresponding figures for England only were 61 per cent and 8 per cent. In the regions containing the largest concentrations of urban population, rates of provision were higher still: more than five in every six authorities in the North West region and Greater London were making special provision.

In detail schemes vary greatly, but the basic characteristics of each type in 1985 may be summarized as follows:

Price concessions for all users. Most general price concession schemes offer the use of facilities at reduced prices (mostly half normal price) at specified, usually off-peak times. Several are restricted to school term times only. However, as a policy development officer of Birmingham City Council said, 'The unemployed are unemployed all day every day.'

Price concessions for the unemployed (and, in some cases, other specified target groups). Over two-thirds of these schemes apply only to the unemployed, but in the remainder concessions are extended to one or more of the following target groups: pensioners, single parents, the disabled, students, those on work experience schemes, and other 'disadvantaged' groups. Many require proof of unemployed status, usually in the form of an unemployment benefit card (UB40) shown in order to gain entry at the cheaper prices. Around one in nine schemes encompass the family and dependants of unemployed people.

The nature of the concessions offered varies among schemes. Nearly one in five offer free use to the unemployed, and one in four apply at peak, as well as off-peak, times.

Organized sessions. These consist of one or two activity sessions per week, usually with basic coaching and a choice of activities available, either free or for a token charge. Most are intended specifically for unemployed people, but a few are open to other target groups.

Concession cards. Commonly known as 'Passport to

Leisure' schemes, these provisions are a packaged form of price concession through which users purchase, or are given, a card or 'passport' valid at specified facilities for a specified period. Twenty-five of the 65 schemes operating in 1985 were aimed at the unemployed as the sole target group, 16 of these extending also to the families of the unemployed. In some schemes concession card holders can obtain sports gear at reduced prices from local shops, and in one case concessionary access to some private sector facilities is also included. The local authority concerned had sold the idea through the promise of good publicity for the commercial operator, and the fact that the unemployed users would be making a contribution to fixed costs.

Sports leadership. These schemes offer a programme of activities, mostly for a range of target groups, especially unemployed youngsters. Some are available free of charge, others involve a small payment. All offer supervised sessions, some with formal coaching, but mostly for casual participation. Most schemes involve a substantial element of 'outreach', with sports leaders actively promoting participation by contacting members of the target groups through other organizations (e.g. drop-in centres), at their homes, or in streets and shopping centres. Swimming, football, five-a-side, basketball, table tennis, badminton, canoeing, weight training, and keep-fit classes make up major shares of the programmes offered, and in some cases competitive leagues have been established for some activities. While most schemes are confined to sports provision, a few contain a non-sporting element, including such provisions as mother and toddler groups, board games, sewing, discussion groups, walks, car and motorcycle maintenance, arts, crafts, and music. Newcastle-under-Lyme Borough Council's Newcastle Recreation Project, for example, is mainly a sports project but includes bingo, and plans to add monopoly, classes, art, cookery, and guitar lessons to its programme. Halton Borough Council's Daylight Leisure scheme contains a substantial arts element, with an arts development worker part-funded by Merseyside Arts.

The scale of operation ranges from just three or four staff members, to over 60 in the Newcastle Recreation Project. Most schemes provide activities at several venues and have their own transport and sports equipment. Virtually all have attracted financial help from other agencies, in particular from the government training agency, the Manpower Services Commission for the funding of staff, and from the Sports Council. Staff supported by the Manpower Services Commission are usually funded for a single year only, and are recruited from the ranks of the unemployed.

THE AIMS OF THE PROVIDERS

Providers' aims in directing schemes of provision towards particular target groups may relate to the group(s) concerned and their (assumed) needs; to the use and management of facilities; and to other, extraneous, reasons. Fewer than one in three local authorities in the 1985 review had sought guidance from elsewhere in developing their policies and provisions, and consultation with unemployed people was very much the exception rather than the rule. Even with published evidence accumulating on the experience of the earliest-established schemes, most new initiatives were set up in isolation, without recourse to the expressed needs of local people and organizations, or the experience of other local authorities addressing similar problems and providing similar schemes.

Most providers voice a general concern to 'help' the unemployed, by 'meeting their needs' and furnishing physical, social, and psychological well-being: reducing boredom, developing life-long interests, providing the opportunity to meet people, developing community spirit, enabling the unemployed to become involved, and developing a sense of belonging. Some authorities are more specifically concerned to ensure that price will not prevent participation.

Most schemes of provision, even if open to all sectors of the community, intend that the unemployed be their prime target, though in these cases a 'hidden' target, in order to avoid segregating and stigmatizing the unemployed. Comments from policy development officers involved in running such schemes included the following:

> There is evidence that the unemployed do not wish to be singled out for special treatment as a group even though the purpose may be benevolent . . . also [the authority thought it] wrong to ask people to undergo the indignity of producing evidence of their unemployment in order to qualify for the cheaper rate.

A concerted effort was made to avoid 'labelling' the

163

unemployed and the emphasis [was] placed on
integration, e.g. shift workers could attend with
unemployed people.

> The unemployed deserve to be integrated into sporting
> activity. It should not be necessary to treat them as a
> separate and different group.

A few authorities are concerned not so much to help the
unemployed, but to divert them from 'hanging around' and
'turning to bad things':

> To help relieve boredom . . . and attract the younger
> unemployed from cafes, street corners, etc.
> (policy development officer)

In some cases, especially the price concession schemes, the
main aim has more to do with filling facilities than with
catering for the customer:

> To promote daytime casual use.

> To reduce revenue loss.
> (offical council statements)

In a few authorities, although the overt mission is to help
the unemployed, the real impetus has been covert political
pressure:

> The Council offers free use to the unemployed as a
> political gesture.
> (policy development officer)

> It's a bit of a token gesture ... the Council wanted to be
> seen to be doing something.
> (policy implementation officer)

One honest officer reported that his department had set
up a scheme of provision because the neighbouring
authorities were doing something! In general, although with
notable exceptions, officers involved in the implementation
of schemes were more sceptical of their authorities' motives
and more ready to sense the limitations of leisure schemes
as a way of attracting large numbers of unemployed people
or imparting substantial benefits to them.

Others, however, were more positive:

It is probably fair to say that whatever policy is adopted there will be discontent in some quarter, as it is seen as 'insensitive and bureaucratic' or 'wasteful double subsidy' at either extreme. . . . There is a view that concessions are not required since a local authority already subsidises recreation centres, and further that if hardships do exist then they are a matter for national rather than local government concern. This authority, however, takes the view that local needs do exist and that it is inappropriate to wait for central government action.

(policy development officer)

While most authorities feel that sports opportunities for the unemployed are 'a good thing' to provide, their views differ on how best to deliver the service. Several authorities offering concession cards, organized sessions, and leadership schemes are keen to develop a package of activities and a club-like atmosphere in which to participate. Many of those offering leadership schemes are doing so in order to bring opportunities to the target groups in the neighbourhoods in which they live, to offer some structured activity in the form of basic coaching and competition, and to actively encourage newcomers into sport and win back those who may have been put off in the past. Halton Borough Council's Daylight Leisure scheme, for example, as described in an annual report of the project, is aimed at:

the unmotivated, the intimidated, the sports-shy, the 'it looks too much like hard work' types, specifically amongst the unemployed, part time workers, house-wives and young mothers, the disabled, the retired, students and shift workers. . . . People alienated by past experience of sport at school, intimidated by forever changing procedures within recreation centres, huge impersonal sports centres, hostile management attitudes.

The main areas of dissent among authorities are twofold. First, some feel that the unemployed should be separated for special treatment while others are strong advocates of integration. Second, some feel that price is such a barrier to the unemployed that opportunities should be provided free of charge; others, by contrast, argue that people only regard something as worth having if it bears a price.

THE RESPONSE OF THE UNEMPLOYED

Price concessions for all

Few schemes are monitored in a way that identifies the amount of use by specific target groups. Monitoring the usage of Knowsley Borough Council's price concession scheme for a sample week in summer 1986, however, showed that the scheme attracted some 4,043 attendees at the borough's six facilities, with between a fifth and a half of attendances generated by the unemployed, depending on the venue. The population of the borough is 169,000, including 18,800 registered unemployed people. Many of the unemployed users of the scheme have taken up sport as a result of becoming unemployed. They came along initially for 'something to do', and found it gave them a sense of purpose, whether it be keeping fit, acquiring new interests, or acquiring new friends:

> It's cheap and it's something to do to get out of the house. We come every Thursday for about five hours.

> This place gives you a sense of purpose, something to do instead of simply slumping in front of the telly.

> I used to play sport at school but never really liked it. Now I come quite often to do weights and play five-a-side - it's very sociable.

> I appreciate being fit. Being unemployed gives me loads of time to train. I come nearly every day to do weights, run, and maybe play squash.

Price concessions for the unemployed

Several authorities express disappointment at the low take-up of price concessions for the unemployed:

> Enjoyed by the few who use it.
>   (policy development officer)

Insignificant take-up - only 2-3 last week.
(policy implementation officer)

Others, however, report a gradual increase in unemployed attendances, and in some cases regular attendance by established groups of users, with certain venues and activities - notably swimming, football, and weight training - proving particularly popular.

Organized sessions

Levels of attendance, again, are lower than many providers had hoped for. One district reported that when the unemployed did attend sessions, it was in ones, twos and threes. The schemes that fare rather better tend to be those that actively promote a club-like atmosphere, such as Antrim Borough Council's weekly '2 - 4 Club' and those that offer more unusual activities. Stirling District Sports Council's summer scheme, for example, offers mid-week activity breaks (two nights away). As the organizers report:

> We know that these activities will never substitute for work, but they're really to get away from the day-to-day drudgery of the situation they're in ... a way of trying to break through and give them some sort of active interest.
> (scheme leader: designer and implementer of programme)

Concession cards

Though a quarter of the authorities offering concession cards are disappointed at the response to date, most report some successes. In the first year of operating its Leisure Pass scheme, the Royal Borough of Kensington and Chelsea, for example, sold approximately 2,000 passes, three-quarters of them to unemployed people. Unemployed people account for a quarter of Gateshead Borough Council's 11,860 Leisure Card holders. Birmingham City Council sells approximately 24,000 Passports to Leisure annually, 49 per cent to unemployed people. Unemployed users of Belfast City Council's concessionary membership scheme say that the main benefit they gain from taking part is the opportunity to keep fit at low cost. Most feel that the scheme takes their minds off being unemployed for a few hours and gives them a reason to get out of the house. Many users, especially young unemployed men, take their activities seriously, several attending every day for training. Indeed, a marked difference in attitude to unemployment is found between the young unemployed and their elders in the Belfast scheme. Comments typical of the young men were:

> I'm not too concerned about being unemployed.

> I'm not really down in the dumps about being unemployed. You learn to cope.

Older people see things very differently. Only one man over 40 years of age appeared to be content with unemployment; he had been out of work for over 20 years.

Sports leadership

There is a general feeling of success among most of the authorities providing sports leadership schemes. Middlesbrough Borough Council's Sports Motivation Project attracts at least 780 attendances per month (many others go unrecorded), an average of ten per activity session. The population of the borough is 150,000. Registered unemployment is approximately 16,300, representing a rate of 24 per cent. Some of the unemployed users come along specifically to benefit from the coaching available, or to learn a new sport, but more attend as a way of occupying time and getting out of the house:

> You have to do something or you'd crack up being unemployed.

> I come along to get out of the house, otherwise I'd be in the bookie's or down the pub spending my dole money.

The Newcastle Recreation Project (NRP) has 1,300 members; unemployed people make up 36 per cent of the membership, but a rather lower proportion of actual attendances. There are 5,600 registered unemployed people in the borough. The NRP leaders report that it is difficult to attract the unemployed to the scheme, and difficult to secure their regular commitment. Young unemployed women are particularly underrepresented among participants. The unemployed people who attend do so mainly for social reasons, many of them coming along as a group. Most have taken up activities in which they had not participated previously.

Nottingham City Council's Sport for the Unemployed scheme attracts an average of just over 400 attendances per week, 30 per cent of these by unemployed people. Nottingham has a population of 277,200 and registered unemployment is currently 23,000. Activities are provided at 24 venues throughout the city, at a price of 25 pence per session. Twenty-one of the scheme's 51 staff are involved in creche provision, and the scheme has had considerable success in attracting women, who make up 70 per cent of all attendees. Most users feel that the main benefit of attending the scheme is keeping fit. Others mention friendship, the imposition of a time structure, and relief from boredom. For some of the unemployed the scheme has become a central part of their routine:

> I base my life around the scheme really. I suppose it keeps me out of the boozer. I live alone, and the scheme is important to me for company.

Several authorities report achievements over and above the mere generation of attendances:

> Local young unemployed group have been through a community recreation leaders' scheme . . . in inner city area, and now busy coaching local youngsters.
> (policy development officer)

> We feel that the scheme has been particularly successful in assisting the creation and development of clubs and associations within the area, and developing groups which have eventually become self-supporting.
> (policy development officer)

For several users of Kirkcaldy's Leisure Leader project, the scheme had clearly become very important. An unemployed man in his 40s who had been out of work for 18 months had become very depressed. After a year out of work, his wife encouraged him to take up badminton, and he now attended the scheme every day. He said:

> If this place wasn't here I don't know what I'd do.

Some groups initiated by the scheme have moved towards

independent status, including a group of carpet bowls players who formed their own club in 1985 and now enter teams in local leagues.

ISSUES AND CONCLUSIONS

Staff training

Community recreation requires a rather special mix of skills from those who provide it. Sports leaders and motivators need a much broader range of abilities than that typically needed for 'conventional' facility management. Most sports leaders have a sporting background; few have experience of community contact, outreach work, or social work. The problems of recruiting people with such skills and providing appropriate staff training are compounded by the fact that in all schemes virtually all the staff are funded on one year non-renewable contracts through the Manpower Services Commission. Most are recruited with little or no experience of community contact work. Inevitably they take time to settle in to their work, and inevitably their motivation wanes in the two or three months prior to the expiration of their contracts. For the workers concerned, a year is scarcely long enough to acquire all the skills needed for the job in hand; for the schemes, even assuming that new staff are appointed, each year brings a completely 'cold' start, with little opportunity to plan strategically and build upon past successes. There is, of course, a training benefit to the workers concerned, and indeed community recreation provision in the UK would be much depleted were it not for the extent of staff funding provided through the Manpower Services Commission. However, the extent to which staff are qualified to cope with the complex business of promoting awareness, recruiting and motivating users, running activity sessions, providing tuition, and helping users to set up their own self-supporting activities must be questioned.

Community self-help

Several schemes, particularly of sports leadership, include within their objectives the intention of generating leadership from within the community, so that in due course the running of activities can be handed over to users themselves. As a policy development officer of Corby

District Council put it, the authority's aim is to 'innovate and abdicate'.

This is not easy to achieve. Newcastle-under-Lyme Borough Council, for example, has found that in most cases unemployed people are not keen to take on a leadership role, or to commit themselves to turning up regularly. To an extent, of course, there may be little incentive to take on the running of a scheme which someone else is already providing, as Halton Borough Council has found with its Daylight Leisure scheme:

> The attitude is that if Daylight Leisure is there and can do the stuff free, why should the group become independent and have to pay for it?
>
> (policy development officer)

Wrexham Maelor Borough Council has experienced the same problem:

> There is a danger that the leaders become crutches.
>
> (policy development officer)

It is not only the users who can become dependent on schemes; other providers, such as social services departments and government training schemes, can also take them for granted, or try to fob off their own clients to the recreation schemes. Newcastle-under-Lyme Borough Council reported that the Newcastle Recreation Project had been thought of by some organizations as

> a babysitting service for other agencies
>
> (scheme leader)

and Halton's Daylight Leisure scheme was sometimes seen as

> resources to prop up someone else's initiatives.
>
> (policy development officer)

The needs of the unemployed

Virtually all schemes of provision are founded on the basis of assumed need, and the case for their continuity is argued on the basis of assumed benefit. There is nothing inherently wrong with such an approach (although with its lack of clear objectives and measurable targets, it is hardly a model for effective service delivery), as long as there is due recognition that the needs and benefits are largely assumed. Even so, sport and recreation policy for the unemployed must be viewed at two levels: first in the context of inner city and social policy generally, and second in the context of leisure policy. As far as the first is concerned, sport and recreation are not high priorities for most unemployed people, as Wrexham Maelor Borough Council, for example, recognizes:

> Most people want work, they don't want to play badminton. With some of these schemes it's a bit like putting bandages over the symptoms.
>
> (policy development officer)

The sports development officer of Stirling District Sports Council agrees:

> Most of the unemployed are not interested in sport and recreation on a structured, regular, timetabled basis. ... They say they prefer to work out everything else they have to do - day to day chores, jobs to check - and then if they want they might go for a swim. They have their priorities, and for the majority sport and recreation is not one of them.

Except for a small minority - overwhelmingly young and male - who can effectively adopt sport as a central source of structure and satisfaction in their everyday lives, sport and recreation do not solve the problems of being unemployed, nor greatly soothe the experience of unemployment. They are but one ingredient - and not the core ingredient - in a potential policy package for the inner cities.

Within leisure policy, however, especially with its contemporary concern for community, the unemployed are important constituents. The evidence from current provisions is that sport can contribute some enjoyment and some purpose to the lives of some of the unemployed. However, relatively little has yet been achieved for the older unemployed, unemployed women, the unemployed in rural areas, and certain ethnic groups (notably indigenous whites in some inner city areas). With sensitive monitoring and honest introspection about progress and problems, the number of people involved in such schemes could undoubtedly increase, and lessons could be learned about the benefits actually accruing to those who take part. Already there are several different models which can form the basis for further provision, but there are three vital prerequisites for 'success'. First is a willingness to benefit from hindsight, that is to assess critically and build upon the achievements of other schemes, and learn lessons about their planning and management. Second and third, success can only be achieved in relation to stated aims and stated needs. Any formulation of policy and implementation of provision must be prefaced by an explicit statement of aims and as full an appraisal as possible of what (if anything) the target group(s) want. Admittedly, such an appraisal is more than usually difficult in the case of the unemployed, as they are not to found in cohesive, contactable groups, nor do they have seats at the bargaining tables of Britain. None the less, they, and other target groups within our inner cities should be consulted more fully to find out whether the provisions wished upon them are what they would wish upon themselves.

NOTES

1. Unless otherwise stated, all unemployment statistics are taken from the Employment Gazette 95 (3), March 1987.
2. All data on current schemes of provision, providers' aims, and scheme usage and users are drawn from research by Glyptis and Pack, funded by The Sports Council in conjunction with The Scottish Sports Council, The Sports Council for Northern Ireland, and The Sports Council for Wales.

REFERENCES

Archbishop of Canterbury's Commission on Urban Priority Areas (1986) Faith in the City, London: Church House Publishing.
Department of Employment (1987) Employment Gazette 95 (3), March.
—— (1987) Employment Gazette 95 (1), January.
—— (1987) Ethnic origin and economic status 18-29.
Glyptis, S.A. and Pack, C.M. (1987) Local Authority Sports Provision for the Unemployed. London: Sports Council (forthcoming).

Glyptis, S.A., Kay, T.A., and Donkin, D. (1986) Sport and the Unemployed. Final report on the monitoring of Sports Council schemes in Leicester, Derwentside, and Hockley Port, 1981-84, London: Sports Council.

Glyptis, S.A. and Riddington, A.C. (1983) Sport for the Unemployed: a Review of Local Authority Projects. Research Working Paper 21, London: Sports Council.

Rigg, M. (1986) Action Sport: An evaluation. London: Sports Council.

9

COMMUNITY RECREATION: NEW WINE IN OLD BOTTLES

Les Haywood and Frank Kew

INTRODUCTION

In the United Kingdom a number of local government authorities have recently adopted what have been termed 'community' approaches in determining effective policies for the provision of sport and physical recreation. With particular reference to three examples in the cities of Leicester, Sheffield, and Bradford, this chapter identifies the main characteristics of these approaches and offers a critique. In all community sport and recreation initiatives, management processes have been subject to considerable scrutiny and reformulation. In each case the overarching aim has been to develop a greater sensitivity to the needs of the community served by the programmes. This chapter suggests a more radical critique of what community sport and physical recreation may imply and involve. Present community initiatives are deficient because they fail to consider the diverse nature and structures of the very sporting activities that make up the programmes. While community approaches are characterized by the adoption of particular management styles and processes, the context of the programmes has largely been taken for granted and remains untheorized.

It is acknowledged that existing community approaches improve the opportunities for participation by disadvantaged groups, and further allow a greater degree of consultation with clients about their needs. But these approaches do not address an issue that is a central concern for sports theorists - the appropriateness of particular sport and physical recreation forms as instruments of social policy in community and educational contexts. Despite a growing critical literature (Gruneau 1980, 1983; Beamish 1982;

Hargreaves 1982), the question of the nature of sport forms as products and reproducers of particular traditions and values and their current relevance in an era of rapid social change does not seem to appear on this agenda.

This chapter therefore problematizes sports as traditionally or conventionally understood. A model of the nature and structures of sport forms is outlined as a heuristic device to illustrate that sports, the content of community programmes, are manifestly diverse. This diversity includes the particular challenges that are offered, the different ways in which these challenges are conditioned or regulated through rules, and the skills that have been developed as responses to that conditioned challenge. Moreover, the experiences of participants in confronting these sporting challenges are similarly diverse, as are the values which are inherent in different sport forms. It is therefore suggested that a sensitivity to the diversity of sport forms is a critical dimension to any policy that seeks to provide physical activities for those communities who are targeted. The model provides a vantage point for characterizing the content of community sports initiatives, and for providing recommendations for its application in the planning of future interventions in community provision.

REACTING TO COMMUNITY NEEDS: COMMUNITY RECREATION IN PRACTICE

Leicester

In 1986 the community recreation approach of Leicester's Recreation and Arts Department was highlighted as a exemplar of 'best practice' in recreation management by the Institute of Leisure and Amenity Management. This policy is in line with those at national level by bodies such as the Sports Council and the Central Council of Physical Recreation, exemplified by their 'Action Sport' and 'Operation Sport' schemes, and by Community Sports Leadership Award Courses. These initiatives have been adopted in inner urban areas characterized by high levels of unemployment, poor housing, poverty, and industrial decline. They exhibit a concern with the identification of special target groups, increasing opportunities for participation, the training of community sports leaders, and in some cases the adoption of participatory management styles. Leicester's

'Sport and Social Policy' document outlines the parameters of its community sport approach:

1. the identification of inner-city problems - unemployment, poverty, industrial decline, housing, racial disadvantage
2. the identification of specific target groups in need of special treatment
3. a shift in management styles from facility-orientation to client group-orientation
4. the devolution of responsibility down the management structure
5. an emphasis on outreach work and consultation with members of target groups about their perceived recreational needs
6. the injection of fun sessions and new activities

As a means of comparison with the Leicester policy, a more detailed analysis was undertaken of community recreation initiatives in Sheffield and Bradford. In the case of Sheffield, the focus is on city-wide policies. In the case of Bradford, the focus is upon one particular sports centre in the inner urban area of Manningham. This was one of the first centres in England to devise a 'community' approach to sports provision. Subsequently, this approach has been adopted and adapted by other central area sports centres in Bradford.

Sheffield

Local government in Sheffield has for all but two of the past 60 years been socialist. In the 1980s this local state has been at odds with central government on issues relating to financing the council's services - reductions in the national contribution to the local economy being positively counteracted by increases in locally-based income from rates and council rents in an effort to maintain services at existing levels.

Against this background the delivery of local services, including recreation, has become increasingly politicized in the last decade. Since 1980 there has been a deliberate campaign to use recreation as a tool to tackle problems of inequality, and provision has targeted disadvantaged and 'problem' groups: the unemployed, women, ethnic minorities, young people, the poor, the elderly. A major feature of this campaign since 1982 has been the adoption of 'community recreation' as a philosophy and method of working. During the past 18 months this approach has been formally incorporated into the management structures and processes of the department, not only as a means of improving service delivery, but in order also to delegate decision-making downwards among community recreation officers and play leaders.

Outreach

Community Recreation in Sheffield is the responsibility of one of the four assistant directors in the Recreation Department, together with a staff of 20 patch-based outreach community recreation officers and play leaders. The role of this team is to reach out to communities within their 'patch' or area in order to determine and develop local interests, and to make the fullest possible use of existing community facilities in order to meet these latent needs. The approach is thus not primarily based on facilities owned by the city council, but seeks also to utilize other underused resources such as redundant works, playing fields, and social facilities in the private sector.

Consultation

In line with Sheffield's policy commitment to community involvement in the decision-making process, the major characteristic of the community recreation approach is that of consultation. Community recreation officers, working through existing community networks, seek to involve people in the planning and programming of recreational activities. Typically this embodies such work as consultation on the siting and nature of play spaces; devolvement of responsibility to community groups to operate and manage sports facilities; and liaising with other agencies such as schools and sports clubs in order to maximize recreational opportunity for local residents.

Finance

In support of this policy, the Community Recreation division has received increased staffing and resourcing despite an overall climate of financial constraint upon local government spending. This funding has also permitted extensive subsidization of access to facilities and activities. For example, the unemployed, pensioners, and young people are eligible for a free 'Passport to Leisure' providing free facilities in off-peak time.

Community Sport

Potential clients have been contacted by outreach workers through existing voluntary community networks and in community settings such as 'drop-in' centres. These clients include the unemployed, youth, the elderly, ethnic minorities, and women. There has been an attempt to determine the needs and desires of these groups in terms of the range of sports demanded, and activity programmes and locations have been devised in consultation with the clients themselves. Outreach workers have thus taken the role of animateurs in generating enthusiasm and turning latent demand into manifest activity by matching up clients with resources and raising the awareness of like-minded potential participants. Examples of this process are the formation of 'women's only' groups for swimming, archery, and judo. There has also been some effort to widen the range of activities available to the community, making available certain "more exotic" sport, not normally easily accessible to disadvantaged groups e.g. canoeing, snorkelling, archery and climbing. There does not however appear to be any underlying rationale for the selection of activities appropriate for use in a community context - essentially the approach to activity is pragmatic, based on what people say they want and what can be provided from existing expertise and resources.

Bradford

In 1978 the local authority working party on inner city deprivation identified the Manningham area as one of the most deprived in the district and noted the gross inadequacy of provision for leisure. Levels of unemployment are high and housing stock is of poor quality, with a high incidence of overcrowding and limited space. This working party, aided by funding from the Urban Aid Programme, provided the impetus for Manningham Sports Centre to be built on a piece of derelict ground which earlier had been designated as a 'kick-about' area. The centre opened in November 1980 as the flagship of community recreation in the district.

Bradford Recreation Division's policy for the centre is 'to make Manningham Sports Centre a part of the community-based facilities which will provide a programme of activities reflecting the recreational, social and cultural needs of the community'. Hence from its inception the programme was characterized by 'reactivity' - providing sport and recreation activities in order to respond to the expressed needs and interests of clients. To realize this aim three tasks were identified:

1. to foster closer links with other social services in the area, e.g. housing, health, education, careers, and to learn from their knowledge of the area
2. to establish a dialogue with community groups and to learn about their needs in terms of sports and recreation. For this, staff had to deploy communication and outreach skills and be able to feed back information and share interests
3. to establish credibility and create a particular identity among potential centre users; to undermine preconceptions about local authority leisure services, for example that they are expensive, mainly for the middle classes, and, in the managers words 'a bit like school'.

As has already been argued, the emphasis on presentation rather than considerations of sports activities themselves is a characteristic feature of community recreation. In Bradford, activities are therefore organized with the following in mind:

1. informality - minimize the imposition of structuring activities
2. no provision of 'courses' which necessarily require attendance over a period of time, predetermined scheduling, and a financial commitment by participants at the beginning of that period
3. pay as you enter, for single sessions
4. no booking in advance (although this has been discontinued lately as pressure of usage rises)

In keeping with the ethos of open access, management has resisted the establishment of both user schemes and user committees. The first was deemed a hurdle to participation in that it required bureaucratic measures which would deter potential users. User committees were seen to be inappropriate since they would be dominated by vocal, politically sensitive, and mainly white community groups. These would not provide an adequate representation of the expressed interests of the local community although they would claim to represent the real interests of that community. In short, the management policy has been to revise deliberately the position of administrative and bureaucratic procedures which might detract from the 'reactive' style of the community recreation programme. This commitment to reacting to community needs requires continuous reappraisal of policy and of provision. According to the present management, the period 1983-85 was characterized by a failure to sustain credibility with the community, an inflexibility with respect to the choice and scheduling of activities, and a decline in attendance. A subsequent reappraisal of the centre's objectives met with notable sucess.

Acting on the advice and experience of other social services, management decided that there was little point in providing recreational activities for Asian women. This decision proved to be erroneous, as 'women only' sessions have been extremely successful in attracting Asian women to sessions on aerobics and self-defence.

The unemployed were targeted by providing specific sessions. These sessions have now been discontinued because they were dominated by a particular ethnic group drawn mainly from outside the immediate locality. The provision of additional 'unemployed sessions' scheduled at different times met a similar fate despite alterations to the way the sessions were structured. Therefore, the decision was taken to discontinue the sessions altogether. The overall result is that more unemployed people use the centre and these are drawn mainly from the local community, especially Asian males. This illustrates that targeting particular disadvantaged groups has the unanticipated effect of stigmatizing those people deemed to be worthy of special leisure provision.

THE LIMITS OF REACTIVITY

In Leicester, Sheffield, and Bradford, the community recreation approach is characterized by a shift in management structures and processes from a facility-based provider-orientation to a consultation-based client-orientation. The aim is to break down perceptual barriers to participation by identifying community needs and subsequently providing for them. As we have seen, flexibility, reactivity, open access, and informality are key concerns in this process.

However, this policy relies on an implicit assumption that the target population possesses a collective understanding of the range of sports and physical recreation available, upon which an informed choice may be made. Since leisure professionals pursue this reactive policy, they are absolved of any responsibility for providing for sporting activities which may not be within the collective experience of client groups.

If they were not to absolve themselves of this responsibility, leisure professionals would be making a political intervention into leisure provision, merely by problematizing sports as traditionally understood. In short, leisure professionals are confronted with a range of objectively instituted sport forms which are produced (and so reproduced) over time, and they treat these in a relatively unproblematic manner.

A similar issue is outlined by Mennell (1979) in his consideration of the problems in identifying cultural needs. He points up the difficulties encountered by providers working within the 'animation' tradition in moving from clients' wishes to real needs - from the known to the unknown. In so doing he highlights the conceptual limitations of a purely reactive approach to consultation with client groups, and suggests the necessity of going beyond this dimension of needs if opportunities are to be realized for real advances in the ability of people to recognize their potential in culture and recreation.

However, reacting to the expressed interests of client groups does not necessarily preclude the possibility of being proactive. We further suggest that in order to be proactive, community recreation personnel must be sensitive to the differences between sports and physical recreation in terms of their structural characteristics. Torkildsen (1986) has argued that the success of community recreation programming depends on an understanding of the nature of sports and physical recreation. However, his analysis results in a series of crude classifications of sports: for example, those requiring large/small spaces, those with high/low skill thresholds or high/low technical requirements in terms of equipment, those that appeal to younger/older clients or to men/women, and those that are unpopular/popular with different ethnic groups. This is not an exhaustive list, and clearly community recreation programming must incorporate these issues in order to mount effective provision. But these classifications represent a constrained understanding of the nature of sporting activities - one that is limited to either a consideration of the organizational and management issues posed by providing particular sports, or the acknowledgement that sports differ in their appeal to different client groups.

There is much more to the nature of sporting activities than this analysis allows. In order to be proactive in providing for community recreation, leisure personnel must acknowledge that the nature and structure of individual sports are crucially different from one another. Once this is understood, community recreation personnel could offer a range of sports experience that would not necessarily be offered if a purely reactive approach were followed, while still working within the given constraints of finance, facility, and expertise.

Indeed, these issues are not restricted to community recreation programmes. Any assessment of the nature, function, or place of sports and physical recreation in contemporary society must be based on an understanding of the range of social processes that together comprise what we conventionally call sports. What differences in experiences do these sports offer? How are these experiences differentiated one from another?

A fundamental first step, therefore, in providing for community recreation is a rethinking of the nature and structure of diverse sport and physical recreation forms. This applies also to other initiatives in public sector provision and programming if a closer integration of sporting experiences and individual needs, however defined, is to be accomplished.

Few recreation providers to date have taken this necessary first step. This is possibly due to the acceptance of a commonsense understanding of 'sport'. More probably, however, it relates to the lack of any adequate method of analysis and classification of heterogeneous sports. Consequently, the following model might sensitize community recreation professionals to the diverse nature of experiences provided in and through sports.

THE DIVERSITY OF SPORT FORMS

The model for exploring the basic properties of sport forms (Figure 9.1) draws to some extent on earlier typifications (McIntosh 1964; Caillois 1961; Best 1980). However, we have tried to go beyond the level of 'motivation to participate' that characterizes most other analyses in order to work through in detail the consequences of the initial challenges inherent in all sport forms.

What sports have in common is that they consist of a contrived (often arbitrary) problem which somehow has to be solved through the deployment of a range of psycho-motor skills performed by individuals and/or groups. This basic consistency in sports has led to its perception as a unified whole; what it masks is in fact a series of profound differences among and within groups of sports. These differences flow from the fact that the contrived problem at the heart of sports takes a variety of forms; that the conditions imposed upon solutions to these problems are manifold; and that the psycho-motor responses to this matrix are drawn from the whole range of human action capacities.

In order to determine the nature of these properties, we suggest that the variety of sport forms should be compared and contrasted by posing the following questions:

1. What is the nature of the <u>challenge</u> - the basic problem to be solved?
2. What sorts of <u>conditions</u> are imposed upon this challenge?
3. What is the nature of the <u>response</u> resulting from the conditioned challenge?

The <u>challenge</u> takes one or two fundamental forms; it is either <u>environmental</u> or <u>interpersonal</u>. Environmental challenges (usually to do with gravity or friction) may be subdivided into those posed by a <u>natural</u> phenomenon (e.g. ice, rock, water) and those that are essentially <u>artificial</u> (e.g. trampolines, hurdles). Both natural and artificial challenges may be further categorized, in Best's terms, as <u>purposive</u> or <u>aesthetic</u>. This is a specific use of Best's distinction (which in its original form is applied more generally) in that in some activities, for example, canoeing, the outcome is central; in others, however, as in gymnastics, the style of performance is crucial. While recognizing that outcome and style are linked to varying degrees in different

Figure 9.1. Structural properties of sports forms

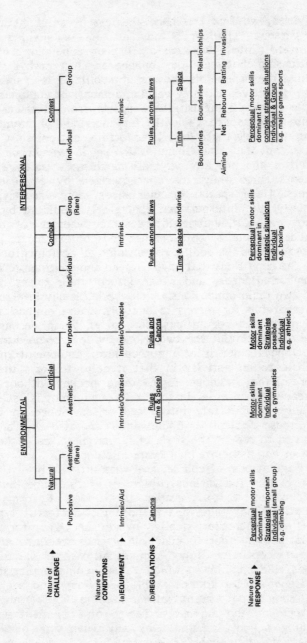

activities, we find this none the less a useful distinction. Interpersonal challenges may also be subdivided (after McIntosh) into two basic forms, depending on the relationship between the opponents. In combat sports, striking the opponent's body or immobilizing it in some way is the objective, and only varying amounts of equipment and simple rules distinguish these sports from a crude fight. Combat sports are typically for individuals, team fights being relegated these days to entertainment per se. Contest sports, on the other hand, may be individual or group activities and in many ways are much more contrived than combats since they are characterized by a variety of targets. Here spatial circumstances differ greatly; and, crucially, the interpersonal struggle is mediated by some object (e.g. ball, shuttle) interposed between the opponents. What is common to both combat and contest sports is that the outcome is the goal towards which all action is focused.

The conditions that have evolved and continue to evolve around challenges, and which inform their exact nature, have two main dimensions which, while clearly interrelated, are separable for means of analysis. These dimensions are equipment and regulations, the latter being perhaps the more interesting of the two. None the less, some discussion about the former is also appropriate. Equipment may be intrinsic to an activity in that it helps to form the very nature of the challenge; for example, hockey without sticks is clearly a nonsense. In this sense equipment is usually an obstacle, deliberately introduced or developed to create gratuitous difficulty. Equipment can also be an aid, however, to reduce the scale of the problem, as in the case of ropes and associated hardware in climbing.

Regulations, of course, are what ultimately distinguish sports within the various categories of challenge, but it is also instructive to consider the different forms that regulations may take, and to note that different types of challenge characteristically evoke specific forms of regulation. In order to clarify this issue we have adopted three conceptually (if not semantically) separable terms - canons, rules, and laws - which we use in a particular sense.

Canons refer to acceptable behaviour, and are much more subject to current values, even fashions, than rules. For example the amount and type of equipment used in climbing is not legislated by any governing body, and appears in no rulebook. This information is, however, well known to climbers through informal channels at any given time. Of course, 'sportsmanship' is the most persistent and thorny area in the realm of canons in most sports.

Rules describe necessary behaviour; they are essentially about how to play sport forms (e.g. backward passing in rugby football). They prescribe or establish the limits to one's action within the context of the particular sport.

Laws refer to the laws of the land which underly the rules and canons of sports and which in some interpersonal sports, where violent physical contact is inevitable signify the bottom line - the point beyond which behaviour becomes not merely unacceptable or unruly but unlawful (Grayson 1979).

As one moves from natural environmental, through artificial, to interpersonal sports, a shift from reliance on canons to rules and thence to laws is discernible. The very experience of regulated behaviour, of freedom and constraint inherent in each type of sport is crucially different: the degree of choice, the nature of rewards and sanctions, the consequences of disobedience or conformity.

A further elaboration of the rules of interpersonal sports, but not usually of the environmental ones, is the detailed specification of time and space. Time imposes a boundary around the activity, cutting it off temporarily from other social behaviour; spatial considerations define both the playing area, and in the case of contests, the playing relationship between opponents. For example, contestants may share territory, use it alternately, or attack it. This element of the use of space leads to Mauldon and Redfern's classification (1969) of five major types of game sports, all of which exhibit major differences in form and content even though they belong in the same overall contest category: aiming games, (golf); net games (volleyball); rebound games (squash); batting games (cricket); running or invasion games (football).

The nature of the response to the blend of challenge and conditions peculiar to each sport provides the mixture of psycho-motor skills and strategies employed singly and in co-operation with others which are the manifestations of sports as they are experienced by participants. These skills and strategies may be further subdivided on such bases as 'closed' (motor-dominant)/'open' (perceptual-dominant); fine/ gross; locomotion/propulsion; co-operation/deception. It is sufficient to suggest again that the experience of the individual player varies significantly from sport to sport.

Figure 9.1 displays the challenge, conditions, and response of any given sport form within one of the broad categories (environmental/interpersonal) and compares it with other forms both within and outside that category. In this way the major variations in the conception and execution of each form become readily apparent. Some activities have been suggested in Figure 9.1 as examples. It is clear that some activities hold a central position between environmental and interpersonal challenges - athletics is a good example - and that there is a tendency for environmental challenges to take on a marked interpersonal flavour as they are influenced by the wider competitive culture that infuses modern sports.

CONCLUSION

In Great Britain there is considerable disquiet in the education service that traditional school sports are not relevant to the needs of many who are provided with a physical education. The key argument is that traditional sports foster a kind of elitism which effectively bars most children from gaining satisfactory experiences from school sport. The main response is to downplay competitive structures and to provide 'recreational' programmes in a wider range of sporting activities. In this provision, choice seems to be a major factor, coupled with an 'ethos' that cultivates a noncompetitive attitude towards participation, with an accent on individual enjoyment. In effect, this policy resonates well with the community recreation programmes discussed above. Meritocracy and elitism are out; mass participation and 'relevance' are in.

However, whether one perceives these aims as being laudable or misconceived, there is a failure to address the issue of what sorts of experiences are inherent within different forms of sport. Such a failure is starkly demonstrated in programmes designed to provide alternatives to elitist sporting structures, while utilizing activities which, by virtue of their inherent characteristics, demand competition (on the basis of merit) between participants. To play badminton, for example, is by definition to engage in a competitive zero-sum activity. The game has no sense unless participants try to win. Hence, the very structure of the activity compromises the particular aims which some physical education personnel want to advance.

Louise Bricknell (1986) argues that modern sport is trapped behind a mask of outdated, out-of-touch values.

British sport is riddled by class domination, gender and racial oppression. She concludes:

> Only by learning to question dominant values and ideologies of these sports will pupils ... learn to question their existence ... by adopting their own sporting values and experiences, they will start to see that a different society with different meanings, beliefs and values can develop.

This argument is, of course, in line with those critical analyses of sport in capitalist society cited briefly in the introduction. Contemporary strategies to provide alternatives to what are perceived as elitist school sports exhibit similar characteristics. However, there is little evidence of any sustained analysis of the disparate structural properties of sport in the initiatives either of education or the leisure profession.

Education, we would argue, is one field in which adoption of our model for the analysis and classification of sport forms would expand traditional horizons about the nature and role of sport. Leisure providers and policy-makers, working with special populations or target groups in multicultural urban contexts, should employ this model and other analytical methods of enquiry in order critically to inform and develop sports provision. Examples of the application of the model in such contexts could take the following forms:-

1. Drawing on existing data on the range and nature of sports and physical recreation sponsored by the local state, the model could be used to explore relationships between the structual properties of sport forms and levels of funding accorded to different sports. Which categories of sports are favoured, which excluded? What are the implicit or explicit functions assigned to particular forms of sport which justify their subsidization by the public sector?

2. An examination should be undertaken of sports and physical recreation forms adopted by selected target groups such as ethnic minorities, women, the elderly and the unemployed. What forms of basic sports challenges appeal to such groups? What are their structural properties and what sort of social relationships do these sports entail? Compare these findings

with public sector provision in order to discover areas of match and mismatch, and to develop future policies accordingly.

3. Community approaches to sports provision demand critical thinking if they are to be effective. The model provides a tool for assessing the role of competition in sports; only interpersonal sports are inherently competitive in a confrontational sense. It therefore provides a framework for approaching sports creatively - adapting, modifying, inventing new challenges and new conditions; it also helps the provider to understand aspects of social change in sports; what are the basic properties of new sports, as opposed to the old 'industrial' sports which are in decline?

Community sports leaders working within such frameworks would be enabled to develop their own understanding of the nature of sports and to offer to clients a range of experimental creative alternatives to existing sports provision. These in turn could be monitored and compared with traditional activities in terms of participation data and client satisfaction.

These are only indications of possible courses of action which become available to recreation providers and policymakers when they adopt such an heuristic device for the analysis of sports. The particular demographic, social, and economic conditions that have developed in Western European cities in the late twentieth century demand new initiatives and new thinking about leisure policies. There have, however, been few tools available to the policymaker in pursuing this reappraisal, and much policymaking has been ad hoc and under-theorized.

This adoption of a model to understand the diversity of challenges, conditions, and responses in sports and physical recreation is an essential element in such a reappraisal of sports policy. Moreover, the development of similar critical analysis of the nature of other leisure forms is also necessary and desirable.

REFERENCES

Beamish, R. (1982) 'Sport and the logic of capitalism' in R. Gruneau and H. Cantelon (eds), Sport, Culture and the Modern State, Toronto: University of Toronto Press.
Best, D. (1980) Philosophy and Human Movement, London:

George, Allen and Unwin.

Bricknell, L. (1986) 'Outmoded Sports', Sports and Leisure 27 (2): 24-26.

Caillois, R. (1961) Man, Play and Games, Glencoe: Free Press.

Grayson, E. (1969) 'Crimes of soccer violence', Police Review 77 (February).

Gruneau, R. (1980) 'Freedom and constraint: the paradox of play, games, and sports' Journal of Sport and Social History 7 (3).

Hargreaves, J. (1982) Sport, Culture and Ideology, London: Routledge & Kegan Paul.

Hoberman, J. (1984) Sport and Political Ideology, London: Heinemann.

McIntosh, P. (1964) Sport and Society, London: Macmillan.

Mennell, S. (1979) 'Social Research and the study of cultural needs', in J. Zuzanek (ed.) Social Research and Cultural Policy, Waterloo: Otium Publications.

Torkildsen, S. (1986) Leisure and Recreation Management, London: E. & F.N. Spon.

SECTION THREE:
LEISURE AND SOCIO-SPATIAL STRUCTURE

After having highlighted in the first section the (national-local) political dimensions in terms of which urban leisure programmes are developed, and having looked at the more practical dimensions involved in the production and use of leisure facilities in the second section, this last section focuses on the spatial dimensions involved in urban leisure developments. In doing so the contributions explore the consequences of shifts in urban economic and social policy for the spatial distribution of public and private leisure facilities.

Because of cuts in central government expenditure on a range of public facilities and because of rapidly changing patterns of employment, many agencies of local government are attempting to refurbish and redevelop the inner city areas. Governments, faced with high rates of un-employment, particularly among the young and ethnic minorities, seek to attract private capital and higher-income groups and direct public expenditure to develop tourism, usually within the historic central city core. Central government, too, has encouraged such initiatives by making available funds to local authorities as well as by overruling local governments and their planning procedures to open up defunct heavy industry areas to market forces and development by private capital.

The following chapters explore how market forces find their expression in spatial forms, with particular attention to land use. In most of the areas studied, the rapid demise of primary industries has meant unemployment, a deteriorating built environment, and collapsing infrastructure of public services. Leisure plays a central role in plans for economic regeneration.

John Spink's contribution argues that land with a recreation function cannot compete with land serving industrial, commercial, or retailing functions. Consequently, recreation (in the form of pitches belonging to professional football clubs) is under pressure from capital for higher returns or profit. Clearly, the argument also holds for land use associated with other spatial-extensive leisure forms. The local authorities, and the public sector in general, will be under increased pressure to release land to the private sector, thereby limiting public control over its future development.

Jean-Michel Dewailly's chapter examines the opportunities for and constraints on outdoor recreation in the Lille region of Northern France. The land use is predominantly multifunctional in an urban area that is suffering from deindustrialization, unemployment, and social deprivation. He documents the 'institutional jungle' surrounding the planning and development of outdoor recreation resources, while highlighting the autonomy of numerous local communes. Although certain policy initiatives have met with some success, the planning process has failed to understand and meet the needs of the local multiracial population.

Myriam Jansen-Verbeke analyses tourism and recreation development plans in ten middle-sized Dutch cities. She outlines the intuitive marketing approach of local authority planners and the organizational and financial constraints within which they operate. Local tourism plans are not developed on the basis of a clear identification of the nature of their product or of their position within the market in relation to the target groups they construct. Nevertheless, short-term plans are currently under way, awaiting a fuelling by national funding.

Hans Mommaas and Hugo van der Poel's chapter traces the way in which leisure is a site for social divisions in major Dutch cities, with flourishing leisure lifestyles for 'gentrifiers' and 'reserves' for the marginalized and deprived. They tease out the ways in which private capital, local state initiatives, and leisure lifestyles meet to provide leisure opportunities for some and constraints for others. Indeed, their chapter provides a useful overview of many significant issues of both leisure and leisure policy within an urban context.

10

URBAN DEVELOPMENT, LEISURE FACILITIES, AND THE INNER CITY: A CASE-STUDY OF INNER LEEDS AND BRADFORD

John Spink

This chapter seeks to examine the relationship between processes of urban development and the availability of leisure facilities within the inner city. It relates the forces that structure land use in central areas of cities to the specific circumstances of parts of inner Leeds and Bradford, West Yorkshire.

LAND USE STRUCTURE AND INNER-CITY LEISURE FACILITIES

Within West European cities, leisure and recreational pursuits are as commodified as any other land-using activity and thus form an integral part of the real-estate structure of metropolitan areas, subject to the prevailing dynamics of investment, disinvestment, and development decisions. Since the land market tends to transfer sites and buildings to their most profitable use, a broad pattern of land uses has become established based in general, on competition between activities for limited urban space.

The pattern of land use thus established tends to reflect and reinforce the pattern of land values within the city, as demand for urban spaces is derived from the profitability or utility of sites. This potential for profitability or utility has classically been represented (see Figure 10.1) in the form of bid rents for property. This approach, derived from Alonso in the 1960s, makes simple assumptions about declining density and intensity of use away from a single city nucleus, and implies a free-market operation of land.

This type of neo-classical, equilibrium approach to the allocation of urban land use has been criticized extensively by neo-Marxists (Harvey 1973; Roweis and Scott 1981) for its oversimplified assumptions and its neglect of the realities of real estate submarkets, the sequential allocation of urban space, and the diversity of interests present. Its usefulness as an heuristic device is that it broadly represents the relative financial strength of competing land use and explains the intensive, largely commercial development of city centres. These uses have historically dominated the core, giving way outwards to nineteenth century industry and high density residential areas which have characterized the British inner city (Balchin and Kieve 1985).

Figure 10.1. Generalized bid-rent surface for urban areas

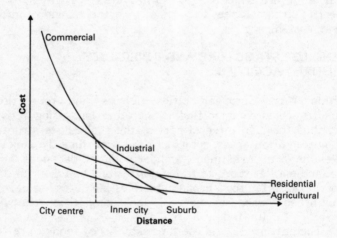

Leisure facilities range across the spectrum of bid rents and land values, being diverse enough functions to reflect either profitability or utility. Certain commercial operators are thus able to occupy central city sites based on the intense profitability of their provision (see Table 10.1) while other facilities, less profitable or operated less intensively, are located at a corresponding distance out from the central area, until at the periphery, extensive recreational uses can outbid agricultural activities. This market-structured pattern of leisure facility provision is, of course, modified by history and public intervention. It should, however, alert us to the nature of commercial land use and the dynamics involved. With rising rents due to growing demand for urban land, each of the land-use activities can be expected to relocate outwards, and commercial pressures ensure that redevelopment, when it occurs, is usually to a more intensive and profitable use of space.

Table 10.1. Land-use zones and leisure uses

Central area	High rents and land values
	Intensive and competitive
City core	land uses
	Commercial uses dominate
Central business district	Commercial leisure facilities are market-based, intensively and profitably operated
	Public leisure facilities are heavily subsidized
Inner city	Lower rents and land values
	Lower density of land use
	Mixed land uses in transition between core fringe and residential areas
	Some commercial leisure activities but smaller scale, less intensive in operation
	More extensive leisure facilities due to historic inertia or lower land values

Source: Compiled by the author

These latter processes form the crux of the problem for inner-city leisure facilities. In postwar British cities, demand for land has remained high and the scarcity value of urban land has consequently increased rapidly. As inflation has increased prices, land and property have been regarded as attractive long-term investments, reflecting the capitalized value of future rents. Real estate used by institutional investors in this way has maintained values even in neglected inner-city areas. Investors have chosen land rather than manufacturing industry as the target for investment. Thus, while improved transport links have made more suburban land accessible, thus reducing bid-rent gradients in theory, in practice the prospect of potential profits in the city centre has ensured a high value even for derelict land.

Planning intervention in Britain has tended to restrict the supply of available land and hence has ensured continuing high urban land values, encouraging owners to expect and await a price representing the potentially most profitable use. While rents have been more variable outside central areas, leading some authors to assume a serrated pattern of values rather than rent gradients as Alonso envisaged, urban land values in general (see Figure 10.2) have continued to increase (Evans 1983).

Figure 10.2. Serrated bid rents

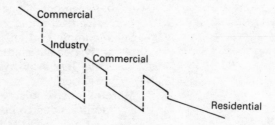

The preference of financial institutions for property investment in the belief that rents will increase faster than inflation has had self-fulfilling consequences in exchange terms. Between 1962 and 1980 in Britain, property capital values on offices, shops, and industry increased from an index base of 100 to 880, while the Financial Times all-share index rose from 100 to 227 and the retail prices index increased from 100 to 462 (Balchin and Kieve 1985: 73). This has ensured high land and premises costs in all urban areas, even, paradoxically, in derelict inner areas, encouraging borrowing at notionally high values and prompting owners to retain title in the expectation of future profitable redevelopment. It is within or against this real-estate context that inner-city leisure facilities must operate (Lawless and Brown 1986: chap. 14; Adams, Baum, and MacGregor 1988).

As the supply of central land is finite and inelastic, each increase in demand has led to proportionately greater increases in land value. The major property boom of the early 1970s and each succeeding upturn has increased prices to successively higher levels and encouraged commercial redevelopment farther from the centre. These supply-related features of macro-economic structure have impacted on the micro-economic aspects of land use in the inner city.

While urban land values have soared, other factors have arisen, radically altering the social and economic character of the inner city. National and international changes in economic structure have meant a catastrophic loss of employment in manufacturing, amounting to over 2 million jobs between 1960 and 1981, 80 per cent which were in London and the major conurbations (Balchin and Bull 1987: 99). This deindustrialization has been particularly severe for inner-city populations where rationalization of production, increasing capital intensity, and the closure of traditional large factory plants have led to massive job losses and urban disinvestment on a scale exceeding that of other European cities, except perhaps within the Franco-Belgian coalfield (Van den Berg 1982; Kitchen 1986; Balchin and Bull 1987). The structural collapse of traditional employment has been matched by massive social changes.

The inner areas of British cities have experienced a net loss of population for over 30 years, with the largest conurbations recording the greatest rates of population loss. Between 1971-81, inner London boroughs lost 25 per cent of their population while Glasgow lost 22 per cent and Manchester and Liverpool 16 per cent, to processes of decentralization and suburbanization (Lawless and Brown 1986: Chap. 8). Employment decline was in fact even more rapid than population loss and the end result has been a selective decentralization of population, with the younger, more skilled, higher-paid, and affluent groups moving out of inner-city areas. Despite some metropolitan gentrification, this has left most British cities with intra-urban divisions between the inner city and suburbia that are greater than any gap between regions or the 'north' and the 'south'.

Selective population changes have left a residual population in inner areas who are disproportionately elderly, drawn from ethnic minorities, from the low-paid or unemployed, and who occupy poorer housing with more rented accommodation. The characteristics of this population, its low levels of educational attainment, poverty, higher incidence of disease and increased death rates, large numbers of handicapped, high rates of delinquency and crime, and higher proportion of one-parent and larger families have tended to encourage 'social pathology' approaches to the area and its occupants (Balchin and Bull 1987: 119).

Socioeconomic structural change has thus left an inner-city concentration of vulnerable and disadvantaged groups in most British cities, paralleled in Europe by Rotterdam and Wien and differing from the more suburban distributions found in Goteborg, Koln, Paris, and Strasbourg (Drewe 1983). This concentration of the unemployed and elderly can in no sense be seen as a 'leisured society' since so many of its members exist at or below official definitions of poverty.

Leisure facilities within the inner city are thus subject to the joint pressures of urban development processes, which maintain relatively high rents and land values despite an atmosphere of cumulative decline, and a resident local population impoverished and disadvantaged. Commercial viability is thus rendered marginal or impossible and only a limited range of facilities can persist in such an economic climate. Historically, inner cities have been less well provided with active recreation facilities than other urban areas. Redevelopment has also tended to diminish the number of halls and sports facilities available, forcing up costs for disadvantaged participants (Department of the Environment 1977). The price sensitivity of inner-city residents and the links between sports participation and income present real problems for the commercial maintenance of leisure facilities, while the falling tax/rate base and declining support for local authority spending from central government means that greater public intervention is increasingly unlikely (Gratton and Taylor 1985; Balchin and Bull 1987).

All these factors portend further problems in the future provision of inner-city leisure facilities.

INNER-CITY LEISURE FACILITIES: THE EXTENT OF THE PROBLEM IN CENTRAL LEEDS AND BRADFORD

As has been shown so far, policymakers working within the context of the inner city are likely to be faced with a restricted recreational infrastructure, due in part to the nature of historic development of these areas, their recent neglect, and their increasingly limited appeal as markets for leisure commodities.

Pressures for redevelopment further tend to threaten the retention of the limited range of economically marginal and residual leisure land uses remaining there. These circumstances form the context for urban policy which is now explored, using examples from disadvantaged parts of central Leeds and Bradford, West Yorkshire.

The inner districts of Hunslet and Girlington have been selected to exemplify the nature of the problem and the processes operating locally. Within the cities of Leeds (population 690,000) and Bradford (population 350,000) respectively, each of these two districts forms part of a central core of high-density terraced housing, built in the nineteenth century, adjoining industrial zones. The areas have traditionally housed working-class populations employed in textiles, transport, printing, or engineering, which developed a long-established pattern of local loyalties, lifestyles, and values characteristic of urban populations in the industrial north of England, as extensively recorded elsewhere (Hoggart 1958). This was the established population that has been disrupted by the socioeconomic changes detailed in the previous section.

Today the Girlington district contains about 8,500 people forming 2,800 households, the majority of which occupy housing within a designated General Improvement Area. The 1981 census recorded population characteristics matching those expected for inner-city areas. It recorded

201

higher levels of economic inactivity than the rest of the city (40 per cent in Girlington to Bradford's 36 per cent); more New Commonwealth-born residents (21 per cent to 7 per cent); larger families with three or more children (15 to 9 per cent); more single-parent households (8 to 6 per cent); more retired people (14 to 12 per cent); greater representation of Social Class IV and V households (33 to 19 per cent); and limited representation of Social Class I (1 to 3 per cent).

Similar statistics were collected for the Hunslet area of Leeds in the 1981 census. Here, economic inactivity was found for over 40 per cent of the population of working age; there were more pensioner households (27 per cent); and many households dependent on local facilities due to lack of motor transport (73 per cent of households lack a car).

Surveys of shopping and leisure facilities were made in the area bounded by the major roads of Toller Lane and Thornton Road, Girlington (see Figure 10.3), and in the vicinity of Dewsbury Road, Leeds (see Figure 10.4). The findings are included as Tables 10.2 and 10.3 and show the consequences of the poverty experienced by the majority of the local populations. Even given the distortion of some 'through trade' attracted from the major radial roads which form the bulk of shopping streets, the pattern of facilities recorded bears testimony to the exigencies of low-income lifestyles.

There are large numbers of small shops in both districts which reflect the local demand for second-hand clothes and furniture, as well as the standard corner-shop staples of groceries and vegetables. A number of bakeries in the Girlington area have 'day-old' shops attached to them, and many shops in the Dewsbury Road area of Leeds have closed or appear to be operating unprofitably.

Leisure facilities are limited in both areas. The bulk of free time outside the home is catered for by public houses and working men's social clubs. Each area has a bingo hall in operation, along with a few betting shops. The video shops in the Girlington survey are mostly Asian-run and the stock reflects families reinforcing their cultural links and attempting to strengthen their children's use of 'mother tongue' (Pryke 1986). Overall, the surveys reveal the limitations of commercial provision of leisure and recreational facilities given the restricted effective demand of an impoverished local population. Thus the pattern of inner-urban land use reflects pressures of commercial

Figure 10.3. Girlington District, Bradford

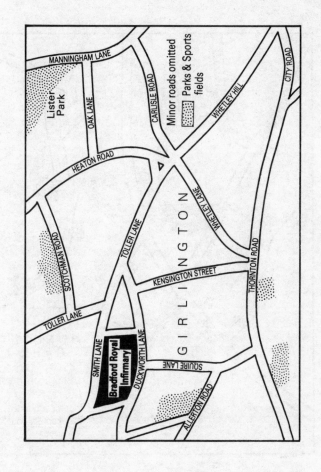

Figure 10.4. Hunslet/Dewsbury Road District, Leeds

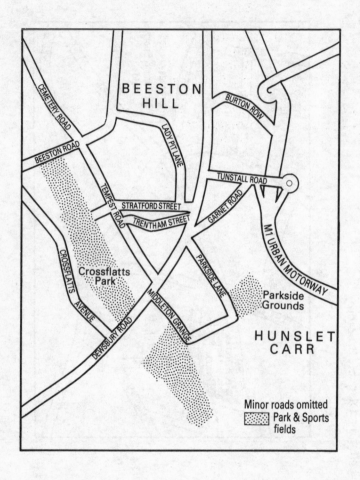

Table 10.2. Facilities in the Girlington District, Bradford

Area	Facility	Number
1, 2	Post office	3
1, 2	Bank/Building society	2
1, 3	Launderette	6
1, 2	Supermarket	2
1	Hairdresser	1
1, 2	Butcher	4
1, 2, 3	Off-licence/grocery	17
1, 2, 3	Newsagent	4
1, 2, 3	Baker	7
1, 2, 3	Greengrocer	7
1, 2, 3	Clothes	10
3	Furniture	1
2, 3	Electrical/TV	3
2, 3	DIY/Decorating	7
2	Shoes	3
2, 3	Second-hand goods	12
2, 3	Working Mens and social clubs	4
1, 2, 3	Public house	7
3	Bingo hall	1
2, 3	Betting shop	3
3	Amusement arcade	1
2	Recreation ground	1
1	Allotments	1
2, 3	Video library	5
1, 3	Garage/petrol	3
1, 2	Chemist	3
1, 2, 3	Fish and chips	4
1, 3	Other hot foods	8

Source: Compiled by the author.

Area key: 1 = Duckworth Lane; 2 = Thornton Road;
3 = Whetley Lane.

Table 10.3. Facilities in the Dewsbury Road area, Leeds

Area	Facility	Number
1	Post office	1
1	Bank/Building society	5
1	Launderette	1
1	Supermarket	1
1, 2	Hairdresser	5
1	Butcher	2
1, 2, 3	Off-licence/grocery	6
1, 2, 3	Newsagent	6
1	Baker	4
1, 2, 3	Greengrocer	5
1, 2, 3	Clothes	5
1	Furniture/carpets	5
1	Electrical/TV	5
1	DIY/Decorating	5
1	Second-hand goods	3
1	Finance/Insurance	2
1, 3	Empty shops	4
1	Various shops	5
1	Working Mens and social clubs	4
1, 2	Public house	5
1	Bingo hall	1
1	Betting shop	1
1	Library	1
1	Recreation ground	1
1	Allotments	1
1	Park	2
2	Sports centre	1
1	Garage/petrol	6
1	Chemist	2
1	Solicitor	1
1	Estate agent	3
1	Taxi office	1
1, 2	Fish and chips	4
1, 3	Cafe	4
1, 3	Other hot foods	3

Source: Compiled by the author.

Area key: 1 = Dewsbury Road; 2 = Hunslet Hall Road; 3 = Burton Road.

competition and the relative unattractiveness of leisure investment in such areas.

The Dewsbury Road district also exemplifies the additional problem detailed in the first section of this chapter, that of the pressures of commercial redevelopment reducing the range of local recreational facilities. This area of Leeds was formerly the home of Hunslet Rugby League Football Club (RLFC), a small professional rugby league (jouer à treize) club, occupying extensive grounds off Parkside Lane (see Figure 10.4).

Several economists have detailed the current problems of professional sports clubs in Britain. With soccer attendances falling from a postwar peak of 41 million in 1948-49 to 16.5 million in 1985-86, and the need to rely increasingly on sponsorship, the economic base of football and other professional clubs is likely to be insecure (Gratton and Taylor 1985: Chap. 12). For many inner-city clubs the size and nature of their traditional local market, in terms of population, is of crucial importance and in reality is likely to represent declining potential demand. The decline in attendance at grounds, so many of which are situated within inner-urban working-class districts, has been ascribed to alternative leisure activities with soccer representing an inferior good; changing fashions and lifestyles as patterns of cultural reproduction change; fear of violence; poor quality of play; and even (and less convincingly) to the degree of uncertainty of outcome (Jennett 1984; Walker 1986; Jennett and Sloane 1985; Sloane 1980; Haywood 1983).

By the time of its closure in July 1973, Hunslet RLFC, like many poor clubs, was unattractive from all these standpoints, yet its closure was largely due to development pressures. In this way it prefigures the current circumstances of a range of urban clubs. Professional clubs may close simply because their support dwindles, since their product is unattractive, and insufficient funds are available to keep them viable (e.g. Bradford Park Avenue closed after leaving the Football League in 1970). Football unprofitability has been a factor for some time with only 18 of the 92 clubs having current assets in excess of their liabilities. Yet recent pressures for development may even bring about the demise of relatively successful clubs in due course. (Chelsea Football Club of the 1st Division will have to buy out the development company, Marler Estates, which has taken over ownership of the club for an estimated £25 million in order to retain its Stamford Bridge ground.)

Leeds and Bradford

Table 10.4. Closure of professional sports clubs

1. Unsuccessful or uneconomic clubs →	unprofitable activity (often in areas of economic decline) →	requires subsidy from directors or local authority, e.g. Wolverhampton, Leeds, Halifax, Oldham, etc.

and/or

2. Clubs sited in areas of economic growth →	development pressures →	requires protection from takeover of shareholding by development company or real estate entrepreneurs e.g. Chelsea, Fulham

Source: Compiled by the author

While professional sports club directors are now expected to run their clubs as a costly hobby, not achieving capital gains or dividend payments as from normal firms (Gratton and Taylor 1985: 240) it is clear that the present depression and declining attendances will tempt many to follow the lead set by Hunslet RLFC in 1973. Then two-shilling (10p) shares in the club became worth over £2.00 each, on the sale of Parkside Grounds (used since 1888 for rugby and cricket) for £330,000 to a development company for building a warehouse complex. In order for this profit to be realized, the local community lost a club which, as a founder member of the Rugby Football League, had been in existence for 91 years, and had won the Rugby League Cup in 1934, and the championship in 1938 (Yorkshire Post, July 1973).

The loss of such local leisure and recreational facilities is particularly significant for disadvantaged inner-city areas. Not only is the existence of the club a public good, but any playing success is important in bringing prestige to depressed populations who identify with their club's success (e.g. Sunderland; see Derrick and McRory 1973). The

208

'Football and the Community' scheme showed what could be achieved using the focus of local sports clubs to involve working-class participants in active recreation (Gratton and Taylor 1985: 250), although its long-term benefits have been questioned (Ingham 1987). Above all, such local clubs are crucial in image-building since they represent community attachment and involvement, and their presence in a national league comes to signify the spirit of the place. Their locality, in a sporting embodiment, brings much-needed prestige to disadvantaged and alienated inner-urban communities.

In the case of Hunslet, the football club was revived the following season through the initiative of local business people. It played as New Hunslet, and in 1987 achieved promotion to the 1st Division of the Rugby League once more. However, Parkside Grounds were developed and lost from leisure use, and Hunslet's current sporting triumphs take place in another part of the city, as part of a ground-sharing scheme designed to assist the finances of the once-mighty Leeds United soccer club which has itself fallen upon hard times.

Hunslet's experience in the loss of a major facility and the poor level of commercial provision in inner districts, paralleled by Girlington, represents the extent of the problem facing urban policymakers.

INNER-CITY LEISURE FACILITIES: THE POLICY OPTIONS

Evidence of the operation of urban processes in the inner districts so far examined is not reassuring, since development pressures show every sign of reducing still further the already narrow range of commercial leisure facilities. The paradoxically high land values still maintained within disadvantaged areas, as discussed earlier in this chapter, ensure that any redevelopment is directed towards commercially more successful, non-leisure ends, serving a market beyond that of the local population. The profits still to be made from land and property development are a strong incentive to develop sites, particularly in cases like that of Hunslet RLFC, where a marginal or uncommercial facility can be replaced, bringing 'windfall' benefits to the directors. Extensive sites like sports grounds are, of course, particularly vulnerable to development pressures since they comprise some of the best locations in the country for accessibility and centrality, and above all, are sizeable pieces of building-land. One of the obstacles to redevelopment in inner-city areas, in addition to high costs, the need to reclaim sites, building costs, and so on, is the small size of land parcels available. Several studies have revealed the attractiveness of larger sites (Nicholls et al., 1982), ideally represented by sports grounds. The value of such properties is enhanced accordingly, and they are thus even more vulnerable, since these are the very sites currently used less intensively. The evidence of growing pressures affecting professional clubs, factory-sponsored teams, and even public authorities, to dispose of such valuable and undermaximized assets suggests that such leisure spaces are likely to diminish. Development pressures will thus tend to reduce still further the already scarce inner-urban amenity spaces available to a local disadvantaged and less mobile population.

Increased reliance on market forces has been a long stated objective of current government in Britain. As a 'New Right' or liberal-individualist administration (Dunleavy and O'Leary 1987), the Thatcher government has, in a series of measures, encouraged the sale of public assets like underutilized land and leisure facilities into the property market. It has attempted to encourage greater reliance on private provision of facilities and suggested privatization of public provision and contracts, like those for the management of local authority-owned sports centres, wherever possible. In such a political climate there has been little central state support for notions of protection of vulnerable spaces or populations through subsidies or land-use controls. Indeed, local authorities that have overtly resisted market tendencies have been threatened with the imposition of urban development corporation (UDC) powers over parts of their areas, similar to those imposed on Merseyside or London Docklands. These corporations, consisting of government appointee management, represent an expansion of the expensive, small-scale 'enterprise zone' initiatives, applied to urban areas from 1981 onwards, possessing wider powers of management and centrally directed land allocation (Balchin and Bull 1987). Their remit is to operate according to market criteria on the allocation of land, which in urban areas is likely to preclude leisure uses from a major role, other than in the case of features like marinas or water sports centres, which can form an attractive backdrop to up-market owner-occupied housing.

There are several parallels in this approach to inner-city development with those of the British government's activities within the housing sphere. In housing, local authority provision has been extensively privatized both as individual units and entire estates, grants for new building and refurbishment have been reduced, and the public have been encouraged and directed by tax concessions and lengthening council housing waiting lists into the private sector of owner-occupation (Malpass 1986). The consistent attitude of central government has ensured the spread of this ideology to all aspects of service provision, so that leisure and recreation cannot be isolated from these general tendencies. The same patterns of suburbanization and social polarization in terms of resource allocation and access are likely to be perpetuated as profitability and market support become the central features directing government policy.

Local authority urban planning initiatives could perhaps be expected to act as a bulwark against the encroachment of development forces within the inner city. A strong argument can be made for exclusionary zoning to protect vulnerable land uses and users, in the case of industry or leisure (Heikkila and Hutton 1986). Indeed, due to political expediency - the electoral power of the residential voter - land-use zoning controls do operate most extensively to protect private householders' utility and externalities within residential areas. However, when operating in inner areas with few facilities and little public open space, planning controls have been much less successful. The British Development Plans System was established to fulfill a largely regulatory and reactive role, and responds to private development initiatives which generate most urban change and necessarily reflect and reinforce market-centred tendencies (McKay and Cox 1979).

Such a position has been reinforced by current legislation, with the areas of planning jurisdiction limited or reduced through the creation of enterprise zones, urban development corporations, or simplified planning zones. Planning in a reactive rather than an initiatory capacity can do little to generate new leisure and recreational facilities. Attempts can be made using local plans, like the South Leeds or Manningham Local Plans, to co-ordinate public sector land uses and even to direct, corporatively, local authority spending budgets, but most of the plan objectives remain pious hopes given the power and direction of market forces necessary for implementation. In a competitive land market, less competitive uses can receive little support from a planning system which, for professional and political reasons, is increasingly coming to accept an ideology of facilitation, of the primacy of development, and the paramount need for job creation. Indeed, radical critics would suggest that from the first, urban planning has been established to legitimate and mystify the operation of urban real estate; and has, by its interventions, in fact served to reallocate resources regressively in its protection of property values, householders, commuters, and city central land values (Kirk 1980).

Local authority spending could, through differential allocation, be used to reverse the tide of inner-city disadvantage and deterioration. Positive discrimination in council spending might be used to develop new facilities in less well-endowed areas of the city. Certainly, initiatives like the South Leeds Sports Centre and the Manningham Sports Centre are significant features, just beyond the boundaries of this chapter's study areas. Further provision of these well-supported facilities could reverse the pattern and image of inner-city disadvantage. However, one of the major urban initiatives of this government has been to reduce the necessary funding in rate support grants allocated to local councils, from over 60 per cent of local authority expenditure in the 1970s to under 50 per cent in the 1980s (Balchin and Bull 1987: 104). In the light of such reductions, and with half of local authority recreation budgets being spent on parks and open spaces, which are not necessarily ideally located, it seems unlikely that local authority spending in the 1990s can correct the present resource imbalance (Gratton 1984).

In conclusion, it seems that few of the institutions involved in policymaking and intervention can, in an era of limited public spending, make much impact on the land-use problems of leisure in the inner city. Reductions in public spending have increased the power of commercial interests in the allocation of vital community resources. The present government's commitment to the market suggests that in future only private consortia would be encouraged to develop facilities in inner-urban areas. Even if such facilities were built they would, for market reasons, need to attract a city-wide catchment and thus, like so many of the employment initiatives, serve simply to encourage suburbanite commuting into the inner city, although for a different purpose.

Private consortia based within the inner-city

communities might provide better scope for initiatives acceptable to the Thatcher government. Instead of channelling funding through local authority agencies, co-operative developments centred on ethnic communities might attract sufficient public funding support to allow developments similar to the Ramgharia Sikh Sports Centre which has been developed on Roundhay Road in inner Leeds.

More generally, the only instances of central government spending significantly affecting resource allocation have been in the form of 'social expense' spending following urban disturbances (Kirby 1985). Given the allocation of City Action Team spending and its extension in 1986, cynics might suggest that riot has been more potent in attracting funds than the ballot box. In West Yorkshire the Chapeltown area of Leeds, which had experienced disturbances in 1985, received a share of the additional £8 million, while Bradford, with a relatively quiescent ethnic population and just as real problems, was ignored.

Without such funding the inner city seems condemned to operate not only as the barracks of the disadvantaged population of the reserve army of labour, but to suffer an expanded constraint on the quality of life beyond the employment sphere into that of leisure and recreation. Local authorities seem unable, and central government unwilling, even to extend powers for the protection of existing facilities, let alone the generation of new recreational space. The problem of the inner city remains that of those in greatest need receiving least assistance from the public or private sectors.

REFERENCES

Adams, C.D., Baum, A.E., and MacGregor, B.D. (1988) 'The availability of land for inner city development. A case study of Inner Manchester', Urban Studies 25; 65-76.

Balchin, P.N. and Bull, G.H. (1987) Regional and Urban Economics, London: Harper & Row.

Balchin, P.N. and Kieve, J.L. (1985) Urban Land Economics, London: Macmillan.

Department of the Environment (1977) Recreation and Deprivation in Inner Urban Areas London: HMSO.

Derrick, E, and McRory, J. (1973) 'Cup in hand: Sunderland's self-image after the cup', Centre for Urban and Regional Studies, Working Paper no. 8, University of Birmingham.

Drewe, P. (1983) Population Studies no. 7, Strasbourg: Council of Europe.

Dunleavy, P. and O'Leary, T. (1987) Theories of the State, Basingstoke: Macmillan.

Evans, A.W. (1983) 'The determination of the price of land', Urban Studies, 20: 119-29.

Gratton, C. (1984) 'Efficiency and equity aspects of public subsidies to sport and recreation', Local Government Studies, March/April, pp. 53-74.

Gratton, C. and Taylor, P. (1985) Sport and Recreation: An Economic Analysis, London: E. & F.N. Spon.

Hargreaves, J. (ed.) (1982) Sport, Culture, Ideology, London: Routledge.

Harvey, (1973) Social Justice and the City, London: Edward Arnold.

Haywood, L.J. (1983) 'Sport and cultural reproduction', Newsletter Supplement, Leisure Studies Association.

Heikkila, E. and Hutton, T.A. (1986) 'Towards an evaluative framework for land use policy in industrial districts of the urban core', Urban Studies 23; 47-60.

Hoggart, R. (1958) The Uses of Literacy, Harmondsworth: Penguin Books.

Ingham, R. (1987) 'Problems in implementing good ideas: Football clubs and their communities', Leisure Politics Planning and People, Leisure Studies Association.

Jennet, N. (1984) 'Attendances, uncertainty of outcome and policy in Scottish league football', Scottish Journal of Political Economy 31 (2), June 1984.

Jennet, N. and Sloane, P.J. (1985) 'The future of league football', Leisure Studies 4 (1): 61-86.

Kirby, A. (1985) 'Leisure as commodity: The role of the state', Progress in Human Geography 9 (1): 64-84.

Kirk, G. (1980) Urban Planning in a Capitalist Society, London: Croom Helm.

Kitchen, T. (1986) 'Inner city policy and practice', in K.G. Willis (ed.), Contemporary Issues in Town Planning, Aldershot: Gower.

Lawless, P. and Brown, F. (1986) Urban Growth and Change in Britain, London: Harper and Row.

Malpass, P. (1986) The Housing Crisis, London: Croom Helm.

McKay, D.H. and Cox, A.W. (1979) The Politics of Urban Change, London: Croom Helm.

Nicholls, D.C., Turner, D.M., Kirby-Smith, R., and Cullen, J.D. (1982) 'The risk business ...', Urban Studies 19: 331-41.

Pryke, J.M. (1986) 'Inner city health problems in Bradford', Unpublished BA dissertation, Bradford and Ilkley Community College.

Roweis, S.T. and Scott, A.J. (1981) 'The urban land question', in M. Dear and A.J. Scott (eds), Urbanisation and Urban Planning in Capitalist Society, London: Methuen.

Sloane, P.J. (1980) Sport in the Market, London: Institute of Economic Affairs.

Van den Berg, L. and Drewett, R. (1982) Urban Europe: A Study of Growth and Decline, Oxford: Pergamon.

Walker, B. (1986) 'The demand for professional league football and the success of football league teams ...', Urban Studies 23: 209-19.

11

OUTDOOR RECREATION AND DEVELOPMENT IN THE LILLE AND BASSIN MINIER REGION (NORTHERN FRANCE)

Jean Michel-Dewailly

With the increase in free time witnessed over the last few decades, outdoor recreation has become increasingly important as evidenced, for example, by the development of hiking, jogging, urban marathons, golfing, riding, tennis (indoor and outdoor), sailing and wind-surfing together with other more traditional and/or seasonal practices: bathing, football, rugby, cycling, fishing, hunting, etc.[1] These activities need space. Either they become sole land-users (golf courses, sports grounds, stretches of water) or they 'co-habit' with other functions to which they remain subordinate. Hunting, hiking, and riding in rural areas and forests do not prevent the principal function of production of these areas. This chapter focuses on the use of land for such recreational purposes by the local/regional population in the evenings, at weekends, or on excursions.

These activities and the spatial framework in which they are situated are of increasing economic significance. During an economic crisis, leisure, more than other sectors of industry, may be able to generate jobs. Connotations of modernism and a high standard of living are associated with outdoor recreation and the space which supports it. In popular consciousness, the outdoors = nature = green spaces = quality of life = social status (e.g. golf). This contributes greatly to the mental images attached to a town, a region, or an activity. For example, the IBM head office for northern France has decided to settle in a magnificent private park in close proximity to the largest recreational green space in Roubaix. This provides just one example of ways in which the economic benefits of provision for outdoor recreation have taken on a new importance. There may be fierce competition between locations that wish to be able to provide the most attractive living environment for potential investors. Outdoor recreation, however, may generate conflicting pressures. As a necessarily spatial element, outdoor recreation constitutes an essential component of any planning policy, and both highlights and is itself a source of, spatial conflicts. For these reasons geographical researchers have become increasingly interested in the phenomenon.

France seems to have discovered later and more slowly than its neighbours in Northern Europe the importance of a planning policy that takes space into account in a reasonable and appropriate manner. However, although the need to accommodate outdoor recreation in spatial plans is now acknowledged, it cannot yet be said that this is being done satisfactorily everywhere. The primary aim of this chapter therefore is to illustrate how outdoor recreation fits into a space which is already charged with multiple functions. After briefly describing the spatial characteristics of present land use, we will look at the tiers of government involved in recreation planning and at how they intervene. Finally, an overview of some important ongoing projects will help to give a more complete view of the workings of the system.

THE REGION OF LILLE AND THE COAL FIELDS: AN UNFAVOURABLE ENVIRONMENT FOR THE PRACTICE OF OUTDOOR RECREATION

An old industrial region

The five arrondissements in question constitute the demographic and economic heart of Nord Pas-de-Calais. The problems experienced here in economic, social and environmental terms are particularly acute. Table 11.1 illustrates some characteristics of the region and the concentration of its population. Approximately 2.3 million inhabitants, 60 per cent of the region's population, are located in less than a quarter of its area. Almost 95 per cent of the urban population live in approximately 600 inh.Km² and this is concentrated within only 287 of the 413 communes that constitute the area concerned.[2]

Although the population is almost entirely urban, the region is not entirely urbanized. However, for the purposes of our analysis we will focus on urban agglomerations and rural fringes, since our concerns lie with outdoor recreation planning for the majority, urban population.

Table 11.1. Main characteristics of the Lille and Bassin Minier region

Arrondissements	1	2	3	4	5	6	7	8
Lille	87,947	1,126.1	1,280	125	89	703.5	9,008	96.6
Douai	47,659	244.1	512	64	37	744.7	3,814	88.4
Valenciennes	63,480	360.3	568	82	59	774.1	4,393	94.2
Lens	27,839	332.2	1,193	39	37	713.8	8,518	99.7
Béthune	67,394	277.2	411	103	65	654.3	2,691	89.3
Total	294,319	2,339.9	795	413	287	712.6	5,665	94.95
Part of the Nord Pas-de-Calais region	23.7%	59.5%						

Source: Compiled by the author.

Note: 1 = surface in ha; 2 = population in thousands; 3 = density in inh./Km²; 4 = number of communes; 5 = of which urban communes; 6 = average surface of a commune; 7 = average population of a commune; 8 = percentage of urban population.

The five arrondissements listed in Table 11.1 incorporate the most significant elements of regional industry and include sites experiencing many of the acute economic, social, and environmental problems that have resulted from extractive industrial activity and from subsequent economic recession. In coal fields that have been exploited for 250 years there remain only five working pits, but more than 200 colliery spoil heaps and hundreds of hectares of industrial waste land. The decline of the iron and steel industry in the Valenciennes-Denain area has also added significantly to the problem of waste land. In the Lille-Roubaix-Tourcoing built-up area (also referred to as Metropole Nord), the crisis of the textile industries has led to the closing down of numerous factories. These three pillars of regional industry have only partially been replaced by industrial reconversion and the development of the tertiary sector. In short, the area bears closer resemblance to sites of industrial decline in other countries, such as the British 'black country' than it does to the rest of France.

Around these urban and industrial areas, the nearby countryside is relatively unattractive in terms of recreation. There are no large picturesque sites. Almost every area is dominated by intensive agriculture established throughout the centuries by means of land clearance and improvements of the watery plains (Lys, Scarpe). The afforestation level is very low (4.85% with 14,300 hectares of forests, of which only 6,834 represent established forests). The valleys of Scarpe and especially Sensée incorporate marshland which is more often than not 'colonized' by hundreds of caravans, bungalows, and cottages generally of relatively low aesthetic value. The rest of the rural space is suffering from widespread encroachment by urban expansion. As for the cities themselves, they offer very little outdoor leisure space: $16m^2$ per inhabitant in Lille, $10m^2$ in Roubaix and the Western coalfield, $17m^2$ for the whole of the Communauté Urbaine of Lille (which is largely attributable to the new town of Villeneuve d'Ascq which has $43m^2$).

A disadvantaged population

In such an environment the population does not have much going for it, especially as a relatively large part of the population is in the lower-income category. With a 13 per cent unemployment rate in 1985, Nord Pas-de-Calais is the second worst among the French regions. In the coal, textile, iron, and steel industries, there is a large percentage of foreigners, especially from North Africa. For example, in 1982 Roubaix had a 21.7 per cent immigrant population, of which more than half come from North Africa. The immigrant population often has families larger than those of the indigenous population, which has itself an above French average family size. The low level of professional qualification of the French and immigrant workers employed in traditional industries gives them a relatively low income. Motorization and mobility are consequently more limited among these sectors of the population. However, because of the poor quality of the urban environment, they tend to inhabit low-grade housing: rows of run-down workers' terraced houses and high-rise council estates. These groups are perhaps most in need of opportunities for access to the greenscape. As for the middle and upper classes, although they have easier access to outdoor recreational spaces, they generally go further afield (French Côte d'Opale, Belgian seaside resorts, Avesnois) because there is little to be offered in close proximity to the conurbation. In order to understand how and why this situation has developed, however, it is necessary to examine the level and location of existing outdoor recreation provision and to establish who the principal decision-makers are in the leisure planning system.

POLICYMAKERS AND THE MEANS OF DECISION-MAKING

A large number of decision-makers are involved in the planning process for outdoor leisure activities.[3] Before studying their roles and the nature of the organizational framework within which they operate, it is necessary to set out the conditions within which planning activity takes place.

The lack of information, definitions or standards of provision in the outdoor recreational fields

The researcher may lack reference points within which to locate an analysis of recreation planning practice, but the situation for the planner is perhaps even more confused. Outdoor recreation planning in France has tended to be conducted with little reference to guidelines or even to data on existing provision, as can be illustrated by the following examples.

Responsibility for green and outdoor recreational spaces has come under the auspices of communes (except for voluntary, and rather rare, delegation to a supra-communal authority). There is no overall listing of these spaces and therefore no statistics nor follow-up on the supra-communal scale. Intercommunal collaboration sometimes exists in the form of a 'syndicate' in the establishment of leisure space; but even so, such an arrangement does not cover all the recreational space in the communes that are members of the syndicate. A more precise listing of real available resources should therefore be carried out for the member communes. This difficulty has increased since 1982 when decentralization legislation was enacted which strengthened communal power: previously, reports concerning new green and leisure spaces went through departmental offices of the Ministère de l'Equipement. Since 1982, this practice has diminished.

The need for a precise listing is not made easier by a preliminary question concerning two definitions:

1. What is 'outdoor recreation'? In France there is no official definition of this activity applicable in an administrative framework. Hence the study of outdoor recreation, planning, and policy becomes problematic.
2. What is 'green space'? Is it a privileged (but non-exclusive) territory for practising outdoor leisure? It is in the interest of communes to inflate their statistics and adopt rather broad definitions if they wish to be considered as being 'green'. Consequently, the figures given in Table 11.1 should be revised downwards, because not all supposedly green spaces have any real recreational function. For example, areas planted with trees around car parks, cemeteries, flower beds or grass verges at the sides of roads and motorways, land on university campuses or belonging to hospitals or public authorities, bits of grass at the corners of streets or in the middle of roundabouts, are all examples of 'green space'. Certainly this extends the surface area, but has only an aesthetic function and is not for outdoor recreational purposes.

There are virtually no standards of reference for a potential leisure space policy, as in the Netherlands or the United Kingdom. In these countries, one can distinguish different categories of outdoor recreational space according to function and distance from home.[4] Of course, such standards would have to be adapted with care but they would make it possible to evaluate existing, potential and desirable land use. As a target for 1970, the OREAM Nord proposed 15m²/inh. for urban fringe parks and 10m²/inh for urban green spaces as the minimum needs to be taken into consideration; to these must be added areas of forest and countryside.[5] However, there is a potential conflict here between the highlighting of needs that are wider than local (the realization of which would require a concerted planning policy across communes) on the one hand, and a jealously guarded autonomy which communes all claim. It is not surprising, therefore, that of the 6000 hectares identified as necessary, only 2,500 (approximately) exist, of which about 1,000 were created between 1975 and 1985. At that rate, the shortfall in recreation space would not be met before the year 2020! In 1977 OREAM Nord published 'Elements for outdoor recreation and tourism in Nord Pas-de-Calais development policy', which reiterated these data and which should have been followed up by a plan for recreational development. Nothing happened!

In spite of this vagueness concerning the nature and goals of outdoor recreation planning and despite the tendency of organizations to empiricism, or to act in an ad hoc manner, policymakers have achieved some positive results. However, let us first outline the organizational structure and responsibilities in the field of outdoor recreation planning.

The policymakers

As seen in Figure 11.1 project decision-making, planning and management involves several tiers of government operating in various organizational configurations.

Central state intervention in this field of policy is in the form of defining general legislation which in part concerns leisure spaces. For example, instructions for the Schémas Directeurs d'Aménagement et d'Urbanisme (SDAU) from 1967 onwards followed by the Plans d'Occupation des Sols (POS), have obliged communes to provide green space. More specifically, the state created the Parcs Naturels Régionaux from 1967; the first of them was in Saint Amand, between Lille and Valenciennes, in 1968. It has also established a procedure for helping the reconversion of industrial waste land in the coalfields into leisure areas (among other things), thanks to the creation of the Groupe

Figure 11.1. Lille and Bassin Minier region administration and planning structures

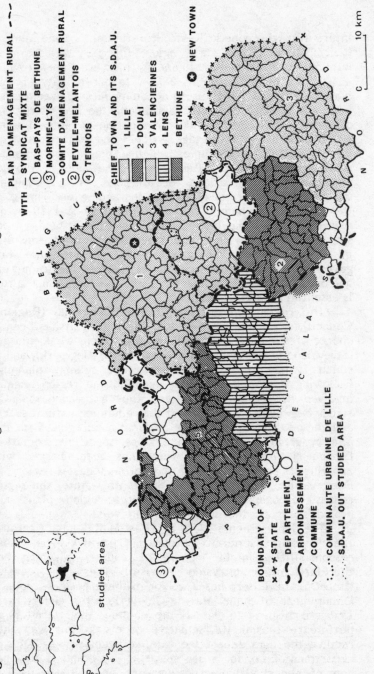

PLAN D'AMENAGEMENT RURAL ⌒⌒

WITH — SYNDICAT MIXTE
① BAS-PAYS DE BETHUNE
③ MORINIE-LYS
— COMITE D'AMENAGEMENT RURAL
② PEVELE-MELANTOIS
④ TERNOIS

CHIEF TOWN AND ITS S.D.A.U.
1 LILLE
2 DOUAI
3 VALENCIENNES
4 LENS
5 BETHUNE

★ NEW TOWN

BOUNDARY OF
╳╳╳ STATE
DEPARTEMENT
ARRONDISSEMENT
COMMUNE
COMMUNAUTE URBAINE DE LILLE
S.D.A.U. OUT STUDIED AREA

10 km

studied area

BELGIUM

NORD

PAS DE CALAIS

Interministériel pour la Restructuration de la Zone Minière (GIRZOM). In 1984 a state-region joint plan was drawn up within which particular financing measures are provided during the IXth Plan (1984-88) in favour of gîtes ruraux (vacation farms), light leisure accommodation, river tourism and, only in Nord Pas-de-Calais among the French regions, of 'bases' - fenced-off outdoor recreation and leisure areas, which were in great shortage. In 1976 the state started the Pays d'Accueil programme, which makes it possible for small regions like the Bas-Pays de Béthune to develop amenities for recreational destinations: hiking, camping, caravaning, gîtes ruraux, farms, inns and so on. Thanks to the Plan Vert, which it has encouraged since 1980 in the region, the state has helped in the creation of public green space too, although more in aesthetic street operations than in leisure spaces. Throughout these actions, the state government pushes forward policies, defines the framework and brings funds to other partners who use them. Such a role is essential in large operations.

The region, through the Conseil Régional (Regional Council), is a major partner too. Since 1975 it has been in charge of the Parc Naturel Régional, which it has enlarged (St. Amand is one of three parts of the existing park), and to which it has given broader tasks of country planning. Following the Mellick Report in 1977, the region became involved in 'social tourism' and thus a balance must be struck between conservation of the remaining natural spaces and their accessibility to the regional population. With this aim in view, it created in 1978 a specific association, Espace Naturel Régional, which has been charged with applying its policy in well-defined areas (coastal region and Parc Naturel Régional). With the central state, the region shares responsibilities in joint state-region plans and provides help at other infra-regional levels.

The departements (Nord and Pas-de-Calais) act through the Conseils Généraux (County Councils). They have responsibilities in the sphere of country planning and therefore of countryside tourism. They can develop departmental leisure bases, as for example has been done in Olhain hear Béthune. Pas-de-Calais in 1978 and Nord in 1979 are the first to classify the whole of their territory as périmètre sensible (a 'sensitive zone'). In this way they receive the taxe départementale d'espaces verte (TDEV, a departmental tax for green spaces). This amounts to 1 per cent on almost all construction work, and must be used to acquire green and natural spaces which have to be open to the public. The General Council has the right of compulsory purchase which has enabled them to acquire some woodland sites around the urban areas.

The communes are the most important agents for recreational development within their constituency. They can act alone when creating strictly communal recreational areas, like the Prés Duhem base in Armentières or the project under way in Seclin. But they also have a great number of different types of association with various partners:

1. Syndicat Mixte (Joint Committee), as in Bas-Pays de Béthune, which is responsible for the countryside planning, including recreation.
2. Comité d'Aménagement Rural (Countryside Planning Board) which is responsible for the same problems, although in a less restricting structure.
3. Syndicat Intercommunal (Intercommunal Joint Committee), such as those which generally group together several communes for GIRZOM-type bases. In the coalfields, six of the nine existing bases are managed by intercommunal syndicates grouping from two to six communes.
4. Communauté Urbaine de Lille (Lille Urban Community), participating, for example, in the Syndicat Mixte du Parc Naturel Regional.
5. The 'new town' special procedure, which made it possible for Villeneuve d'Ascq to be endowed with a 180 hectare urban park, comprising a 50 hectare stretch of water and several old farms reconverted for recreational activities.

Quasi-public sector organizations also have an important role. The Office National des Forêts is responsible for forest management, the creation of light amenities (tables, benches, paths); the Agence de l'Eau for creating stretches of water integrated in leisure areas, like that in the Prés Duhem in Armentières or in Villeneuve d'Ascq's Parc Urbain; and the Houillères Nationales (coal board) for selling industrial waste land or participating in its development.

The private sector also plays a role, even if a minor one. The Chambers of Commerce and Industry or of Agriculture are members of Syndicats Mixtes (Parc Naturel Régional, Bas-Pays de Béthune). Protection societies are formed and consulted about the protection of nature in

225

recreational sites (e.g. SATIS in Sensée Valley). Private individuals can open up private spaces to the public through various agreements concerning woods or footpaths for example and they create many small leisure amenities which become integrated into broader procedures.

This rather rapid glance at the policymakers in leisure planning does not lead one to conclude that there is any real, rational, overall coherent development, especially given the lack of necessary information for a true evaluation of the situation: few or no statistics, little research into the wishes of the local population and their activities, and no precise definitions to work from. It is perhaps more accurate to speak of recreational amenities created with the help of 'available money' of people in high office, or because of fortuitous circumstances, rather than to refer to the impact of any real, comprehensive plan. In this situation, it is the communes which are responsible for land-use policy and consequently are the main policymakers: thus nothing can be done without their consent. As a result, ten years were necessary to elaborate the new charter of the Parc Naturel Régional (finally promulgated in 1986). The delay resulted from the difficulty of getting a large number of partners, including some 167 communes to agree. Add to this the various elections, internal squabbles, slow pace of public authorities, even within joint communal structures, to act, and the ten year delay is easy to understand.

SOME POSITIVE BUT PIECEMEAL RESULTS

The 'institutional jungle' that governs planning and the uncertain bases upon which it is built has managed despite its complexities to achieve some favourable (albeit limited) results, as seen in Figure 11.2.

The main results

Over the last 20 years outdoor recreation has improved in this highly urbanized area. Listed below are important achievements.

Officially created in 1986 as one of three parts of the Parc Naturel Régional du Nord Pas-de-Calais, the Parc Naturel Régional des Plaines de la Scarpe et de l'Escaut was the next step after the founding in 1968 of the Parc Naturel Régional de Saint Amand-Raismes. It covers 52 communes, 45,240 hectares and has about 175,000

Figure 11.2. Main outdoor recreation amenities

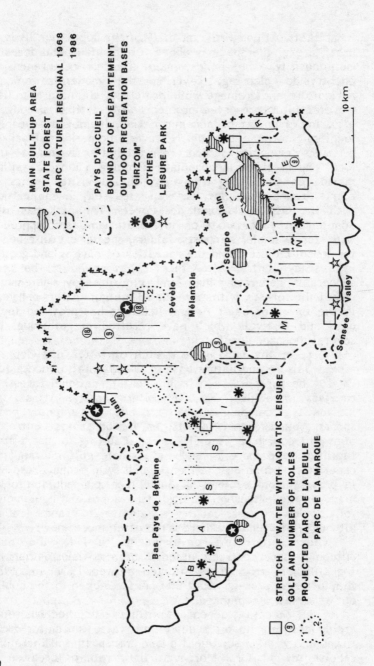

MAIN BUILT-UP AREA

STATE FOREST

PARC NATUREL REGIONAL 1968
                                    1986

PAYS D'ACCUEIL

BOUNDARY OF DEPARTEMENT

OUTDOOR RECREATION BASES

"GIRZOM"

OTHER

LEISURE PARK

STRETCH OF WATER WITH AQUATIC LEISURE

GOLF AND NUMBER OF HOLES

PROJECTED PARC DE LA DEULE

       "   PARC DE LA MARQUE

10 km

Bas Pays de Béthune

Pévèle – Mélantois

Scarpe plain

Sensée Valley

Lys plain

inhabitants. Although the majority of the population lives in urban areas, the space is above all farmland and forests. Consequently, the park's main aim is comprehensive countryside planning, covering the modernization of agriculture and drainage while protecting the natural milieu (several natural reserves, problems with fertilizers, hedges, etc), improvement of accommodation, helping old people, local commerce, and so on. However, the park's authorities are also developing outdoor recreational activities for the local and neighbouring population: hiking, riding, a sailing marina on the Etang d'Amaury, guided visits, grants to sports grounds, camping, caravan sites etc., in conjunction with the Office National des Forêts. The park has also adopted an educational or interpretation-based approach with, for example, signposts, folders, special exercise books for school children, and the reception of classes and groups in a study centre. Altogether it has proved to be very successful, generating high (and sometimes over-intensive) use of the forests, with more than 3 million visitors per year in the forest of Saint Amand itself. It has provided topic days and festivals which have resulted in gatherings of several thousand people.

Despite the lack of a stretch of water, the departmental leisure and nature base in Olhain is also successful. On 104 hectares (close to a 300-hectare national forest) it receives more than 500,000 visitors yearly. Attractions include two camping-caravan grounds, a swimming pool, sports grounds, tennis courts, an indoor sports centre, a mini-golf course, a keep-fit course, catering for short-stay facilities, and more recently a six-hole golf course (the creation of which on chalk grasslands with orchids resulted in protest from ecologists). Some mention should also be made of the extensive facilities (ski slopes and equipment) for the lowest cross-country ski centre in France (180m) although unfortunately there is not often much snow!

Other interesting developments include the nine outdoor leisure centres created in the coalfields as part of the GIRZOM programme. Started betwen 1974 and 1980 they offer at present about 300 hectares open to the public out of some 1,500 planned.

Their success is dependent on their siting because some are located on old pit heads or on waste lands, far from towns and without sufficient public transport, and therefore receive few visitors. Moreover, their rate of creation is rather slow: reclaiming areas which include marshland or suffer from problems of mining subsidence, turning over colliery spoil heaps which still have some market value (for thermal power stations or public works), and razing old industrial factories spread over dozens of hectares needs more time and money than the creation of such centres on virgin agricultural land. To all this has to be added the problem of communal boundaries, which complicate matters considerably.

Many communes have managed some outstanding achievements on their own territory. For example, leisure bases have been created around stretches of water excavated by the Agence de l'Eau for regional water needs: in Armentières, 40 hectares of water out of 110 hectares of leisure area: in Villeneuve d'Ascq, 50 out of 180 hectares. The first has entrance fees and offers variety while the second is free but lacks variety. They receive large numbers of visitors from urban areas during the spring and summer. Other towns such as Wattrelos, Seclin, Mons-en-Baroeul, Douai, Bruay-en-Artois and Douchy have equipped smaller or more traditional green spaces with some children's games and leisure amenities. They also attract crowds but on a smaller scale. On the other hand, the entertainment park begun in June 1985 in Lomme (in the suburbs of Lille), intensively equipped and confined to a small area without either trees or stretches of water went bankrupt as early as September of the same year, probably because of its low attraction level and high admission charges, which generated few visitors.

Dispersed amenities that offer new outdoor leisure areas or foster access to rural spaces should also be considered. This is best illustrated in the case of the Bas-Pays de Béthune, where the Pays d'Accueil policy has made it possible to weave a rather close and coherent network of recreation zones. Hiking and bridle paths have been opened too. However, a lot of new urban green spaces, although important for aesthetic reasons and the general improvement of the urban environment, have done little to improve outdoor recreation. With the exception of the urban park in the new town of Villeneuve d'Ascq, only 275 hectares of green space were created in the 86 communes of the Communauté Urbaine de Lille from 1970 to 1982. This serves to underline the paucity of provision. By pouring out of their immediate environment (to coast, Belgium, Avesnois, etc.) or by immediately invading new forms of local provision, the region's population are demonstrating the shortfall in local provision within the region. Some hope, however, does exist.

Hopes, projects, uncertainty

In addition to small or medium-sized projects involving several communes, and the continuation of the projects under way (especially the Parc Naturel Régional, the GIRZOM programme), decisions on two other large projects are still pending.

First, between Lille and Lens, the Parc de la Deule along the Deule valley, proposed by OREAM as long ago as 1968, would incorporate stretches of water created by the Agence de l'Eau (520 hectares) with wooded spaces (620 hectares), sports and games fields (600 hectares) and 1,140 hectares preserved for agriculture but with light amenities such as paths and benches. All in all, 2,880 hectares ideally located close to the urban population would provide a large recreational area and various leisure activities, while improving the image of an environmentally damaged region. Apart from some very occasional initiatives in one or two communes, this Deule Park has not as yet been considered a priority in the region. Nevertheless, it would go a long way to solving some of the above-mentioned shortages. However, so far no political power has yet given its backing, although this is hardly surprising with 17 communes, several intercommunal or joint committees, the Communauté Urbaine de Lille, two departements (counties) and one region all involved in the decision-making process. Competition has also come from other large money-consuming projects, such as the Parc Naturel Régional for the region and the underground (public transport scheme) in the Communauté Urbaine of Lille. All this, together with a lack of intercommunal political will to establish the Parc de Deule project, has inevitably delayed the scheme.

A similar although smaller (800 hectares) project is the Parc de la Marque on the southeastern fringe of Lille, also proposed by OREAM. For the same reasons - inter-organizational complexity and lack of political will - it failed. However, it has recently been considered again, pushed this time by Villeneuve d'Ascq, which is concerned to strengthen its image as a green and high-tech town (a new town with an urban park, research centres, two universities, an automatic underground transport system, the Bull computer factory, etc.) to attract investors. A major benefit of these two projects would be to generate stretches of water and forest land so badly needed for the urban environment and for the local urban population for outdoor recreation purposes. But the size of the projects, the physical complexity of carrying them out, the number and more or less divergent interests of concerned partners, both on economical and political levels, and the unfavourable economic outlook all generate little optimism about the implications of these projects in the immediate future. It would seem that neither the urgency of meeting social needs nor the potential economic benefits to be obtained by gathering greater levels of outdoor recreation provision are sufficiently well understood by the public authorities concerned.

CONCLUSION

Some significant outdoor recreation projects have been completed with little apparent delay in the last few decades. However, these have emerged from a complex policy framework which on the whole has failed to meet adequately the needs of the local population. Nevertheless, such provision as has been made is based on an emerging awareness of the necessity for this kind of space. Responsiveness to this greater awareness of regional recreation need is, on the one hand, running into financial restrictions due to the economic situation, and on the other, being slowed down by the decentralized system of local responsibilities. This situation hinders all attempts at designing and obtaining outdoor recreation spaces, on a scale appropriate to the recreational activities and levels of usage envisaged. There is no overall planning authority in this field. The countryside has increased its recreational function, but it can only partly meet the demand. Large urban fringe leisure provision is deficient throughout the region. Densely populated communes simply do not have the space to provide for outdoor recreation and have no means of imposing their requirements on smaller neighbouring communes that have the necessary resources. It would seem then that the provision throughout the local, regional and national government structure has sought to foster decentralized responsibility without clearly assessing whether strategic planning for wider than local needs can still be effective. The system of recreation planning established has resulted in dysfunctional spatial allocations.

Perhaps a new comprehensive regional tourist development plan, announced in February 1987 and linked to the Channel Tunnel of which the region expects much, will modify this situation.[6]

NOTES

1. I thank Jan Rembowski for revising this text.
2. The INSEE (Institut National de la Statistique et des Etudes Economiques) considers as urban any commune of more than 2,000 inhabitants, or which is an integral part of a grouping of at least 2,000 inhabitants, even if the member communes have themselves fewer than 2,000 inhabitants.
3. We have of necessity had to be brief here about French planning. For further details, see specialist texts.
4. Compare, for example, the standards recommended by the National Playing Fields Association and other British associations.
5. Organisation Régionale d'Etudes et d'Aménagement de la Metropole Nord, part of the Ministère de l'Equipement, had as its remit to elaborate a development plan for Nord Pas-de-Calais. Created in 1968, it was closed down in 1983.
6. Further details concerning time, space, and geographical problems on the subject touched on here can be found in J.M. Dewailly (1985) Tourisme et Loisirs dans le Nord-Pas-de-Calais, Lille: Société de Géographie de Lille.

12

INNER CITIES AND URBAN TOURISM IN THE NETHERLANDS: NEW CHALLENGES FOR LOCAL AUTHORITIES

Myriam Jansen-Verbeke

INTRODUCTION

The main objective of this chapter is to reveal the views of local authority planners on the current planning process leading towards local tourism and recreation development plans in several Dutch towns. Strategic planning of recreation and tourism on a local scale is in many ways a real challenge for the municipal planners, who are beginning to experiment as tourism marketeers. The current interest in urban tourism resources is largely inspired by the economic benefits from tourism. Yet tourism is no longer the well-defined responsibility of a single specific municipal service and it now involves, in one way or another, almost every branch of local authority administration. The main reason for this is that the entire urban core is presently looked upon as a recreational environment and as a tourism resource.

The process of generating a new strategic plan for urban core areas, as an integrative framework for recreational and tourism development is obviously one of trial and error, of ad hoc decisions and short-term views; it is a process which is unfolding.

This review of contemporary planning in Dutch cities could contribute to a discussion of similar situations in other West European cities. However, the planning process analysed here is now in rapid evolution and therefore likely to be subject to change. Nevertheless, the topicality of the subject is a good reason for reviewing the development of this process, identifying the limitations of the organizational structures, and evaluating the opportunities being created by a wide range of local initiatives.

The primary source of information for this review is a

questionnaire sent to administrators in key positions within several local authority departments. In addition, reports issued by municipal services dealing with local recreation and tourism development have been reviewed. Several questions, especially those seeking views on future development, were too demanding for a written response and subsequently a number of interviews were conducted. Answers to the questionnaire therefore have been supplemented by interview data where appropriate. The results of this data collection will be presented in a relatively full description in order to provide an appraisal of the role of local authority planners in the development of recreation and tourism in urban core areas.

Many different approaches to the subject of city recreation and tourism development are possible; for example, consideration of the supply side of facilities, of commercial prospects, of consumer behaviour, consumer images, and so on. However, this discussion will focus predominantly on the role of decision-makers, among whom local authority planners play an important role.

FOCUS ON DUTCH INNER CITIES

In order to make a comparison between different local plans dealing with tourism and recreation development in urban core areas, ten Dutch towns have been included in this review: Arnhem, Breda, Deventer, Dordrecht, 's Hertogenbosch, Kampen, Middleburg, Nijmegen, Zwolle, and Zutphen. Their location and some indication of their importance as tourist places is illustrated by the map included (Figure 12.1). None of those towns really has a long-standing tradition in tourism, but what they all have in common is an historical central core area. This valuable type of historical heritage, which is being widely rediscovered as a tourism resource, can be seen as providing a key focus for the tourism ambitions of cities (Jansen-Verbeke 1986a). A number of important historical buildings concentrated within the urban core area was once considered a major problem in terms of urban conservation, but this is now appreciated as a valuable asset for tourism marketing (Ashworth and Voogd 1986).

For a long time, many historical parts of the inner city lay dormant in the shadow of renewed commercial areas, with the exception of some very well-known monuments, churches, guildhouses, and so on. Tourist attractions in the inner city were identified for visitors and promoted as isolated points of interest. This approach to urban tourism policy and management is rapidly changing in favour of a more integrated approach. Tourism is now seen as an integrated urban element incorporated into the functional and morphological urban texture. In some ways this is a return to historic city tourism of the past. Some cities, with a long tradition in tourism, have been selling themselves as a whole for many generations. Nowadays the idea of integration seems to be the key to success in tourism and recreation development plans.

The problem of integration of recreation and tourism in the urban context has two distinct dimensions. First, on the level of the urban structure and organization, the functional relationship between recreation, tourism, and other urban facilities and commercial sectors needs to be examined. This relationship also displays a well-determined spatial aspect (Ashworth and de Haan 1985). A well-known example is the problem of imposing a tourism and/or recreation function on an inner-city area which has traditionally had a different function, such as a residential area. Both local inhabitants and tourism planners may be ambivalent about this kind of policy development (Jansen-Verbeke 1986b). Second, from the point of view of the inner-city visitor, whether tourist or other, integration of tourist attractions in the urban network of commercial activities and catering facilities such as outdoor cafes is usually positively valued. Indeed, the spatial integration of tourist attractions and other facilities leads to higher expenditures by tourists while visiting the inner city. Since in the final analysis this is the main objective of tourism promotion policies, a spatial and functional integration of tourism and recreation within the urban texture is certainly a primary challenge for those concerned with local tourism development.

Planning for recreation and tourism development in the inner city requires a strategic management of resources and this implies much more than an original or aggressive promotion slogan (Jansen-Verbeke 1988). All of the ten towns included in this review are at the moment seriously engaged in producing a development plan for urban tourism and recreation. It should be noted that these towns are at different stages in the planning process. Furthermore, although the ten cities chosen for this exploratory study have many characteristics in common which may allow some generalization of the problem, each is also unique in terms

Figure 12.1. Tourist cities in the Netherlands

Selection of tourist places according to <u>Classification of tourist places in the Netherlands</u>

Ministry of Economic Affairs classification applies to cities and buildings:

- ● Unique setting
- ● Important setting or unique element
- · Modest setting or interesting element

Inner Cities in the Netherlands

Legend of the map	(1) Town	(2) Major tourist elements
4: Unique setting	Amsterdam	Old centre. Numerous monuments

3: Important setting or unique element	Alkmaar	Historic centre. Old Dutch town.
	Delft	Ancient Dutch town. Numerous canals.
	Deventer	**Old centre. Marketplace.** **Churches.**
	Enkhuizen	Historic town.
	Franeker	Old town. Canals. Townhall.
	Gouda	Old town. Church. Eglise.
	's Gravenhage	Binnenhof and surroundings. Churchs. Streets and alleys
	s'Hertogenbosch	**Medieval centre.** **Cathedral.**
	Hoorn	Historic town. Harbour.
	Kampen	**Old town. River site**
	Kinderdijk	Numerous mills.
	Leeuwarden	Large old town.
	Leiden	Historic town. Canals Churches.
	Maastricht	Old town. Churches. Market places.
	Middelburg	**Historic centre.** **Abbey. Townhall.**
	Utrecht	Churches. Streets. Canals.
	Veere	Old town. Harbour

2: Modest setting or interesting element	Dordrecht Breda Arnhem Nijmegen Zwolle Zutphen	(63 towns)

(1: Interesting element)	(69 places or elements)

_____ 10 towns included as case studies.

of regional setting, urban morphology, and most importantly, in terms of its image as a possible tourist destination. Discovering the nature of their uniqueness is basically a task of local tourism marketeers when positioning their product on the tourist market, but their image of the 'tourist city' is often biased by virtue of their professional involvement or by the mere fact of being employed within a specific municipal service.

THE ORGANIZATIONAL FRAMEWORK

The main purpose of these development plans is to improve the functional and spatial integration of tourism and recreation, including many other aspects of urban leisure, such as culture, sports, parks, etc. The accent is explicitly on the organization of the supply side of facilities. Given existing local government structures, the idea of integration and its spatial realization seems utopian. Traditionally, welfare services, including recreation, sport, education, health services, and youth services, are clearly separated from departments responsible for economic development such as commercial services, tourism and public services.

But what happens when the boundaries between recreation, sport, culture, and tourism sectors are no longer obvious, when a diffusion of responsibilities is taking place? There are many instances of changing uses - for example an urban park is rediscovered as a possible location for tourist attractions and events, or a historical monument is used for recreational or social uses by locals (Ashworth and de Haan 1986).

Can local government structures adapt in order to initiate an integrated approach to recreation and tourism? The answers of respondents on this issue reflect the dispersion across different service departments of responsibilities concerning recreation and tourism. In some communities predominant responsibility for co-ordinating leisure and tourism policy is given to the economic development department but more frequently, departments responsible for welfare services, such as environment, recreation, sport, are mentioned as taking the leading role. The involvement of public services and urban planning departments usually comes into action at the moment of implementing specific plans or projects. Occasionally the information services, including the local tourist board, are mentioned as being actively involved in generating tourism and recreation plans.

The fragmentation of the municipal organization over numerous departments, all dealing with different aspects of tourism and recreation, is very much seen as an obstacle to that construction of an overall development plan. The more people involved, the greater the risk is that no consensus can be obtained, that views of decision-makers will differ from one another, or that establishing a community of interests is unrealistic and that departmentalism will prevail.

There are at least three solutions to this organizational problem. The most frequently cited was a continuation of the fragmented approach to recreation and tourism, with one or other department taking a lead in the planning process. This is in fact the situation in several towns. Another response was to install a co-ordination committee, working group, or even an interdepartmental service with a clear brief to prepare a local development plan. Even in those towns where such a co-ordination committee has been initiated, the dominant influence of a particular department can still be traced in the philosophy of the plans. Nevertheless, this initiative can be considered as a step forward towards integrated recreation and tourism development plans.

A third solution, only mentioned by respondents from 's Hertogenbosch and Breda, was the procedure of integrating local plans for recreation and tourism in a regional framework. In such circumstances recreation and tourism are placed in the context of the regional (outdoor recreation) plan. Obviously, this will incorporate a different set of elements and factors, and the focus on such plans is not explicitly on the historical core area and its tourist assets; resources are evaluated in combination with outdoor recreational facilities and other tourist attractions in the urban fringe area. As a consequence, the discussion on tourism and recreation development takes place at a different level.

Within the organizational structure of regional recreation boards (Recreatieschappen), which traditionally organize and plan outdoor recreational facilities, there is now a marked tendency towards a more commercial approach, thus bringing closer the objectives of regional tourist boards and regional recreation boards. The question is which of these governmental boards, or which combination of them, is capable of realizing an overall plan including tourism and recreation (Ashworth and Bergsma

1987)? It is beyond the scope of this analysis to estimate the effects of this trend; furthermore it would certainly be a premature judgment. Several local authority planners saw no reason at all for shifting local problems and responsibilities to regional authorities. With the exception of 's Hertogenbosch and Breda, all the other towns included in the study considered the task of a development plan for local tourism as the responsibility of local authorities.

Given the variety of organizational frameworks, it is perhaps not surprising that questions concerning how local planners started the procedure towards an overall plan were answered very differently. The fairly recent and unexplored task of drawing new plans could have been a real incentive to initiate research projects investigating the characteristics of tourism and tourists, of recreational behaviour, of local potential, and assessing all these aspects in the broader context of leisure in a changing society. In some towns, local government includes a research department appointed as a bureau of statistics of human geographical research or a general research department. Although the number of scientific researchers working in these services tends to be rather limited, it can be concluded that where such facilities exist, there is a platform for the launching of an integrated planning process.

Some municipal departments have been doing research work on matters related to tourism and recreation in their inner city. Usually, a first exploration into the urban core as a leisure setting is followed by research projects on specific aspects such as leisure patterns of the local population, participation in cultural activities, and a critical evaluation of the local authority's image building policy (Zwart 1987). This wide variety of subjects, some farmed out as research contracts to advice bureaux or university departments, contributes to an efficient framework within which a local plan for recreation and tourism can grow. Informed action programmes for local development of recreation and tourism are now gradually developing from these research results.

As one can see from the list of municipal reports and research projects, there is some variety in the topics of research projects. Some are restricted to a feasibility study of one specific tourism project, some venture into an overall recreation and tourism research project covering the entire urban core area. A closer look at those reports reveals approaches that vary considerably. This is a reflection of local priorities and the attitude towards the research of local decision-makers and planners.

The time constraints under which those overall plans are developed are hardly conducive to a long-term research programme. Generally, the practice adopted is simply to collect up-to-date local information, often by means of brainstorming sessions with decision-makers, to proceed eventually to some small-scale research projects, but generally to rely strongly on commonsense knowledge and short-term views of local planners. The rationale given for this approach is that local authority planners are in the best position to judge the local situation and that research investments are unproductive and too time-consuming.

One may conclude therefore that local authority planners facing the challenge of drawing up a tourism and recreation plan are unlikely to seek scientific research on the subject. They are more likely to consider their knowledge of the local situation as preferable to lengthy research programmes, and as a better political instrument than scientific reports. The start of the planning process lies with the municipal professionals, inspired (and limited) by their personal and professional backgrounds, and relying strongly on their own intuition.

THE ACTUAL PLANNING PROCESS

Despite the range of views on the starting point for tourism plans and on the desirability of supporting research, most local authority planners were convinced of the necessity to initiate or to proceed with a local development plan. Even where such a planning process has not yet begun, local planners and decision-makers are well aware of its potential.

In the ten towns studied, the tourism planning process has clearly reached different levels of progress. An outline local tourist-recreation development plan has been accomplished in Dordrecht, Middleburg, Kampen, and Zwolle. Elsewhere it has been presented as a partial plan, for example in Nijmegen, where economic issues are predominant. In the case of Breda and 's Hertogenbosch the plans are to be presented as part of a regional plan for recreation and tourism. This leaves the communities of Arnhem and Zutphen, where the planning process is underway, and Deventer, where the tourism planning process has yet to begin in earnest (although this situation may have changed by the time of publication). However, despite this variation in levels of maturity in the planning process, one can evaluate the anticipated merits of such plans and identify some key issues that have emerged in their initiation and development.

The incentive most frequently mentioned is the fact that such a plan can be used as a lever for obtaining national funds for local tourism projects. This is clearly a short-term move and a very questionable one, since national financing capacity is severely limited. A further benefit claimed is that this planning process is an effective vehicle for encouraging an integrated pllicy in recreation and tourism, and also represents a framework in which disparate activities and initiatives can be bundled together in order to promote local tourism more efficiently.

Some of the respondents regarded this planning process as a useful way of stimulating political awareness both of local potential and of local problems in tourism. Evaluating resources also implies that a priority can be given to certain developments or at least that a balance of strengths and weaknesses can be established. Thus the major advantage of a development plan is that it functions as a framework within which action steps can be taken and responsibilities delegated.

None of the respondents awarded these plans a long-term significance; rather, they cited largely short-term benefits. Some reservations were expressed by respondents about the absence of feasibility studies in the approach to planning. Some local planners also expressed concern that short-term gains were being sought which may be dysfunctional in the longer run since they might subsequently lead to a reaction of inertia. Relatively few respondents mentioned the problems that could arise by producing plans and promoting a tourism and recreation policy without full support of the local inhabitants and local trading interests.

Identification of urban tourism resources

The first difficulty encountered by local planners and decision-makers was the need for a consensus on the elements, facilities, and characteristics which their city has to offer tourists and recreationists. What is the nature of local tourism resources as elements of a 'tourism-recreation product' (Jansen-Verbeke 1985)?

The realization of a development plan requires consensus between decision-makers and planners on the urban elements contributing to the local tourist product. It is usually not a problem to indicate the strongest tourist attractions of a city, for this can invariably be deduced from the actual success in terms of numbers of visitors. Yet even here there is a remarkable difference in the way local planners identify the local tourist product.

As expected, the historical setting of the inner city, its typical morphology and its collection of historical buildings and monuments, is generally appreciated as a primary element of the local tourist product. The historical heritage was the most regularly cited feature on which to develop local tourism promotion policies. The interesting point is to see which additional features or attractions they consider to be 'worth a visit'.

The list of elements suggested in the answers on the questionnaire can be complemented with other elements described in the municipal reports. However, some interesting conclusions can be drawn merely by looking at the spontaneous reactions of respondents. Some municipal authorities are primarily seeking to capitalize on their regional situation, which means they are looking to combine landscape attractions in the surrounding area to attract more visitors and stimulate more frequent visits with their urban core. Nevertheless, considerations about the attractiveness of the rural or natural surroundings of the city generally come in second place. Looking further into the typical urban elements, museums are considered to be of a substantial importance in attracting visitors to the inner city.

When questioned about the present meaning given to urban tourism, respondents answered by reciting the calendar of local events. A large number of events are planned as tourist attractions, varying in scale, topic, and organization. For one reason or another urban tourism seems to be strongly associated with such events and festivities. The recent success of newly promoted events and the financial benefit of such promotions for the local merchants seem to support this approach. Last but not least, shopping facilities, markets, and entertainment facilities within the urban core were also considered to be elements of the local tourist recreation product.

This last item can be seriously questioned, for shopping facilities and markets are not really typical of any particular place. At most, the historical setting of shopping areas and markets or the local scenery can be seen as unique and attractive; retail shops and department stores in the urban centres belong to a large extent to national or even international chain stores, presumably offering no real motivation for visiting one town instead of another.

There seems to be a great degree of similarity between the views of the different municipal planners concerning the importance of local events and attractions. Only exceptionally is reference made to the attractiveness of the surrounding region.

Evaluation of local strengths and weaknesses

The views of individuals in different community services and from the different local authorities about future perspectives were canvassed. Confusion about the strength and nature of tourism attractions obviously results in a speculative approach to future development. The real challenge lies in developing strategic views, based on short- or long-term goals. In the wide variety of answers and ideas, two lines of thinking can be distinguished; product improvement and product enlargement.

Product improvement is seen in terms of consolidating the existing facilities and investing in their quality. This policy often results in planning for a better functional and spatial integration of existing resources and implies only minor additions or alterations in the urban core. A small example of this could be the relocation of visitors' car parks in order to create new traffic flow patterns in the city, thus bringing visitors into closer contact with the historical core areas and other places of interest. Another example of product improvement could be the introduction of a flexible system of opening hours for museums, shops, historical monuments, even for some tourist attractions. Other minor adaptations such as improving signboards and signposting or urban walks may prove to be effective. Most of these suggestions imply only minor financial investments.

Product enlargement, in terms of adding new elements of importance to the local tourist product, seems to describe more clearly the present attitude of local tourism promoters. Remarkably, questions about future developments almost always led to mention of a range of new initiatives for events and festivities. The present success of events in attracting visitors, together with the fact that the organization of events allows for an efficient private-public partnership, would seem to explain this. Usually, no important or permanent environmental alterations are required. In addition, financial risk can be minimalized by the flexibility of events and festivities which can adapt to new demands and fashions. Furthermore, characteristics such as location, time, and organization can fairly easily be altered.

In general, ambitions for enlarging the present tourism product tend to be inspired by the situation along a waterfront, by the presence of a city harbour, canals, and rivers incorporated in the urban landscape. Those areas of traditional crafts and industrial activities have to a large extent lost their original function and gone through a period of decline. Nowadays those areas are being rediscovered as a potential tourism asset. In a variety of ways, plans are now being conceived for a tourism revitalization of those waterfront areas. It happens that such projects usually involve large financial investments, often because of the expensive nature of the physical infrastructure and because the process of decline was such that an important upgrading of the area is required.

Another element of product improvement which seems to be popular with local planners is the enlargement of hotel capacity. Arguments referring to positive developments in congress tourism, combined with estimates of shortages in the availability of specific categories of accommodation, are, in general, not yet based upon prospects in the market.

It is apparent therefore that all suggestions about product enlargement should be the subject of feasibility studies and market research. When simply brainstorming about future possibilities no realistic limit was placed on the potential market for urban tourism by planners and policymakers.

Respondents were somewhat more realistic when questioned about difficulties to be encountered in realizing tourism market potential. Nevertheless, the problems mentioned tended to be more related to organizational and financial barriers rather than to structural shortcomings or weaknesses of the tourism-recreational resources.

The lack of an integrated and long-term policy for tourism and recreation is, of course, related to the problems of a fragmented organizational framework. As a consequence, local authorities lack any real programme of corporate priorities, a fact which can only serve to stimulate further ad hoc solutions and projects. Such a situation is an effective barrier to the development of long-term planning because there is no consistency of policies. The financial shortage of community funds for tourism and recreation, as one might expect, represented a further barrier to development, although in some towns the lack of political support for tourism development was the major inhibiting factor.

The indifference of local entrepreneurs and merchants, sometimes accentuated by the lack of interest from local inhabitants, reinforced the fact that tourism and recreation tend to rate rather low on the scale of political priorities. In addition to financial and organizational problems, tourism development plans encountered some structural problems. The accessibility of historical areas to visitors requires a well-balanced city traffic plan and parking policy.

Important choices have to be made between accessibility for local residents and conservation of an attractive urban landscape for visitors. Pedestrian areas, outdoor cafes, evening entertainment, street activities are all questionable policy options. The reaction of urban inhabitants must be given serious consideration (Jansen-Verbeke 1986b). The actual location of tourist attractions in the inner city area was frequently mentioned as a general point of weakness of local recreation and tourism. This problem is of course linked to the characteristics of accessibility: it underlines the need for urban pedestrian routes and, above all, of finding ways to integrate existing tourist attractions more closely into the urban texture.

Finally, the general shortage of hotel accommodation for tourists was cited as a negative factor. Changes in the location policies in the hotel sector have led to changes in the number and price categories of hotels in the urban area. New hotels have been located in urban fringe areas along motorways and main access roads, whereas hotels have tended to disappear from the inner city or are to be downgraded. The market need for such facilities remains questionable. In terms of the balance of local strengths and weaknesses, local authority planners tended to make judgments along very similar lines and in similar terminology. This does not come as a surprise, since a number of urban problems are indeed comparable. As to the shared terminology employed, it leaves the impression of a lack of insight into the needs of specific locales.

Estimation of the market situation

The marketing approach adopted can be evaluated more closely by questioning the views of local planners and decision-makers on the market situation of their tourist product. Referring to their competitive position in the tourist market came as rather a surprise, or at least demanded some second thoughts. Indeed, the simple question 'what has this city to offer more than a neighbouring or similar historical town?' proved to cause some difficulty.

An attractive historical core area, a lively shopping centre, an attractive waterfront, good accessibility by road and public transport, interesting museums, exciting events, and lively festivities, which they all have in common, can hardly be seen as a discriminating factor for attracting visitors. So what more is there? At this point in the discussion, local authority planners tended to look outside the walls of their city and find additional arguments in the characteristics of the surrounding region.

This question led logically to the critical point of the image of their city as a tourist place. Having no real tourism tradition, this is of course the starting point for every tourism promotion policy. Apparently, very little is known about the image of the urban cores of Dutch cities as tourist places, apart from some rare studies (Dietvorst 1987).

The process of image-building as a key to urban tourism is yet to be explored. To some extent the underestimation of image-building as a promotion priority also explains the fact that well-defined views on the market position were difficult to trace. Not all respondents could produce a realistic view of their position with regard to other nearby tourist attractions and places of interest.

The above line of questioning was intended to uncover their views on distinct groups among existing and future urban visitors. Knowing that very little empirical research has been carried out on the subject of inner-city visitors and target groups, the answers invariably constituted a series of personal views. Sometimes reference was made to the results of local surveys. Indeed, the estimated importance of visitor groups in the city, their motives, and their appreciation of the local tourism recreation product were very much a matter of speculation. In general, the primary target group for urban tourism was the day-tourist. This assumes that the trend of day-trips, of sightseeing tours, or just a day out for fun shopping, will continue. Distances in the Netherlands are so small that almost every town can be considered as a destination for a day out. This even applies to some parts of the neighbouring countries, Belgium and Germany, where further market potentials may be assumed.

Much attention was also paid to the group of guests and holiday-makers in the region staying in hotels or on camp sites in the surrounding area. These were seen as an important group for urban tourism. This also included sailing/canal traffic, cyclists, and hitch-hikers. Nevertheless, the emphasis on these potential market segments is questionable.

Another assumption made by tourism planners was that of an increasing interest in cultural activities: more participants in guided urban tours and more visits to museums, even though such a trend seems unlikely according to some recent survey results. However, the market fragment most regularly cited is that of hotel guest and congress tourist, since their pattern of expenditure means a real stimulus for the urban economy. This area of the market is nevertheless limited in size and intensely competitive.

In conclusion, the profile of inner-city visitors remains rather vague and identification of target groups was primarily based on intuition rather than on marketing research.

Promotion policies

The vagueness concerning target groups obviously affects the way promotion policies are initiated. Nowadays, promotion of the local product is a task which demands considerable mental and financial investment. Promoting urban tourism, traditionally the main and only task of local and regional boards, has now become a working field of different municipal services.

The lack of co-ordination between the existing organization and several newly created promotion teams was pointed out in interviews as a serious handicap. It is perhaps remarkable that the majority of towns came to the conclusion that in addition to existing local and regional tourism boards some kind of a promotion team needs to be installed in order to strengthen the relationship between local government and the private sector of local merchants, hotel owners and pubkeepers.

In principle, the basis for future development of private-public partnership in the recreation and tourism sector has been laid. In practice, this evolution had led to an even more fragmented organization structure concerned with promotion policies. Probably the main advantage of promotion teams lies in their potential for providing a financial stimulus. Local government resources for tourist boards are often insufficient; by developing a joint venture with the private sector, new prospects for promotion are offered.

In response to questions about how local tourism promotion should be reinforced, the answers given were rather vague although respondents were fully aware of the problems involved with tourism promotion. Within the organizational structure, there seems to be a gap between the local planners and the promoters of the product. It is beyond the scope of this review to analyse this structural problem of local government policy. A preliminary conclusion could be that intensive communication among the community services involved in tourism provision improves the chances of promoting and realizing particular tourism development schemes.

A crucial question in relation to promotion policy concerns views on target groups. Following the lines of the previous discussion, it seemed logical to ask about the promotion programmes oriented to specific population groups. As a rule, promotion was not directed at specific target groups, which means that there was no philosophy explicitly developed on this subject. This is perhaps typical of a marketing approach which is still in the phase of product identification, rather than being concerned with the actual and potential users of this product.

In some towns, however, more precise views had been developed on interesting target markets. Several reasons were mentioned for aiming at specific groups, despite the fact that the identification of target groups often lacked any empirical support. This absence of data, however, did not prevent promoters developing a promotion policy aiming at specific population groups. Several respondents came to the conclusion that holiday-makers in the region provide interesting market potential. It was assumed that 'cultural tourists' would be important for the future of urban tourism. Similarly, the population group over 55 years of age was also cited as a target group. Thus, views on target groups for promotion and marketing are unsupported by any data, and promotion policies displayed a lack of strategic co-operation between tourist boards and local planners.

CONCLUSIONS

The introduction of local tourism strategies is at an early stage of development in the Netherlands. This review has sought to highlight some of the opportunities grasped, difficulties experienced, and the nature of policymakers' and planners' thinking at local level. In doing so a range of potential benefits and problems have been highlighted. Not all the respondents were convinced as to what priority should be allocated to the development of urban recreation and tourism. Nevertheless, according to most local urban planners, the development of recreation and tourism merits greater support from local authorities. The economic effects of tourism are slowly being appreciated. For a long time the multiplier effect of tourism was only seen as profitable for the catering sector and to some extent for the local retail trade. Views are changing and the possible multiplier effect is now appreciated in much wider context: not only can local employment be stimulated by tourism, but there is also considerable potential for upgrading urban areas. This means improvements of the urban infrastructure, a higher quality of facilities, and better profitability for local trade, all elements which are assumed to improve the overall quality of the urban environment. Certainly, these benefits will also be appreciated by local inhabitants. Growing awareness of local resources by inhabitants and by interested investors, could result indirectly in an attractive image of the town: a nice place to live, to work, and to visit and an interesting location for commercial investments.

Questions about drawbacks of tourism promotion led to some interesting reactions. Promoting tourism and investing in tourism development plans may downplay more important social issues. The greatest concern of respondents was the possible effect on the urban environment and its residential function. How large is the carrying capacity, physically and 'emotionally', of urban residential areas in terms of visitors? At what point does tourism, or flows of tourists, in urban contexts become a problem for local residents? There is more to this issue than the problem of traffic and parking arrangements. Views on these future issues are still very hesitant. The most frequently mentioned negative effect, so far, is related to traffic problems.

In the present stage of tourism development in the inner cities, problems of overcrowding, of pollution of the urban landscape, and of erosion of the historical heritage still seem very far away. None the less, some respondents had serious reservations about the long-term effects of intensified tourist activity and were in favour of tourism development plans that take account of conservation concerns and local residents' wishes. Concern about the future seemed to increase in direct proportion to the progress made in the planning process. Most of the towns reviewed, however, are only starting to realize their tourism development plans. Thus it might be argued that promoting local tourism and recreation should not be seen as an aim on its own, but as a means of improving the environmental quality for local inhabitants as well as for visitors.

The interviews with local planners and decision-makers incorporated a question about the role of scientific research as a basis for their planning task. This question was intended to draw some information about future research in the field of urban recreation and tourism. A distinction can be made between research projects conceived at the start of the planning process, which could result in some fundamental insights into trends of behaviour, and problems and research projects mainly seen as an evaluation of a selected policy. In principle, the results of such a research programme could provide directions for future planning processes but the practice proves to be very difficult. Making local development plans for recreation and tourism is currently a hot topic, so the pressure placed on local planners hardly leaves them the time to worry about more theoretical aspects of the problem.

Research as a starting point for the conception of development plans is frequently seen as irrelevant with regard to local problems and issues. With some exceptions, a more pragmatic approach based on commonsense assumptions and local knowledge is generally preferred. The benefits of investing in research were seen simply in terms of eventually obtaining more convincing support for political arguments.

Research on urban recreation and tourism was, however, seen as useful or even necessary under certain conditions.

1. First, research projects should be programmed as short studies directly dealing with well-defined local problems, and should lead to precise instructions on how to proceed in local developments of recreation and tourism.

2. Market research could serve to indicate specific target groups. The lack of hard information on this subject was repeatedly mentioned. General views on market segmentation cannot always be applied to the local situation, for recreation and tourism attractiveness of a particular city may be relatively unique.
3. Although support for research was rather low among several respondents, all respondents agreed that development plans for recreation and tourism should at least be subject to feasibility studies.

All three research stages are essentially project-linked, and include the establishment of technical feasibility, appraisal of financial investments, identification of the required action programme, and eventually an estimate of economic and social costs and benefits. Almost all local planners pleaded for adoption of economic priorities in this field, rather than accentuating the social or physical implication of tourism developments in the urban environment.

These views fit very well into the current political pattern, but do foster a certain risk by omitting long-term strategies. Plans for urban recreation and tourism are short-term exercises of planners and decision-makers. The future of urban recreation and tourism, placed in the wider context of social processes in inner cities, remains a primary challenge for social scientists. The question remains, however, whether such research efforts can bridge the serious gap between marketing philosophies, market planning techniques, and marketing concepts and bureaucratic philosophies, professional planning techniques and administrative practices.

REFERENCES

Ashworth, G. and Bergsma, J. (1987) 'New policies for tourism: opportunities or problems', Tijdschrift voor Economische en Sociale geografie 78(2): 151-55.

Ashworth, G. and Voogd, H. (1986) 'Marketing van het Europes erfgoed', Plan 9: 28-34.

Ashworth, G. and de Haan, T. (1985) 'The touristic - historic city: a model and application in Norwich', Field studies 8 (GIRUG Groningen).

—— (1986) 'Uses and users of the tourist - historic city; an evolutionary model in Norwich', Field Studies 10 (GIRUG Groningen).

Dietvorst, A. (1987) 'De toeristische attractiviteit van Nijmegen', in J. Borchert and J. Buursink (eds), City Marketing en Geografie, Amsterdam/Nijmegen: Netherlands Geographical Studies, pp. 122-37.

Jansen-Verbeke, M. (1985) 'Inner city leisure resources', Leisure Studies, 4: 142-57.

—— (1986a) 'Inner city tourism: resources, tourists, promotors', Annals of Tourism Research, 13(1): 79-100.

—— (1986b) 'Recreational behaviour and attitude of inner city dwellers: some issues of a case study', Tijdschrift van de Belgische vereniging voor Aardrijkskundige studies 2: 239-59.

—— (1988) 'A marketing approach to urban recreation and tourism' in Leisure, Recreation and Tourism in the Inner City: An Explorative Study (in press).

Jansen-Verbeke, M. and Dietvorst, A. (1987) 'Leisure, recreation and tourism: a geographic view on integration', Annals of Tourism Research 14(3): 361-75.

Zwart, A. (1987) 'Het imago van Dordrecht', in J. Borchert and J. Buursink (eds), City Marketing en Geografie, Amsterdam/Nijmegen: Netherlands Geographical Studies, pp. 149-62.

13

CHANGES IN ECONOMY, POLITICS AND LIFESTYLES: AN ESSAY ON THE RESTRUCTURING OF URBAN LEISURE

Hans Mommaas and Hugo van der Poel

INTRODUCTION

Although it is always dangerous to attempt to identify new episodes in history (which all too often appear simply as an effort to add a touch of novelty or realism to a text), it is perhaps not too much to say that during the 1980s Dutch cities are going through a new phase of development. Superficially, at least, one can discern some transformations which, when linked to more general political, economic, and thus spatial developments, support this claim.

Thus for instance, within the core of larger cities, where shopping areas had been transformed in the 1970s into pedestrian precincts, shops have become 'consumption palaces' reflecting the latest in 'fun shopping'. Old and more or less neglected blocks of housing are transformed into modern and luxurious apartment buildings or exclusive hotels, sometimes with the aid of varying degrees of state intervention, and intended for a new generation of gentrifiers. Often only the old facade remains to form part of a cosmetic history. Although taken as a whole the number of pubs and restaurants is decreasing, inside the central core of cities their number is increasing. New plans are being developed and realized for modern opera houses, new town halls, larger theatres and concert halls, and tropical swimming pools. City councils seem to be involved in a growing competition to revitalize their inner city. Part of this forms the aspiration to transform inner-city regions into what have already been called 'recreation reserves', developing (often in public-private partnerships) all kinds of projects promoting the inner city as a leisure resource.

At the same time, however, and in those same cities, public spending on social programmes has been decreasing.

Youth centres or local community centres have closed down or have had to make do with less staff. Public libraries are raising their prices in order to meet decreased public funding. Expenditure on green areas for the more suburban parts of cities has been reduced. Programmes for the renovation of housing built in the outskirts during the 1960s have rarely been completed. In some modern suburban working-class areas deterioration has set in quickly. It looks as though major shifts are taking place in the political and economic context of city development, leading to new social and spatial segregation and new private and public cultures.

As the foregoing suggests, within these developments leisure plays an important role. The issues involved can be analysed partly as leisure issues, not simply because the lifestyles, for example of gentrifiers, are identified in part by leisure tastes and activities but also because leisure forms a major focus for planning and investment in modern processes of revitalization. In this chapter a preliminary attempt is made to theorize upon these changes in city development, paying special attention to the related reorganization of urban leisure.[1] From the outset it should be clear that in doing this, it is impossible to deal with all relevant dimensions of the processes involved.[2] The focus of this chapter will therefore be on changes within the sphere of urban leisure policy and the sphere of urban leisure lifestyles. Both in turn will be related to more general developments in the sphere of capital accumulation.

The term 'urban leisure' is a rather vague one. Used as an analytic concept it raises the obvious question of whether or not there is such a thing as 'urban leisure' clearly differentiated from 'rural leisure'. It would seem to cover a whole range of different facilities and practices from 'hanging around' to squash, pop music, or the arts. It might therefore be considered a rather deceptive or chaotic concept (Sayer 1982), unifying activities which are clearly differentiated by participants. However, the term 'urban leisure' can also provide an object of research, covering as it does images of the relationship between the urban or the city and types of leisure, images which are reproduced in novels, policy, or marketing programmes, newspapers, and so on. Used as such, urban leisure does not relate to distinct theoretical or analytical meaning, but rather remains part of political, economic, or everyday practice. It is in this way that the term will be used in this chapter.

SETTING THE STAGE: THE MODERNIZATION OF THE CITY

In the postwar period, Dutch cities saw tremendous changes in economic, political, sociocultural, and spatial relations. In the economy the postwar period up to the 1960s saw a new era of industrialization which fed a period of economic growth. This was fuelled by a combination of factors: economic opportunities created by the destruction of capital during the war; the postwar Marshall programme; and a culture of consensus concerning broader economic and political developments. This consensus was loosely organized around the concept of the welfare state, a culture shared by political parties, employers, and trades unions.

In the 1960s and 1970s, however, this was followed by a period of deindustrialization. Due to a new and more intensive phase in capital accumulation (resulting in disinvestment in manufacture and new investment in the service sector) and because of the rapid expansion of Keynesian policy, new employment from this period onwards was largely restricted to the fields of finance, administration, information exchange, and public services.

In the 1950s and 1960s the state became heavily involved in subsidizing all kinds of social programmes, such as outdoor recreation, sports, media, and the arts.[3] This was part of a deliberate policy aiming at the modernization of the Dutch economy and society. The Dutch population had to be transformed into a highly educated, socially, economically, and geographically mobile and flexible population. Part of this policy formed the transformation of a community-based organization of local spaces and populations into an individual, or family-based organization, thus consciously aiming at what Castells (1983) has rightly characterized as the 'disconnection of people from spatial forms'.

Although during the postwar era state policy continued to be dominated by the Christian Democrats (with the exception of the period between 1973 and 1977 when Social Democrats held sway in the cabinet), one can discern (especially after the 1960s) a steady 'deconfessionalization' of the Dutch electorate. (Deconfessionalization is the process whereby support for political parties on the basis of religious affiliation is eroded.) This was expressed ultimately in an attempt by the Social Democrats during the period 1973 to 1977 to develop a Welfare Act, which in its original form would have meant a political institution-alization of the transformation of Dutch sociopolitical organization. Thus the traditional pillarized (segregated along religious lines) network of community-oriented and quango-like welfare institutions gave way to a modern professional, secular, and decentralized network of client-centred public services.

The physical correlate of these modernizing tendencies can be traced in two major developments: a spatial redistribution of economic enterprise and a radical development of new housing estates. Seen from the urban perspective, the redistribution of economic enterprise resulted in a spatial decentralization of manufacture and a spatial centralization of service-oriented industries. The new housing estates (the majority consisting of houses built with public financial aid but managed by quango-like housing societies) were constructed within the former periphery of towns, with the segregation between working, living, and recreation areas as a leitmotiv while at the same time reflecting old images of the 'green village'.

The migration into suburbia during the 1950s and 1960s of white, family-oriented, middle-class, employed residents, having the money and the desire to move to green areas with modern housing, originated mostly from the areas of housing built between 1890 and 1940. During the 1960s and 1970s these middle-class suburban migrants were followed by working-class groups, when welfare programmes were developed to give lower-income groups better access to public or council houses. As a result, new working-class suburbs developed, dominated by high-rise housing. The houses left behind were demolished to give way to office buildings, traffic lanes and/or parking lots, or were split up to provide living space for groups of 'marginal gentrifiers' (Rose 1984) like students and artists or to that growing group of Mediterranean migrant workers and inhabitants of former colonies.[4] Most of these people were not able to move to modern suburbs because of low income or rules connected to the housing distribution programmes (which gave priority to small families and local residents) and/or because they preferred the ambience of the inner city, the proximity of facilities, and the availability of houses that were both cheaper and more suited to single-person or large households.

Taken together, these developments implied a growing differentiation between the core areas of cities (some being upgraded as locations for offices or areas with an historical interest, some being downgraded to slum-like zones) and the expanding suburban areas (the living quarters of the white, married, and employed).

Within this complex modernizing process, urban leisure as such played a minor role. With the organization of leisure split between public and private sectors and different segments (e.g. sports, recreation, tourist, media, and cultural provision), each having its own rationale, urban leisure did not form a major focus of public or private attention. The term itself was hardly ever used. There were, however, two exceptions. First, urban leisure formed a comprehensive focus of public attention within debates and programmes taking place up until the late 1960s relating to the moral education, predominantly of factions of the urban working class, who were considered to be ill-equipped in cultural terms to enter the age of modernity. Their lifestyle, organized around the principles of closed communities and open families, did not match modern planning norms, in which the population was assumed to organize its life according to principles of open communities and closed families, thus stimulating modern spatial mobility. Hence research was carried out and programmes were developed to 're-educate' these so-called 'anti-social' groups of people, sometimes even by forcing them to move to special parts of cities in which their entire life (including their leisure) would be subject to control and intervention (Dercksen and Verplanke 1987). Second, urban leisure formed a comprehensive focus of attention within debates and programmes (also taking place until the late 1960s) concerning urban youth, which centred on themes like commercial leisure (youth visiting dance halls, pubs, and cinemas), pop music, sauntering through the streets, the freedom youth experienced (in relation to their parents, teachers, and youth workers) and sexuality. As was the case with the 'anti-social' factions of the working class, mass youth had to be transformed morally in order to prepare them for the coming age of modernity, in which they could easily fall victim to the seduction of modern wealth and freedom (Meijers and du Bois-Reymond 1987). In concluding, one could say that whenever the term 'urban leisure' was used, it predominantly formed part of public debates and of public programmes concerning the moral order in an age of modernization. The city and thus urban leisure represented the hallmarks of modernity.

258

THE ECONOMIC CRISIS OF THE LATE 1970s:
LEISURE FOR THE UNEMPLOYED

Since the mid-1970s there has been increasing attention paid to the urban problems of large cities. As a prelude to the economic crisis, with population growth slowing,[5] cities were confronted with a narrowing financial base for raising revenues with which to provide urban facilities and housing programmes. In these circumstances the rapidly deteriorating economic situation of the late 1970s had a severe impact. Unemployment rates soared as did the demand on public services, particularly with respect to social security programmes. These developments implied financial losses for local governments,[6] not only because their revenues declined, but also as a result of losses made on public investments in land allocated for industrial development which failed to attract private investment. Problems were aggravated by cutbacks in the financial support of local government by the central state, which adopted a more monetarist policy.

The effects of the economic crisis for the social and spatial distribution of (un)employment in urban conurbations are not difficult to understand. Unemployment first of all struck those already holding jobs or destined to have jobs within the older labour-intensive industries. Hence a rise in unemployment among manual workers and unskilled school-leavers had a disproportionately negative effect upon ethnic minorities. Thus, because of city development policies in the 1950s and 1960s and the related distribution of the population across urban space, there was an increase in unemployment within traditional working-class inner-city regions and, subsequently, also within working-class suburbs.

After this first phase in the rise of unemployment, a second stage can be identified in which unemployment spread to other groups. Because of public expenditure cuts on all kinds of programmes, especially welfare and maintainance programmes, unemployment began to affect not only manual labour in the public sector but also young artists, students of social and cultural sciences, welfare workers, and teachers. This created a kind of frustrated class of intellectuals or cultural mediators.[7] Notwithstanding the fact that, while unemployment lasted, those involved found themselves in equally marginal economic circumstances, there were (and still are) major differences

259

among the unemployed, relating to different ethnic, gender, age, and class backgrounds. These differences have expressed themselves in different reactions to a situation which has been characterized as one of 'suspended animation' (Willis 1983b).

Bourdieu's analyses of the judgment of taste (Bourdieu 1984) and Foucault's analyses of the production of subjectivity (Foucault 1978) can be helpful in discerning, very generally, two different kinds of response to unemployment which over time have had an important influence on the reproduction of 'urban leisure'.[8] The first can be called the 'culture of stylistic resistance', the second the 'culture of derivative consumption'. Both are expressed primarily by youth.

By the term 'culture of stylistic resistance' we refer to groups of fomer (white, male and female) students of welfare, social sciences, the arts, education, the media and so on. Educated during the 1970s, identifying themselves with the world of socially concerned cultural mediators (i.e. the world of educators, social scientists, publicists, artists, etc.), having grown up within economically rising middle-and/or working-class milieus, they shared leftist political sentiments. They regarded their way of life during unemployment as making a virtue out of necessity, putting into practice long-shared, politicized aspirations and perspectives. Small-scale manufacturing or service-oriented activities were developed, giving expression to ideas of democratic management, manufacturing autonomy and creativity, social solidarity, environmental concerns, and so on, along with new forms of more or less communally organized households (expressing ideas of female emancipation, collective reproduction, consumption of the necessary), thus breaching conventional boundaries between male and female, work and leisure, production and consumption. They developed a way of life which, on a higher level of abstraction, may be seen not so much as sanctioning a particular lifestyle, as promoting style as a form of resistance against frozen identities (suspended animation) within capitalist production and consumer culture. This culture of stylistic resistance is common to quite different movements such as the early movement for small-scale and environmentally safe enterprise, the gay movement, and punk culture. In spatial terms the culture of stylistic resistance is predominantly situated within inner-city neighbourhoods. Not only did inner-city housing facilities suit best the needs of its members (politically legitimated and stylistically reproduced), but these groups also felt attracted to the liveliness of the inner city, with its 'moving chaos' - the milieu of the urban bohemian.

This culture of stylistic resistance formed a major source of inspiration for many leisure academics writing within the older tradition of the coming of a leisure society. Individuals involved in this culture were considered to be heralds of a new age in which the capitalist division between work (paid and unpaid) and leisure, and between production and consumption would be superseded.[9] During the late 1970s and early 1980s groups of unemployed, sharing a culture of stylistic resistance, could also to some degree count on the sympathy of local social workers and of local civil servants. This sympathy expressed itself in political and financial support for the development of alternative projects on the margins of work and leisure during their period of 'enforced leisure'. Stylistic resistance at least meant people actively making the best of their position as unemployed, being involved in one way or another with public culture (politically motivated resistance being the proof of their involvement), searching for what was considered a meaningful use of their leisure time. They at least did not lapse into apathy, resulting in unpredictable political behaviour.

However, as unemployment continued, attention was directed towards other groups of young unemployed people. They were typified as belonging to a 'lost generation' which ran the risk of losing faith in the existing social order altogether. The major objects of attention here were those unemployed who gave expression to a 'culture of derivative consumption': these were predominantly the less educated, male, working-class youth from different ethnic backgrounds. Having grown up within traditional working-class milieus with rising expectations of the future, and having had less experience of formal education, they tended to identify with the culture of consumer society. Wage work to them would not only mean entering the adult world but also entering fully the world of capable and autonomous consumers, being able to purchase goods that bear the signs of the mature and independent labourer. While unemployed they search for practical ways to deal with the situation. They try to earn some money with (il)legal odd jobs in order still to be able to take part in the exchange of goods and other consumer activities, or they hang around in shopping areas, thus still forming part of the scene of consumer culture, participating in its atmosphere of signs and images in a kind of derivative way (Willis 1983b; Matthijs 1987). Having no job, their normal way into a family life of their own is blocked. After leaving their parental home (already older than is normally the case) they remain single, having to make do with either the council houses offered to them by local authorities in the suburbs of towns (for which most cannot qualify) or with single-room apartments in deteriorating inner-city areas.

In respect of the effects this new differentiation of leisure practices has had on the general image of urban leisure, we must be brief. It has contributed to an already gradually changing fragmentary image of urban leisure in the direction of what Berman (1983) has called a new 'modernism in the streets'. It has contributed to the development of an image of cities 'openly troubled, but intensely alive', stimulating the idea of a new 'urban moving chaos' (Berman 1983). This image has given rise to the impression that urban leisure transcended conventional moral and spatio-temporal distinctions. It came to be seen as a free-floating experience, less restricted by the organization and ethics of work, by tradition, or by norms of usefulness and civilization.

In line with these developments, in the late 1970s and early 1980s, in some cities something like an explicit and integrated leisure policy began to emerge. Most of the time, however, this was no more than what in other cities was conceptualized as a local unemployment policy. Leisure here tended to be used as a new unifying concept in the sphere of welfare work, tying together ideas and images connected with social cultural work, the voluntary sector, the informal economy, city renovation, work projects, daytime sports, and the like. This predominantly reflected the premiss that in the near future labour would disappear as the integrative basis of urban life. Thus comprehensive leisure programmes were to be developed to create a new basis for the social integration of the everyday lives of especially (but not exclusively) young, male, working-class unemployed. Their participation in projects developed for the overlapping concerns of leisure, education, and work, would be instrumental to that aim of integration.

Hence, during this first phase of economic difficulties, urban leisure still formed part of a welfare-oriented policy perspective. To talk about leisure in those days was to talk about unemployment, implicitly or explicitly expressing a concern for social integration.

ECONOMIC PROGRESS: CREATING THE BOURGEOIS PLAYGROUND

Despite the economic crisis and numbers of unemployed, walking through almost any Dutch city with 25,000 inhabitants or more, one finds it hard to avoid the impression that urban life is booming and blooming. During the 1980s urban leisure has gone through an accelerated change in image and policy. A more economically-oriented city development policy style has emerged, aiming at a revitalization of the city. Stress is placed on the importance of creating a leisured atmosphere within the inner cities. Projects, developed in public-private partnerships, are meant not for the reintegration of disadvantaged groups within society, but for servicing the pleasures of the well-to-do. We have therefore seen an explosion of new indoor shopping precincts, pavement cafes, restaurants, and gambling halls, and also of public sector-funded theatres, leisure-related development of the city centre's infra-structure, and the staging of cultural events and festivals.

The City Day held in Rotterdam in 1987 gives a good example of the rationale behind these developments. In the building of the World Trade Centre (built through a public-private partnership between the city of Rotterdam and the city's Chamber of Commerce) the citizens of Rotterdam were invited to discuss the city's future. Leaving aside other remarkable features of this initiative, what was perhaps most surprising was the way this public discussion was organized: it took a form similar to that of the annual general meeting of a firm, one which was trying to sell the 'commodity' Rotterdam. What received most publicity in the newspapers was that part of the meeting was dedicated to the presentation of the results of research into Rotterdam's image as a city in which to live and to work, which had been undertaken by a market research bureau. By the end of the event the public (which in large part consisted of civil servants and other professionals) generally supported the analysis presented and the solutions proposed. The thrust of these proposals was that Rotterdam should attempt to hold on to its acquired market share (in terms of investment and employment) but should also try to attract a larger share of the 'middle-class job market'. It was argued that to modernize its employment structure Rotterdam would have to attract firms active in the areas of banking and finance, high-tech industries, biotechnology, information processing, and the like. In order to attract these types of firms, Rotterdam would need to be seen as an attractive place to live by these new, highly educated, well-to-do employees.

This example is illustrative of the switch in the approach to leisure which has taken place in city policies within only a few years. In the past, urban leisure had hardly ever been an item in city policy. Attention was focused separately on sports, outdoor recreation, the arts, music, schools, libraries, open space, and so on. Whenever leisure per se had been on the agenda, it was within the context of a welfare-oriented policy.

This double change in urban leisure image and policy (urban leisure becoming more institutionalized as a comprehensive policy item and becoming an instrument of economic development) is ultimately linked not only to the shift from a Keynesian to a monetarist state policy, but also to the gradual institutionalization of a new phase in capital accumulation. The reduction of financial support from central government and the increased costs to local government of payment of unemployment benefits has more or less forced local governments into competition with one another to attract new industries and higher-income groups. The tactics of such competition have involved not only giving the industries concerned all kinds of financial incentives and trying to meet the luxurious housing needs of their employees, but also creating a pleasurable infrastructure appropriate to the employees' style of leisure.

What perhaps helped to trigger off this economization of leisure was a report on tourism policy published in 1979 by the Ministry of Economic Affairs, saying that something should be done to try to diminish the deficit of around 5 to 6 billion guilders every year on the national deficit in tourism balance of payments. This report, and the availability of central government grants to explore the leisure and tourism potential of the local region, focused the attention of city boards on the economic attractiveness of tourism developments. This policy initiative in particular reinforced the idea of the city as a kind of commodity to be marketed.[10]

However, the relationship between these political/administrative and economic developments and their actual results (the development of a specific urban leisure policy with a particular spatial redistribution of leisure resources and a restructuring of the rules, norms, or images with which these resources are surrounded) cannot be studied properly without also taking into account the potential leisure practices or lifestyles of those to whom this urban leisure policy is intended to appeal. For instance, it is clear that within modern leisure policy, as with modern city development policies in general, the inner city forms the focus of attention and investment. Of course, this is partly related to a new spatial distribution of production functions, in which sections of modern service industries that contain routine activities are decentralized to the suburbs and prestigious decision-oriented sections are (re)centralized to the city centre. It is also related to the fact that due to former processes of deterioration, inner-city regions now form a favourable place for production or consumption-based investments. However, both merely form conditional opportunities, which by themselves do not explain why the inner city became the focus of a new leisure policy. To complete the analysis, we must include the leisure practices or lifestyles of those who actually make leisure investments within the inner city financially worthwhile.[11]

In the social analysis literature, this new urban lifestyle has been associated with concepts such as 'wealthy gentrifiers' (Rose 1984), 'double-earning households' (Klerk and Vijgen 1984) 'those with more-money-and-less-free-time' (Lakatos and van Kralingen 1985) the 'downtown-oriented' (Engelsdorp Gastelaars 1980), 'individualistic', 'hedonistic', 'postmodern', and so on. It consists of leisure practices which, generally speaking, are outdoor- and inner city-oriented and have, for those participating, high expressive and cultural value. Included in these practices are activities such as visiting exquisite restaurants and pubs with postmodern interiors, museums and music theatres; but also visiting tropical swimming pools, playing squash, and driving a BMW or Golf GTI. The core of those adopting this lifestyle (or its image) as a focus of aspiration form part of a young, middle-class but rising economic elite, deriving its economic resources predominantly from new jobs in information processing industries.

Rose (1984) has argued that this new economic elite differs in at least four respects from the upwardly mobile of the 1950s and 1960s. First, they do not follow the conventional economic life-cycle in which upward mobility formed as the result of years of employment experience. Second, they do not necessarily constitute either single-

265

person households or male heads of families. Third, they can no longer assume single job security and steadily increasing incomes. Fourth, they concentrate, or at least wish to concentrate, in inner-city areas not only because a large proportion of the opportunities for this type of job is concentrated there, but also because these areas have facilities which meet their 'reproductive needs'. For the most part they reside in housing blocks formerly occupied by marginal gentrifiers, but rebuilt as luxury apartments by building and/or investment companies.

With regard to the dynamics of this new urban lifestyle, it should be clear that, as numerous authors have stated before, the production, exchange, and consumption of goods and services, and hence also the consumption of space, are not simply economic phenomena. They are not simply related to strictly functional utility needs, but are always also embedded within a cultural matrix, adding expressive values to what is produced, consumed, and striven for (Featherstone 1987).[12]

Following the analyses of Jager (1986) and Featherstone (1987), both elaborating French social theory (the works of Baudrillard and Bourdieu), this new urban lifestyle can best be characterized as expressing a new petit-bourgeois kind of stylistic consumer culture. Contrary to the traditional working-class and petit-bourgeois culture of necessity and conformity, this culture puts stress upon expressive rather than instrumental or practical values as well as on 'calculated hedonism' and 'coded individuality'. Their practitioners are involved in an ongoing process of aesthetization, adorning not only trivial consumer goods with signs of luxury, modernity, and beauty, but also their bodies with signs of health and confidence. Trying to rise in social status, they combine elements of a traditional bourgeois intellectual lifestyle (stressing the importance of quality, autodidactism, and artistic aesthetization) with more hedonistic consumption-oriented values (pleasure, fun, freedom) - hence the combination of features such as museums and theatres with those of tropical swimming pools and the Golf GTI. As Featherstone has already noted, the practitioners of the new urban lifestyle are 'not so much promoting a particular style, but rather catering for and promoting a general interest in style itself' (Featherstone 1987).

The effect of this rising urban lifestyle on the image of urban leisure is an indirect one. Urban leisure has become part of the ongoing modernization of city life to its postmodern extremes, rendering the boundaries between conventional fields of culture and pleasure, or between art and entertainment, free-floating.[13] The most trivial consumer goods (hi-fi equipment, bathing suits, roller skates, coffee machines) can become the object of an upgrading process of aesthetization. At the same time activities once belonging to the field of culture (visiting exquisite restaurants, museums, theatres) can become the downgraded object of hedonization or marketing. Urban leisure becomes associated with a rather diffuse <u>bricolage</u> of activities. The classification of leisure styles, clearly belonging to the conventional subcultural domain of particular class factions, becomes more and more difficult, a factor which explains some of the problems of market researchers trying to identify their market segments.[14]

The change in the image of urban leisure is clearly stimulated by the fact that this very new urban lifestyle is taken up in urban policy.[15] Perhaps for the first time in recent history a hedonistic trend in urban leisure has not met with a policy response which expresses moral concern. Indeed, the contrary is the case: because of economic interests, local policy has increasingly sought to stimulate the mixture of economic enterprise, culture, and leisure, attempting in this manner to attract the new economic elite to the city. This has involved not only a privately supported aesthetization of urban leisure (e.g. closing down old swimming pools in order to replace them with tropical ones), but also by an economization or commodification (and hence often hedonization) of conventional culture (e.g. cutting down expenses on public libraries, lcoal theatres, art productions, forcing those involved to develop a more market-oriented approach). Within urban leisure policy, in the Netherlands at least, attention has more and more been directed at developing the inner-city area, the inner city being the focus of (post) modern culture.

The consequences of this new policy are showing very clearly. Because urban policy has adopted and legitimated the profiles and potentials of the lifestyle of this new economic elite, thereby also legitimating the economic dimensions involved (the acceptance of making leisure, culture, and welfare objectives the object of market strategies and criteria), the interests of those not having the opportunity to emulate the new economic elite in its pleasures fail to be considered. When the latter start presenting a potential danger for the new leisured image that cities are trying to sell, they are actively removed from view, either by ignoring them, or by physical dispersal (e.g. drug addicts being removed from city centres and dispersed across the city). Hence there has been an increased spatial differentiation in the city over and above that already institutionalized during the 1950s and 1960s, a differentiation that reflects even more strongly the dimension of wealth versus poverty.

CONCLUSION

In the foregoing analysis an attempt has been made to provide an agenda for theorizing recent developments relating to the reproduction of urban leisure. From the outset it should be clear that these developments must be considered in the context of a more general process of urban restructuring.

As is well illustrated in a collection of articles edited by Smith and Williams (1986) dealing with the related issue of gentrification, analysing the process of urban restructuring requires the social analyst to delve into complex theoretical and empirical issues which lie at the heart of many methodological and substantive theoretical debates. Thus, for instance, on a methodological level there is the problem of accommodating structure and agency in the reconstruction of urban redevelopment. The spatial reorganization of capital, the shift from a Keynesian to a monetarist state policy, the emergence of a new middle class, and the associated emergence of a new urban lifestyle, the aesthetization of the built environment, and the economization of urban leisure - these and other developments must be represented as not only the result of structural developments, but also as the result of interventions on the part of diverse groups of knowledgeable and capable actors in the ongoing stream of events.

On a more substantive theoretical level, cutting across the methodological axis, there is the question of which phenomena to look for in characterizing urban restructuring. One can discern perhaps a consensus that analysis of urban restructuring should involve economic, accumulation- and production-based factors, as well as policy- and planning-based, and culture- reproduction- and consumption-based factors. Although, given the capitalist character of Western nation-states, changes in the sphere of capital accumulation are central to an adequate understanding of urban revival and hence also to the economization of urban leisure, it is nevertheless also necessary to focus on the influence of changes in the spheres of state policy and on changes in the realm of cultural reproduction.

To complicate matters even further, in incorporating these diverse factors one must also be aware of the dimensions of time and space not only because every event should be analysed and represented in its proper historical-geographical setting, but also because time and space are intrinsically involved in every act of social reproduction. Therefore it is necessary to pay attention to the different (spatial and temporal) scales on which factors work, to show how local events form the result of the contingent interaction of past and present and of local, regional, national, and even global processes. Consequently, it is also necessary to acknowledge the fact that both the 'user-practices' of leisure participants and the investment and planning practices surrounding leisure facilities always involve temporal-spatial perspectives or dimensions (e.g. concerning the proper time and place to go dancing or the appropriate time and place to invest in 'fun shopping').

The analysis presented here merely touches upon this analytic complexity and the theoretical issues involved. As will be clear, this chapter is more concerned with providing a preliminary indication of the empirical issues which a comprehensive analysis of recent developments in urban leisure should include, than it is with a recapitulation of the results of such an analysis. As such it perhaps reflects the state of the art concerning the theorization of urban leisure within Dutch leisure studies.

Given these limitations, a perspective has been presented here which can perhaps best be summarized as describing how urban leisure image and policy has become part of a neo-liberal/neo-conservative process of modernization. Based upon a new phase in capital accumulation, implying a shift in the economic infrastructure of Western European countries from labour-intensive manufacturing to labour-extensive information processing industries and mediated through a monetarist state policy, hegemonic urban leisure policy has experienced a shift in rhetoric, in objectives, and in criteria of relevance from a predominantly moralizing and integrating perspective to a predominantly market-oriented perspective.[16] The rationale behind this market-oriented approach is strengthened by attempts made by local policy agents to meet central state expenditure cuts and increasing costs related to local unemployment by simultaneously trying to cut expenses and to attract a new economic elite to cities. These two objectives are consonant with promotion of the lifestyle of this elite, a lifestyle which we have characterized as embedded within a petit-bourgeois kind of 'stylistic consumer culture'. Since within this culture conventional fields of leisure, pleasure, and economic enterprise are integrally bound up, it can render conventional cultural and welfare programmes and objectives the object of market decisions, that is reducing their status to that of consumer goods and services.

In terms of spatial relations these developments imply an emphasis put on the (leisure) quality of city centres, more or less at the cost of the (leisure) quality of the suburbs. They stimulate a trend towards a spatial segregation between the pleasure reserves of the economic elite and reserves of the marginal.

NOTES

1. This work forms part of a recently initiated research programme concerning the changing relation between political and economic intervention in leisure. Within this research attention is being focused on the rationale behind these different kinds of interests (economic and political), the kinds of changes which take place between them, the way these changes should be analysed historically and theoretically, and the way these changes are related to the social and spatial distribution of leisure potential and the reproduction of leisure practices of different groups of people.

2. This would require paying equal attention to, for example:
* the restructuring of the process of capital accumulation and its effects on the spatial, economic, and social organization of production; on the related spatial, social, and economic division of labour; on patterns of private and public investment in leisure projects; and the way these effects are related to changes in politics and consumer cultures
* the changes in general central and local policy objectives; the way these affect the relationship between central and local government; the combined

effects on the content of leisure policy; and the way these developments are related to the changes in the sphere of capital accumulation and consumption

* the related changes in the consumption patterns of different groups of the urban population; the lifestyles involved; the way these relate to each other and to changes taking place in the spheres of capital accumulation and politics.

3. These programmes are predominantly promoted by quasi-autonomous governmental organizations.

4. The concept of the marginal gentrifier is introduced by Rose (1984) to refer to all types of middle-income gentrifiers. They are referred to as gentrifiers because their migration to inner-city areas often forms the first stage in the process of gentrification. Smith (1986) argues that this application of the term minimizes the polarization taking place in many gentrifying neighbourhoods between different income groups. According to Smith, the importance of the notion of the marginal gentrifier is not that 'these agents define, or indeed redefine, the gentrification process but it is precisely that they are marginal to a process already defined by its more central characteristics, the change of inner city neighbourhoods from lower to higher income residents' (Smith 1987: 160).

However valid Smith's remarks are, it cannot be denied that in terms of both consumption styles and their effect on property values, these marginal gentrifiers, as an unintended consequence of their migration, create conditions favourable to the process of gentrification. Furthermore, Rose uses the concept simply as an heuristic device. Nevertheless, whether one stresses the 'marginal' or the 'gentrification' dimension, it is an interesting concept.

5. Whereas in 1965 the size of the population was estimated at 21 millions, by 1976 this was adjusted to an estimate of around 15 million (De Gans 1987: 48).

6. Local governments have to meet 10 per cent of the costs of unemployment benefit for the long-term unemployed, a budget item over which they exercise no control.

7. This affected primarily those areas which, during the 1960s and 1970s, with the exodus of their former residents, had been colonized by 'marginal gentrifiers' (students of social science, welfare work, or arts courses). These were often situated close to, or formed islands within, working-class communities.

8. It is not our aim to give a comprehensive overview of the kaleidoscope of consumer or leisure cultures to be found either in the urban context or among the unemployed. Our focus is on those cultural orientations which have had an important influence on urban leisure image and policy.

9. See also Klerk and Vijgen (1984).

10. The 'selling' of cities implies an important role for promotion. Amsterdam's attempt to attract the 1992 Olympics provides a good example of the practices associated with this ideology and of the conflicts it produced. It became quite clear that many of the citizens of Amsterdam thought that the money involved would be better spent on projects of direct benefit to the inhabitants. Others argued that if the Olympics were to be held in Amsterdam, this should be on the basis of the promotion of Amsterdam as it really exists, not on some glossy image of a city of beautiful canals and architecture, devoid of social problems.

11. For a more detailed discussion of the issues involved here, see Smith (1986) and Beauregard (1986).

12. Rose (1984), in theorizing the production of inner-city gentrifiers, emphasizes the point that this phenomenon cannot simply be explained by reference to the fact that inner city housing and neighbourhoods meet the reproductive needs of those groups best. It is also important to note that, in terms of certain cultural codes, living in the inner city can serve certain stylistic needs, that is, it has a high expressive value of its own.

13. See also the collection of texts in Modleski (1986) and Jameson (1983).

14. This does not imply that the class positions would no longer have any consequences for the leisure practices of those involved. Clearly, that is not the case. However, because of the restructuring of both the division of labour and the growing differentiation of lifestyles, the correlation between class and lifestyle becomes less clear.

15. This process is probably facilitated by the fact that a young and rising generation of civil servants is itself party to this consumer culture.

16. This is not to say that within modern leisure policy moral codes do not play a role. However, whereas in the past moral concerns (e.g. in respect of the effects of modernization on different factions of the population) were at the heart of leisure policy rhetoric, more recently morality has become a kind of hidden dimension behind the

interaction between leisure policy and the market. It is implicitly reproduced within the interplay of profitable demand and supply, only resurfacing when deviancy disturbs market relations.

REFERENCES

Abma, R. (1987) 'Jeugd, cultuur en vrijetijd', in E. Meyer (ed.), Alledaags Leven, Vrijetijd Encultuur. Conferentieverslag, Tilburg: Centrum voor Vrije tijdskunde, pp. 361-8.

Akkerman, T. and Stuurman, S. (eds) (1985) De Zondige Riviera van het Katholicisme. Een Lokale Studie over Feminisme en Ontzuiling, Amsterdam: SUA.

Bates, I., Clarke, J., Cohen, P., Finn, D., Moore, R., and Willis, P. (1984) Schooling for the Dole? The New Vocationalism, London: Macmillan.

Beauregard, R.A. (1986) 'The chaos and complexity of gentrification', in N. Smith and P. Williams (eds) Gentrification of the City, London: Allen & Unwin, pp. 35-55.

Berman, M. (1983) All That Is Solid Melts Into Air. The Experience of Modernity, London: Verso.

Bourdieu, P. (1984) Dinstinction. A Social Critique of the Judgement of Taste, London: Routledge & Kegan Paul.

Burger, P. and Burger, C. (1987) Postmoderne: Alltag, Allegorie und Avantgarde, Frankfurt/Main: Suhrkamp.

Castells, M. (1983) 'Crisis, planning, and the quality of life: Managing the new historical relationships between space and society', Environment and Planning D, Society and Space 1: 3-21.

de Certeau, M. (1984) The Practice of Everyday Life, Berkeley: University of California Press.

Dercksen, A. and Verplanke, L. (1987) Geschiedenis van de Onmaatschappelijkheidsbestrijding in Nederland 1914-1970, Meppel: Boom.

Engbersen, G. and van der Veen, R. (1987) Moderne Armoede. Overleven op Hetsociaal Minimum, Leiden/Antwerpen: Stenfert Kroese.

van Engelsdorp Gastelaars, R. (1980) Niet Elke Stadsbewoner is Een Stedeling, Amsterdam: Universiteit van Amsterdam/Sociaal-Geografisch Instituut.

——— (1983) Het Dagelijks Leven in Een Stadsgewest,

Amsterdam: Universiteit van Amsterdam/Instituut voor Sociale Geografie.

Featherstone, M. (1987) 'Lifestyle and consumer culture', in E. Meyer (ed.), Everyday Life, Leisure and Culture. Conference proceedings, Centre for Leisure Studies, Tilburg, pp. 157-68.

Foucault, M. (1978) Dispositive der Macht. Michel Foucault über Sexualitat, Wissen und Wahrheit, Berlin: Merve Verlag.

Galesloot, H. and Schrevel, M. (eds) (no date) In Fatsoen Hersteld Zedelijkheid Enwederopbouw na de Oorlog, Amsterdam; SUA.

de Gans, H.A. (1987) 'Suburbanisatie of compacte stad?' Mens en Maatschappij 62 (1): 44-63.

Giddens, A. (1979) Central Problems in Social Theory, London: Macmillan.

Girouard, M. (1985) Cities & People. A Social and Architectural History, New Haven: Yale University Press.

Glyptis, S. (1983) 'Business as usual? Leisure provision for the unemployed', Leisure Studies 2: 287-300.

Gregory, D. and Urry, J. (eds) (1985) Social Relations and Spatial Structures, London: Macmillan.

Jager, M. (1986) 'Class definition and the aesthetics of gentrification: Victoriana in Melbourne', in N. Smith and P. Williams (eds), Gentrification of the City, London: Allen & Unwin, pp. 78-91.

Jameson, F. (ed.) (1983) Formations of Pleasure, London: Routledge & Kegan Paul.

van der Kamp, T. and Krijnen, H. (eds) (1987) Dagelijks Leven in Nederland. Verschuivingen in het Sociale Leven na de Tweede Wereldoorlog, Amsterdam: De Populier.

de Klerk, L. and Vijgen, J. (1984) 'Cities in post-industrial perspective: New economies, new lifestyles, new changes?' Metropolis '84, Conference proceedings, pp. 52-73.

Kruijt, B. (1987) Stedelijke Netwerken: Groei, Stagnatie en Segmentering in de Randstad. Amsterdam: Rapport van de Voorlopige Programma Commissie.

Lakatos, P.A.M. and van Kralingen, R.M. (1985) Naar 1990, een Kwestie van Tijden Geld, Amsterdam: Elsevier.

Lane, J.E. (ed.) (1985) State and Market. The Politics of the Public and the Private, London: Sage.

Matthijs, M. (1987) ' "Geld maakt niet gelukkig, zeggen ze,

maar mij wel. ..." Overwerk, werkloosheid, consumptiedwang en mannelijkheid', in M. Matthijsen et al. (eds) Beelden van Jeugd. Leefwereld, Beleid, Onderzoek, Groningen: Wolters Noordhoff.

Meijers, F. and du Bois Reymond, M. (eds) (1987) Op Zoek Naar een Modernepedagogische Norm. Beeldvorming over de Jeugd in de Jaren Vijftig: Het Massajeugdonderzoek (1948-1952), Amersfoort/Leuven: Acco.

Modleski, T. (ed) (1986) Studies in Entertainment. Critical Approaches to Mass Culture, Bloomington: Indiana University Press.

Mommaas, H. (1985) Werkloosheid en Vrijetijd, Tilburg: Centrum voor Vrijetijdskunde.

Murdock, G. (1977) 'Class stratification and cultural consumption. Some motifs in the work of Pierre Bourdieu', in M.A. Smith (ed.), Leisure and Urban Society, Salford: University of Salford/Centre for Leisure Studies.

de Pater, B.C. and Thissen, F. (no date) Ruimtelijke Dimensies van Vrijetijdsbesteding, Utrecht: Rijksuniversiteit Utrecht/Geografisch Instituut.

Rose, D. (1984) 'Rethinking gentrification: beyond the uneven development of Marxist urban theory', Environment and Planning D, Society and Space 1: 47-74.

Sayer, A. (1982) 'Explanation in economic geography: abstraction versus generalization', Progress in Human Geography 6 (March): 68-88.

Sennett, R. (1974) The Fall of Public Man. On the Social Psychology of Capitalism, New York: Vintage.

Smith, N. (1986) 'Gentrification, the frontier, and the restructuring of urban space', in N. Smith and P. Williams (eds), Gentrification of the City, London: Allen & Unwin, pp. 15-34.

—— (1987) 'Of yuppies and housing: gentrification, social restructuring, and the urban dream', Environment and Planning D, Society and Space 5, pp. 161-72.

Smith, N. and Williams, P. (eds) (1986) Gentrification of the City, London: Allen & Unwin.

Stuurman, S. (1983) Verzuiling, Kapitalisme en Patriarchaat, Nijmegen: SUN.

Vijgen, J. and van Engelsdorp Gastelaars, R. (1986) Stedelijke Bevolkingskategorieen in Opkomst, Amsterdam: Universiteit van Amsterdam/Instituut voor Sociale Geografie.

White, P. (1984) The West European City. A Social

Geography, London: Longman.

Willis, P. (1983a) 'Jeugdwerkloosheid en kulturele verandering', Te Elfder Ure 27: 619-32.

——— (1983b) 'Youth unemployment: Thinking the unthinkable', mimeograph.

14

LEISURE AND URBAN PROCESSES: CONCLUSION

INTRODUCTION: THE PRESENT AND THE ABSENT

This book reflects the growing and common interest in leisure policies within cities in Western Europe as both national and local governments express an interest in leisure as a vehicle for meeting social and economic urban policy objectives. The focal concerns of leisure policy and leisure research have shifted from issues such as outdoor recreation, recreation management, rural development, or landscape planning to issues related to culture, lifestyle, city-tourism, or city-marketing.

However tempting such a reading of recent developments of revitalization, gentrification, and city-marketing would seem, we nevertheless have to be careful not to simplify matters too far. As Smith and Williams (1986) have argued forcefully in their conclusion to a collection of papers on gentrification, such an analysis would mean losing contact with the complexity of historical and contemporary urban reality. Although it is true to say that in the postwar period urban spatial policies and spatial developments centred around processes of suburbanization, much attention was also directed towards a modernizing transformation of the inner city, concomitant with a major shift within most Western economies from industrial to service-based activities. Indeed, it was this revitalization of the city with its accompanying modernization (some would say destruction) of the living quarters of the old industrial labour classes which actually formed a major factor in producing a move outward alongside the growth of postwar populations. At the same time, it is true that a large number of inner-city areas experienced a new phase of de-investment, leaving a deteriorating quality of life for those left behind - the unemployed, the elderly, and racial minorities.

To capture these processes more generally, and in line with a new interlacing of social theory and human geography (Gregory and Urry 1985), theorizing about social phenomena must take account of their location in space and time. Cities or urban conglomerations in Europe show a marked difference in the way they are affected by recent economic and political changes. Just as in any other type of social development, urban processes are specific to certain periods and certain places, depending on the relation between the local economic or political infrastructures to transformations of a global and national scale. Cities and urban conglomerations are positioned differently within historical time and global space.

Instead of treating the recent attention paid to urban processes within the field of leisure studies, or the growth of interest in leisure policies within local government, as manifestations of an isolated revival of the urban, we would perhaps do better to see them as manifestations within policy and research of a new phase in the restructuring of the urban, leading to new political, economic, social, and hence also spatial relations, which raise new problems and lead to new questions.

The recurring and central argument of this collection, and indeed the rationale behind the project for which this publication is a kind of initial impetus, is that leisure and urban policies demand detailed analysis, not just of cross-national empirical cases, but more so of the interrelation between the general and the specific; not only in terms of relations of time and space but also in terms of the abstract and the concrete, or of the theoretical and empirical.

This demand for 'contextual realism' in recent theoretical debates also features in this conclusion. It aims to draw together some important threads, signalled in the Introduction, developed by the individual chapters and raised by the collection as a whole regarding general developments in urban leisure and urban leisure policy. Second, the conclusion will raise the issue of comparative research, discussing briefly some related methodological and theoretical aspects. Third, it will present a model for organizing comparative cross-national research, projecting ahead some key issues which should be addressed by those interested in urban leisure theory and policy.

LEISURE AND THE URBAN: COMMON THREADS

Organized under three rubrics, the dimensions of the political, the practical, and the spatial, each chapter in this collection has located aspects of leisure policy in distinct historical and spatial settings and worked out the particular trajectory of these policies within urban processes. Nevertheless, reading through the chapters of this text produces inductively a range of common answers to questions of why and in what manner leisure finds its way, sometimes to the forefront, of urban policy concerns in the 1970s and 1980s.

Western industrial capitalism has undergone profound structural changes during this period with regional, national, and international shifts in opportunities for capital accumulation and employment. The boundaries between the primary, secondary, and tertiary sectors of European economies have been redrawn with distinct spatial, political, and social consequences. Cities have been an obvious arena for changes in employment with certain factions of the population benefiting from changes in markets and employment opportunities while others suffer material and cultural deprivation and disadvantage. The economic gains and losses percolate through the structures of class, gender, race, and age as each generation comes to terms with the material and cultural rules and resources it has inherited from the past and out of which the present and future must be made and transformed. Advantage and disadvantage are reproduced by human agency and find their expression in spatial and cultural forms - including leisure. These divisions of class, gender, race, and age may be strengthened or distorted by state policies and it is open to history and social analysis in general to reconstruct and explore the nature and often contradictory direction of state activities and interventions.

It is clear that in doing so, simplistic concepts of the state and/or leisure will not do. Crude characterizations, drawn by naive pluralism or vulgar Marxism, fail to capture the complexity of the state in capitalist societies, particularly with regard to leisure. However, neither will it do to conclude from this that we must either turn to some theoretically uninformed data-gathering (which in terms of theories of knowledge would indeed be impossible, however necessary and informative data can be), or move to some kind of eclectic, middle-range theoretization (which would

279

only· be a means of moving problems to another level of analysis).

Instead we must tease out the complex ways in which the recent restructuring of processes of capital-accumulation has fed ongoing processes of policy formation. This analysis must not lose contact with other relevant constitutive elements of policy formation, for example, the relations between different sectors or levels of policy-making or the resources on which decision-makers depend in developing policies. Nor must we ignore the fact that the state is heavily involved in processes of capital accumulation, indeed perhaps more than ever before. On the other hand, such analysis is also situated within capitalist nation-states, with their own peculiar insulated relation between (transnational) processes of capital accumulation and (national) processes of public redistribution, the second process being dependent on the first (see Giddens 1981). Many contributors trace the shifting ground of leisure policy leading up to just this type of analysis.

During the 1970s the very notion of the welfare state was under ideological attack. Of course, in right-wing circles it has never gained favour because of the confidence placed in the market to resolve the allocation of public, merit or private goods. However, the welfare state has lost much of its appeal for the left also, not only because of the new political realism constructed by dominant right-wing policies, but also because the welfare state had proved to be not as resistant to crisis as social-democratic groups had previously thought, and because the welfare state did seem to produce its own kind of dependencies, a problem for which the left could provide no answer.

At the level of local policy, leisure initiatives, usually in sports and recreation, were regarded as important ways of dealing with the 'enforced' leisure of the unemployed, and as an important element in improving the quality of life of the deprived and the disadvantaged. Such leisure initiatives were consonant with the local political function of meeting the demands of local residents and the electorate. They were fuelled by visions of community development and frequently used at arm's length by central government, which was simultaneously cutting expenditure in conventional areas of social policy such as education, housing, social services, and welfare benefits. It is clear also that there was strong professional support for leisure initiatives (as is also the case with tourism and economic redevelopment initiatives in the 1980s). In certain countries these policies have also been associated with attempts to combat urban disorder, and fear of growing street crime - the violent consumerism of the deprived and unemployed, shopping without money, as they ransacked local shops and fought the police.

By the 1980s the welfare rationales for 1970s' leisure policies were beginning to wear thin in most European countries. A growing body of academic literature suggests that many leisure initiatives have only a limited impact on tackling and redressing social and economic problems. They have certainly not been the panacea that some policymakers and professional practitioners hoped and claimed they would be.

Certainly, the central state during the 1980s has increased its control over public expenditure and in some countries has shifted funding into policies of economic regeneration and tourism, often in partnership with private local capital. Consequently, the local state is under increasing pressure to attract private capital investment and hence employment, to rationalize and market existing public services, and cross-subsidize some services to fulfil unprofitable policy goals. Indeed, some local authorities in Britain look towards an integrated set of local state policies (of education, employment, housing, and leisure) as the only democratic means to resist market forces supported by private capital accumulation and central government policies of monetarism and privatization.

As will be clear from this, the commodification and decommodification of services highlighted in the theoretical writings of Offe (1984) will become the centre of political debate in the 1980s and 1990s, changing the conventional debate over these services drastically, together with the underlying political and professional perspectives and interests.

Another important development could be central government's reliance on increased expenditure on 'social expenses' particularly the police (and perhaps private security agencies) to guarantee some solution to urban disorders and the darker side of consumerism and economic individualism, rather than increased spending in the commodification of public services. We are witnessing a shift away from 'soft' forms of regulation (through provision policy) towards 'hard' forms of regulation (widening the powers of the police, increased police surveillance). Such a policy would reflect a state acquiescence in increased spatial segregation and divisions along the lines of class, gender, and race. The boundaries between safe public and private spaces would be further drawn to the disadvantage of the weak and oppressed. What role leisure professionals, particularly in the public sector, will play in mediating access to production and consumption of leisure remains an open question.

Within the context of these overall developments, several distinct urban leisure policy styles or orientations are in use, sometimes executed alongside each other, often also in direct conflict with each other. In an attempt to disentangle the policy discourse on leisure from the foregoing collection of papers, we can discern six perspectives on the role of leisure in urban policy.

1. First, leisure can be considered as primarily the responsibility of the private or voluntary sector. This is the result either of economic policy objectives to minimalize public sector expenditure and to market public provision, or of a more explicit view that leisure is not something with which the state should interfere. Leisure is defined as a realm of individual freedom, of free choice in which, by definition, the state cannot interfere without compromising its free character (a view which not only ignores existing forms of intervention, but in which civic freedom is confused with freedom per se). Leisure conceived of as a realm of 'pleasure' becomes far too trivial for positive state intervention. In so far as people want pleasure, the market will provide.

2. Second, leisure can form part of a conventional, welfare-oriented public service delivery policy, with specialized local government departments and specialized public sector professionals trying to defend existing resources and provisions and seeking to develop, market, and target existing leisure provisions to increase the partic-ipation of non-users who are constrained by material and cultural disadvantage. Leisure policy forms part of a conventional 'equal access' policy, in which leisure provisions are thought of as vehicles to motivate and facilitate equal participation in (admissible forms of) leisure. As such, leisure policy tries to correct market relations that are thought of either as producing the wrong kind of leisure provisions (commercial forms of cheap amusement) or excluding more disadvantaged groups.

3. Third, leisure can form part of a more entre-preneurial style of urban policy in which it is considered

primarily as a trading service, conducted in a way that will foster profits. Local government can try to profit from leisure either by a general taxation of all forms of local entertainment or, more specifically, by developing leisure services in areas where income can exceed marginal public costs. The profits can be used to cross-subsidize unprofitable but socially desirable forms of provision.

4. Leisure can be seen as an important tool for community development, especially for (unemployed) youth and their integration into legitimate networks of urban structure and processes, or for communities which, because of growing unemployment, are experiencing a deterioration of conventional forms of legitimate social integrations. Leisure provisions are used as vehicles to promote new and legal identities and involvements where conventional ones have become obsolete.

5. Within a more economic perspective, leisure can be seen as an important tool in attracting new sources of income to the city. The public sector, perhaps in partnership with private capital attempts to refurbish and revitalize the historic cores of the cities, strives to represent the historic past and to give the inner city a more leisured, pleasurable infrastructure. This is done in order to attract more tourists into towns, to replace traditional patterns of industrial employment with employment in retailing, tourism, and the service sector, or to attract higher-income groups.

6. Last, leisure can become part of an autonomous cultural policy trying to politicize dominant and popular cultural forms and conventional-cultural policies in order to break down existing forms of cultural domination or cultural classification. This approach will give forms of popular, mass, or particularistic culture an equal chance in public representation. Within this policy the boundaries between leisure and culture are blurred. Cultural expressions become the object of leisure experiences, while at the same time leisure goods and services can become the object of forms of aesthetization.

This classification of styles of leisure policy is not an exhaustive one, nor are the styles as clearly evident in particular cases as they are presented here. However, this classification has more than heuristic value. Its function is to distinguish and trace existing agendas within urban leisure policies, to be able to analyse these in terms of their causes, consequences, and inherited relations in order to understand more clearly why and in what way leisure found its way into urban policy.

Although not written within a common framework of agreed classifications and concepts, several contributions have demonstrated prevailing changes in urban leisure policy and contrasts within leisure policy to indicate the significance of the styles distinguished here. However, before discussing these more extensively in order to develop a model for future comparative research on urban leisure policy, let us first turn briefly to the topic of comparative research itself in order to get an idea about what a model for comparative research should aim for.

INTERMEZZO: 'COMPARATIVE RESEARCH' - IT MAKES A DIFFERENCE

This collection has been gathered as a means of stimulating the development of comparative studies around the topic of urban leisure and urban leisure policy. As such, it does not already form the result of some comparative research project. Indeed, even the contribution that comes nearest to comparative research, that of Franco Bianchini dealing with local cultural policy in Rome and London, does not explicitly explore the two cases in terms of a common problematic which would be required for cross-national comparison. At best, the contributions as they are drawn together in this book can be described as providing material for comparative research.

Conventionally, comparative research describes research which is situated in different nation-states or in different societies. It is research which is completed with a cross-national or cross-societal dimension. However, as Tomasson stated in the first edition of the journal Comparative Studies in Sociology, there seem to be degrees of 'comparativeness'. What is commonly presented as comparative research can range from a systematic comparison of two or more cases of a particular type under a common problematic to single studies of other societies. In fact, according to Tomasson, writing in 1978, this last type (which is far removed from any comparison) predominates. However, beside the fact that much of what is presented under the heading of 'comparative research' is not comparative at all, there are two additional major problems involved in doing genuine comparative research: one relates to the methodology of comparison, the other to the theoretical legitimation of the cross-national.

Authors writing in a more positivistic vein stress that comparative research is really not a specific field of study but represents a more general methodology. From this perspective, there is in principle no difference between comparative cross-societal research and research conducted within a single society. Comparative research involves the application of a comparative method, no matter what the object of the comparison. In trying to verify the relationship between variables (in terms of 'if A then B') a comparison has to be made between cases having A and cases not having A in order to sort out if, given the neutralization of background features by means of randomization or specification, a correlation emerges with the presence or absence of B (e.g. Holt and Turner 1970). According to this view, cross-societal comparative research is the application of comparative method on variables related to cross-societal cases (e.g. variables linked to different national political systems or to different cultures). Indeed, strictly speaking, according to the logical-positivist notion of science, there is no other way to develop general theories about social reality than in terms of a comparative method. If we want to know the influence of A on B, we'll have to compare 'A' with 'not A'.

This is not the place to discuss more generally the logical-positivist notion of scientific knowledge and scientific theory, nor is it the place to present existing alternatives (Manicas 1987). However, it is important to notice that what is commonly referred to as comparative research (also in its cross-national meaning) is largely based upon some vague logical-positivist notion of comparison. While predominantly restricting itself to research in other countries, or to the gathering of material from different countries, this usually is done, however, for the sake of a comparison of some kind.

While there is nothing intrinsically wrong with comparison as such (indeed if used in the broader sense of 'difference' it is hard to see how we can do without it in our perception of reality), some problems can arise with a comparison that restricts itself to a comparison of isolated cases implicitly or explicitly directed towards the formulation of a general law concerning some internal relation within those cases (e.g. a law concerning the relation between the kind of government active in a country or the national economic infrastructure, and the style of local leisure policy). The problem is that such an analysis

Conclusion

distracts from possible relations of reciprocity between the cases analysed. Cross-national comparative research predominantly deals with questions of cross-national differences or cross-national forms of integration or reciprocity. However, if we acknowledge that we live in a world-system in which economic, cultural, and political influences do not halt at national borders, restricting cross-national research to such a comparative perspective is highly inadequate.

Instead of thinking of comparative research as an analysis of particular isolated cases, it would perhaps be better to speak more generally of studies of system integration, which deal with the ways in which phenomena (groups, collectivities, practices) relate to one another, and where these are situated in historical time and global space. Such an approach would draw our attention to relations of presence and absence, to the ways in which certain styles of urban leisure policy are related not just to local circumstances, but, perhaps through these, to more national, global, or historical processes.

A form of comparative research focused on the reciprocal character of phenomena immediately draws our attention to the second problem related to cross-national comparative research. That has to do with the more substantive theoretical problem of the choice of the axis or level of analysis and comparison. If we consider cross national comparative research not just as a way of giving our theories a more general character (in line with a logical-positivist perspective on theory), why then do we cross the state border? The answer should relate to the role of nation-states in the structuring of the aspects of social reality under study. If there is a rationale for crossing the border, it must relate to the fact that in another nation-state things are organized differently or work out differently. Otherwise we could just as well stay at home or engage in cross-regional or cross-cultural (or whatever kind of cross-system) research where we have to cross borders accidentally to reach another region or culture (i.e. another social system). But the other way around, we have to operationalize our problematic in terms of a theoretically informed decision about levels of analysis and comparison. If we want to analyse styles of urban leisure policy, what kind of organizing principles can be distinguished and what would that mean for the differentiation of cases to study in terms of the relevant contexts which define those cases? Do we have to organize our cross-national comparative research primarily along an axis of regions (or cities or conglomerations) with a differing position in the global economic infrastructure? Or should the cases be situated in different national-states, given their importance in mediating the effects of global development to the local/regional level?

Both problems related to what commonly is called cross-national comparative research draw our attention to the role of theory in the process of trying to understand social reality. To analyse developments in the field of urban leisure and urban leisure policy, undisturbed by national, ethnic, or cultural forms of empiricism, we shall have to work towards some theoretical understanding of the relevance of these developments. It is to such a theoretical perspective and its translation into a research model that we now turn.

URBAN LEISURE AND URBAN LEISURE POLICY: FOUR 'LAYERS' OF EXPLANATION

In this book, authors have highlighted various processes of importance in explaining recent developments in urban leisure and urban leisure policy. They include the tensions or debates within the national political landscape (the national discourse concerning questions of leisure, culture and/or welfare) and forms of capital accumulation; the kinds of state policies and relations between the central and the local state; the role of policy executives, demographic developments, relations of class, ethnicity, and age; and the urban patterning of leisure lifestyles. All these processes span the dimensions of the cultural, the economic, the political, and the spatial, thus blurring the distinctive perspectives in theoretical debate often used to analyse urban questions.

These different influences should not be regarded as isolated factors, each separately offering a complete explanation of recent developments. The attitudes of agents of the local state to forms of leisure policy cannot be understood without acknowledging that such people belong to a generation socialized not only within certain styles of policymaking, but also within a specific bricolage of leisure lifestyles, each possessing its own peculiar interests and tastes. The (re)production of this bricolage was and is in turn related to a specific distribution of economic opportunities and to particular national/local leisure/

287

Conclusion

welfare/cultural policies. At the same time, the influence of local state agents in determining an urban leisure policy depends on the resources available to develop such a policy, that is on the amount of local political support or on the economic constraints and opportunities within which the local state has to operate.

Instead of treating the aforementioned elements of explanation as isolated factors, they should be seen as 'moments' within interrelated processes, leaving the task of disentangling those processes in terms of an empirically sound and theoretically adequate hierarchy of influences as to the constitutive elements of local urban leisure policies.

Trying to determine the basic moments responsible for the recent restructuring of urban leisure and urban leisure policy, not just in terms of a quantitative correlation of appearances, but also in terms of a hierarchy of 'structuring capacities' (Giddens 1979), is no easy task. Taking into account the spatial and temporal character of social reality, the following processes can be summed up:

* the positioning of cities or regions within the (re)production of (inter)national processes of capital accumulation and (inter)national divisions of labour
* the positioning of cities within the (re)production of relations between the central and the local state
* the (re)production of relations between the private and the public sector in the restructuring of local space; the power relations, styles of policy, divisions of responsibilities, and types of leisure activities involved
* the (re)production of the local patterns of leisure consumption; the power relations, lifestyles, and axes of differentiation.

This is not to say that whenever we know the characteristics of these processes, we can predict the local style of urban leisure policy. What is argued is that these four processes (representing layers or planes of influences and explanations) are of central importance. They are responsible for the basic conditional opportunities on which such a policy can be developed and as such have a major structuring force.

POSITIONS IN INTERNATIONAL PATTERNS OF CAPITAL ACCUMULATION

From whatever angle changes in urban leisure policies are analysed, be it from local uneven developments for which local policies try to compensate; from the resources available to develop a local policy; from the relation between national and local leisure policy; from the interests and strategies of local civil servants; or from the leisure lifestyles of those towards whom a policy is targeted, one cannot ignore the basic role of international patterns of capital accumulation and the related spatial division of labour. Although cities or regions differ in the degree to which their local economic infrastructure depends on international market relations, they cannot escape the influences of the latter. From designer clothes or audio equipment to local tourist infrastructures, local class relations, and local unemployment programmes - all reflect the ways in which local economies have become a part of a global economy.

International changes in the economic infrastructure, expressed in the West in a shift from production-based forms of capital accumulation to finance-, service-, and credit-based forms of accumulation, have in most cities mentioned in this book effected not only changes in local class relations, in growing numbers of unemployed (unevenly distributed among the population according to class, ethnicity, gender, and age), but also in the development of new and more market-oriented styles of local leisure policy.

However, within this overall pattern of international integration, differences still exist, depending on the specific position of cities or regions within the international division of labour. Industrial cities historically dependent on industrial capital are more vulnerable to a withdrawal of such capital than cities with more mixed economies. Conversely, cities with a service-oriented infrastructure and hence having already attracted some finance-, service-, or credit-based capital, can more easily attract new capital.

Together with the spin-off effect the withdrawal or attraction of capital has for other kinds of investment in land use (e.g. for leisure) and hence for the spatial layout of regions, for the nature and amount of local employment, for demographic developments, and for the revenues of local government, this self-reinforcing process results in what Smith and Williams (1986) have called a 'cruel dialectic of decay and opportunity'. Apart from its impact on the class relations within cities, international patterns of capital accumulation will result in new configurations of prosperous and decaying cities/conglomerations, shifting the economic power balance from one region to another. Widening regional differences may thus impinge on the possibility of cities developing specific forms of local urban leisure policy.

While the analyses presented in this book do not compare different styles of urban leisure policy in terms of the different positions of cities in international economic relations, they do show numerous examples of urban leisure policies taking shape as reactions to local conditions, directly mirroring changes in those relations. Franco Bianchini presents us with Greater London Council's decision in the 1980s on a new kind of cultural policy, partly because it considered the declining industrial working class no longer formed a sound basis for the organization of cultural representation. In Brussels, as Eric Corijn, Dominique Danau, and Livin Bollaert have shown, leisure became a vehicle for strengthening cultural-linguistic difference as the local petty bourgeoisie attempted to defend itself against a decline in its position because of changing national class relations. John Spink, concentrating on changing markets for land use in a rapidly deindustrializing region in West Yorkshire, discusses the policies developed or, better still not developed in relation to these changes. Further chapters show leisure becoming a strategy in attempts to fight forms of urban decay, either to attract new revenues (e.g. by appealing to the leisure lifestyle of the new middle class) or to replace old integrative mechanisms (based on industrial labour) by new ones (leisure as the focus of communal integration).

As all these examples make clear, there is no straight-forward relation between changes in the position of cities or regions within the international division of labour, and the content and style of urban leisure policy. The way in which the one is translated into the other depends not only on the effect of those changes on the local economic infrastructure (leading, for example, to a new division of responsibilities between the local private and public sector and to new local patterns of consumption) but also upon the type of involve-ment of the local state in leisure issues, an involvement again depending heavily upon the national division of respon-sibilities between the central and the local state.

THE RELATION BETWEEN THE CENTRAL AND THE LOCAL STATE

International processes of capital accumulation are not only reflected in a new division of urban regions in terms of economic functions, but in changes in state policies and relations between the central and the local state.

Although different countries have developed their own national political infrastructure and discourse, the economic crisis of the 1970s resulted in a general shift from Keynesian to monetarist state policies. This is not to say that the state is withdrawing from public affairs; that would be too simplistic a view. As suggested earlier, the state does not form an undifferentiated, functional systemic whole. Instead, it seems as though a monetarist shift in state policy can imply both a relative withdrawal from the domain of public services (e.g. welfare, health, social housing, education) and a growing involvement in the private lives of those obtaining social security, widening the power of the police, favouring private investment and ownership, restricting or surpassing the powers of local government. Part of this recasting of state policy forms a rearrangement of the relation between the central and the local state.

Saunders (1984) has described four key dimensions of government activity along which a division of responsibilities between local and central government could be organized. These include:

1. the organizational dimension: the key tension here is between the need for centralized direction and for local self-determination;
2. the functional dimension: the functional division between central and local government is such that the former is allocated responsibility for production while the latter is predominantly responsible for consumption services;
3. the political dimension: the key political tension identified concerns that between the corporate mode of decision-making at the national level and the competitive policies of the local state. Rational planning requires the incorporation or exclusion of conflicting parties, while democratic accountability implies open access to participation in the political process.
4. the ideological dimension: the key tension here is between central government's function in promoting

conditions for the accumulation of profit, and local government's role in meeting local needs.

Although this appears an adequate account of what is going on in terms of the changing division of responsibilities between the local and the central state, the situation is more complex. It remains open to empirical research whether or not this model holds for all local and central state functions, whether the interrelated effect of the different tensions work out the same for all countries and cities, and whether the parties concerned agree upon the model in the sense that they restrict themselves to the responsibilities differentiated.

As is clear from different studies presented here, the model does not mirror the complexities of what is happening in the field of leisure. First, leisure cannot simply be situated in either the field of consumption or the field of production. It spans both halves of the market. Second, as regards leisure, the local state has become more and more involved in attracting new sources of income, not only through stimulating consumption (more tourists spending more money), but also through stimulating production (attracting new types of economic activities, partly leisure-based, by subsidizing investments and developing adequate infrastructures). It is questionable whether these policies can be considered as forming part of the local government's role in meeting local needs. Third, it appears as though this shift to a more market-oriented local policy also leads to changes from more democratic to more directive styles of local planning.

Thus instead of considering Saunders' model as accounting for recent changes in central and local state relations, it can be used to indicate key dimensions in which the local and the central state continuously (re)arrange and contest responsibilities. The outcome of this dispute remains open to empirical research.

In the meantime, it is clear that the organization of local urban leisure policy heavily depends on the outcome of this dispute. Whether leisure is primarily 'politicized' as an instrument for attracting new capital and as such left to the local private sector, or as an instrument for the redistribution of public welfare within the city, or as an instrument in stimulating local cultural representation, will depend on the political agenda set by the state, on the national hierarchy of policy objectives, the related content of national leisure policy, the role of the local state within this policy, the related funds available and the autonomy that remains for local government to develop its own type of leisure policy. Examples of this are to be found in the foregoing contributions. Linda Hantrais traces the content of political commitments, especially among socialist parties in French government, to develop coherent and more decentralized leisure and cultural policies; she highlights the ways these commitments are translated in central and local policies. Fouli Papageorgiou analyses the contribution of Greek central and local government in leisure and cultural development, stressing the way in which the local state, in the absence of a clear central state policy and hence of subtantial funds, lacks a flexible organization to face community problems. Jean-Michel Dewailly gives us a clear picture of a possible dysfunctional effect of the devolution of planning powers to communes, resulting in a reinforcement of inequalities in recreational facilities between different communes. Myriam Jansen-Verbeke has shown how a rapid expansion of interest in the economic potential of local spatial dimensions can be triggered by national programmes stimulating the development of more profitable tourist infrastructures.

THE LOCAL RELATION BETWEEN THE PRIVATE AND THE PUBLIC SECTOR

Local leisure policies rested on clear and conventionally agreed divisions of responsibility between the private and the public sector with regard to different types of leisure provisions. The private sector organized amusement, popular culture, and tourism, while the public sector subsidized and/or organized activities with welfare, health, educational, or cultural dimensions (the arts, classical music, museums, sport, outdoor recreation). Although national and local differences did exist, for instance with regard to the degree in which the public sector felt responsible for leisure, the division between entertainment and moral integration, between pleasure and social reproduction, formed the common parameters on which such difference rested. As such, public policy tried to compensate for the perceived problems or needs from uneven developments, produced through the market. This institutionalized division of labour within the realm of leisure policy formed part of a more general division of

Conclusion

labour between the public and the private sector, a division organized through national and local legislation and policies (e.g. with regard to spatial planning, house building, economic development, investments in transport and traffic, etc.) Based on this formally and informally reproduced division, complete local infrastructures have been developed. They arose not just in terms of organized divisions of responsibilities, in which the parties involved know whom to turn to in case of difficulties and around which professions have developed with their own capabilities to attract finance from either the public or the private sector, but also in terms of styles of policy, policy objectives, policy language, and spatial layouts in land use and activities where everybody knew his or her proper place.

Changes in the position of cities or regions within the international division of labour and changes in the division of responsibilities between the central and the local state have led at the local level to a disruption and restructuring of the institutionalized relations between the private and the public sectors. Faced with decreases in national funding, local governments turn more and more towards local capital in search for funds to finance not just existing provisions, but also (depending on the degree to which production capital has actually withdrawn and service capital could potentially be attracted) to develop new foci for capital accumulation. They are turning from a public policy organized 'against' the market (e.g. developing public provisions to compensate for uneven development and meeting local needs) to a public policy organized 'through' the market (e.g. acting as a market agent, trying to direct investments by contracting out public services, financing programmes in the form of loans, or developing forms of public-private partnership).

As different contributions collected in this book have shown, it is the disruption and subsequent institutional-ization of new types of integration that form another important constituent element in the development of new types of local leisure policies. Depending on the changes taking place in local relations between the private and the public sectors (the new landscape of forms of investment and management policies, the restructuring of local policy along market lines, the restructuring of power relations) this will lead to new hierarchies in leisure policy objectives, new leisure policy styles and instruments, new styles of leisure planning and leisure management, and also to new spatial distributions of new types of leisure facilities. While restructured relations between the private and the public sectors form the medium for organizing new types of leisure policies, the objectives and instruments of these new leisure policies help at the same time to develop and reproduce the relation between the private and the public sectors.

From this perspective, the findings of Myriam Jansen-Verbeke concerning the attitudes of local tourism planners mirror rather closely elements of the changes involved. Triggered by a national policy to subsidize plans for local tourism development, new forms of co-operation develop between the private and public sectors on the local level (creating, for example, close relationships between tourist and recreation boards); this is also reflected in an internal reorganization of local government departments. While welfare and economic departments within local government were formerly separated (mirroring conventional divisions of labour between the public and the private sectors), they now have to look for new forms of integration. A new kind of policy infrastructure is emerging, no doubt a harbinger of influence in future leisure planning procedures (e.g. using feasibility studies instead of public debate as a means of deciding on new projects; looking at museums in terms of their role in city-marketing instead of their role in the transmission of knowledge; blurring existing demarcations between sectors of leisure).

In similar vein, John Spink highlights the consequence of market-oriented national policies on the power relations between the local public and private sectors in determining different sorts of residential land use. Reductions in public spending and specific forms of legislation have increased the power of commercial interests in the allocation of community resources, leaving room for no more than a reactive (instead of proactive) local leisure policy. It could well be that given these institutionalized relations, his suggestion to develop private consortia based within inner-city communities to attract private and public funds for local-initiative projects will figure prominently in future forms of public leisure policy.

THE LOCAL PATTERNING OF LEISURE CONSUMPTION

The final constitutive element in the (re)production of urban leisure policy concerns local leisure consumption. Of course, this is not to say that local leisure policy can be

Conclusion

comprehended as a neutral reaction to local consumption patterns, as if the local state could be conceived as essentially pluralist and concerned with meeting local needs. But neither is it true to say that urban leisure policy would take shape regardless of local patterns of leisure behaviour, as if local leisure policy was a direct reflection of institutionalized economic and political developments. Instead, local leisure policy must be studied as a response to the existing local ways of life, be it because of a desire to profit from them, or because of an implicit or explicit concern to ignore or neutralize them within 'hegemonic' relations, or because of a wish to favour them because of the organized interests involved.

The content of leisure policies for the young unemployed during the 1970s, the programmes and activities involved, can only be understood in relation to the way of life of groups of young unemployed as perceived by local governments. Although all these unemployment policies have taken shape against the background of the consumerism of working-class youth, and were primarily organized through national funding and out of a genuine desire to help, the actual programmes developed can only be understood and evaluated adequately in relation to the local cultural patterns and the way these are problematized, ignored and/or stimulated through local state unemployment policies. The eventual class, gender, ethnic, or age biases involved, the ways of life promoted through the specific content and form of a programme, all these and other, sometimes hidden, dimensions of leisure policies become apparent when we acknowledge the implicit or explicit role of the local fabric of leisure consumption patterns in the development of local leisure policies.

In dealing with this level of analysis, the contribution of Adri Dietvorst has shown the class biases involved in the organization of local projects for the unemployed. Instead of a policy which meets the local needs of the unemployed, the policy, in its effects, reproduces the interests of well-educated groups of the unemployed and the formal economic sector:

> Some of the measures which are part of the unemployment policy seem to fit better in the framework of an implicit strategy of control, to preserve the existing socioeconomic order or to

normalize the existing economic systems, than in the enhancement of unemployed's interests.

At the same level of analysis, the contribution of Sjoerd Rijpma and Henk Meiburg demonstrates how recent changes in sport practices, commonly referred to in terms of individualism or differentiation and rooted in the lifestyle of the young and the well-to-do, resonate in Rotterdam's sport policy, eventually at the expense of the sport practices of marginalized youth.

Of course, there is a difference between signalling the uneven ways in which leisure policies reflect patterns of leisure consumption and explaining them. Such an analysis would involve looking at the relations between different local (leisure) cultures, studying the ways in which differences in leisure consumption are based upon domestic, economic, and political relations, and studying the ways in which cultural differences feed into local leisure policy, mediated and reciprocated by the other levels of influences involved.

A MODEL FOR FUTURE RESEARCH

In conjunction with the different styles of leisure policies mentioned earlier, these four layers of influences/ explanations present something of a model for future research on issues of urban leisure policy. They are summarized in Figure 14.1 below. When linked to the remarks made on cross-national comparative research and hence given the adequate choice of dimensions and styles of comparison involved, this model could even lead to future international studies that would go beyond conventional comparative research.

The model does little more than hint at the structure of such research. Many theoretical questions remain to be solved, such as those related to the conceptualization of the urban or leisure, or those concerning the adequate theoretization of relations between politics and economy or between aspects of economic and cultural relations. Nevertheless, Figure 14.1 presents a model on which such future debate could be founded. It encourages research to analyse the emergence of specific types of urban leisure policies, involving interrelated dimensions of international economic relations, national political developments, and local political, economic, and cultural infrastructures. Such

297

Conclusion

Figure 14.1. Model for international research on urban leisure policy

National political relations
Relations between the central and the local state

International economic relations
Processes of capital accumulation
International division of labour

Urban leisure policy
Forms of conceptualization
Policy instruments
Styles of policy
Policy objectives
Programmes

Local relations between the private and public sectors
Relations of power
Divisions of labour
Styles of policy
Forms of integration

Local leisure consumption
Patterning of leisure cultures

research would have to take place across cities or urban conglomerations, situated differently in international economic divisions of labour and national political configurations. It would involve not only a comparison of isolated cases, trying to determine social 'laws' about the relation of, say, the position of cities in international economic relations and local urban policy, but also an analysis of how the local-specific is related to the international-institutional, of how international and national economic and political developments affect the realization of local forms of urban leisure policy.

Such a move on the effect of forms of international integration only reflects current reality. With Ladbrokes (originally a British corporation) exploring the Dutch market for horse-betting and Center Parcs (a Dutch corporation) exploring the British short-stay holiday market, we have two recent examples of the internationalization of leisure capital. This internationalization of leisure also finds its expression in cross-national or cross-cultural tourism, in the cross-national and cross-cultural mediation of information (satellite television, cross-national publishing, cross-national film and music production and marketing) or even by cross-national migration of labour (e.g. labourers from the Mediterranean countries working in sections of the Dutch leisure industry, migrant workers reproducing their own culture either within their own community or even through the leisure market, as in the case of the recent boom in foreign restaurants). All these cases stress the inadequacy of a leisure research programme organized on a national basis. National or ethnic provincialism only fortifies existing dominant interests. It restrains us from an adequate and valid picture of reality and offers no sound basis for scientific research.

'. . . AND THE DEVIL TAKE THE HINDMOST'

So far the trends identified in this book suggest a further polarization of leisure opportunities for the near future. With the withdrawal of production-based capital, a large industrial labour force has lost contact because of unemployment, with what was considered until recently as a normal way of life. The growing importance of long-term unemployment not only among youth but also among the elderly, indicates a class without employment because of the coincidence of postwar demographic developments and the loss of jobs which suit their education and culture. In some countries research into the consequences of poverty is gaining in popularity again, despite an absence for some decennia.

At the same time the growth in credit, finance, and service-based processes of capital accumulation has given a new generation the chance of quick economic gain. Forming a new target group for the market, their lifestyle, based upon sophisticated commodity aesthetics, features in numerous commercials. City governments are competing to attract this new economic middle class. Parts of shopping areas become dedicated to shops totally devoted to the conspicuous demands of those involved. Although the exact distribution of this uneven development may differ from country to country and from city to city, it nevertheless presents a structural development, based upon the changes in capital accumulation.

Conclusion

With national policies organized along supply-side economics, the local state has become restricted financially, and in some countries even legally, to try to bridge the gap between the privileged and the marginalized. It remains questionable whether leisure programmes are able to bridge that gap. There is a growing body of academic literature which suggests that many leisure initiatives have only a limited impact on tackling and redressing social and economic problems.

While it remains open to further empirical research to analyse what effects more market-oriented leisure policies can or will have on the constitution of urban leisure, it is clear from research presented here that its legitimation as a means of fighting existing forms of urban decay is highly questionable. While existing forms of urban decay are predominantly related to the withdrawal of production capital, leading to an increase in unemployment among industrial workers, new types of policies are oriented towards attracting service capital, based upon another type of employment from which the local industrial working class is unlikely to profit. Local government not only attempts to attract new service capital, but in doing so also tries to attract new groups of employees. In practice, this changing relation between the private and the public sectors will result in a decrease of leisure programmes specifically developed for local marginalized groups. Attention has shifted to programmes attracting new kinds of economic activities and new higher-income groups, who, by their mere presence, will stimulate a rise in prices on the local leisure market (together with an introduction of new and more expensive kinds of leisure activities), leaving the original industrial working class further behind. Beyond the glamour of the bourgeois playground, it seems as though differences will increase instead of being counterbalanced. The crucial question for the future is not so much whether or not urban leisure policies wil be able to deal with the consequences of uneven development, but rather whether we can develop economic policies that will restructure market relations so as to give disadvantaged groups more equal opportunity to meet their economic interests. It is a question that is less audible in current political discourse.

REFERENCES

Giddens, A. (1979) Central Problems in Social Theory: Action, Structure and Contradiction in Social Analysis, London: Macmillan.
—— (1981) A Contemporary Critique of Historical Materialism. Vol 1: Power, Property and the State, London: Macmillan.
Gregory, D. and Urry, J. (1985) Social Relations and Spatial Structures, London: Macmillan.
Holt, R.T. and Turner, J.E. (1970) The Methodology of Comparative Research, New York: The Free Press.
Manicas, P.T. (1987) A History and Philosophy of the Social Sciences, Oxford: Basil Blackwell.
Offe, C. (1984) Contradictions of the Welfare State, London: Hutchinson.
Saunders, P. (1984) 'Rethinking local politics', in M. Boddy and C. Fudge (eds), Local Socialism, London: Macmillan.
Smith, N. and Williams, P. (eds) (1986) Gentrification of the City, London: Allen & Unwin.
Tomasson, R.F. (1978) Introduction, in Comparative Studies in Sociology. An Annual Compilation of Research, vol 1, Greenwich: Jai Press, pp. 1-15.

INDEX